T0352914

HITMAN
FOR THE KINDNESS CLUB

High Seas Escapades and Heroic Adventures of an Eco-Activist

Captain Paul Watson

Groundswell Books
Summertown, Tennessee

Library of Congress Cataloging-in-Publication Data available upon request.

We chose to print this title on sustainably harvested paper stock certified by the Forest Stewardship Council®, an independent auditor of responsible forestry practices. For more information, visit us.fsc.org.

MIX
Paper from
responsible sources
FSC® C005010

Printed in the United States of America

Groundswell Books
an imprint of BPC
PO Box 99
Summertown, TN 38483
888-260-8458
bookpubco.com

Disclaimer: This work depicts actual events in the life of the author as truthfully as recollection permits. The experiences and views expressed in this book are solely those of the author.

ISBN: 978-1-57067-412-9
E-book ISBN: 978-1-57067-805-9

28 27 26 25 24 23   1 2 3 4 5 6 7 8 9

I have no concerns for the media spins

and the lies and falsehoods they scatter.

May the future forgive my ecological sins,

for all other sins don't matter.

Dedicated to Aida Flemming,
the founder of the Kindness Club,
and to my children and grandchildren:
Lilliolani, Tiger, Murtagh, Gemma, and Tommy.

CONTENTS

	Introduction	1
1961	**Beaver Tales and BB Guns**	3
1964–1965	**My First Rodeo**	11
1968–1969	**A Boy Goes to Sea**	16
1970–1971	**People's Park**	22
1972	**Eighty Days, Eighty Dollars**	27
1973	**Hoka Hey**	32
1973–1975	**No Tanks, I'm Heading to Turkey**	36
1975	**Eye of the Cachalot**	40
1976	**Urban Warfare**	45
1976	**Shepherds on the Labrador Front**	50
1977	**Brigitte Bardot and the Media Circus**	55
1978	**Butcher of Uganda**	61
1979	**Painting Baby Seals**	67
1979–1980	**Sinking the *Sierra***	74
1981	**The Ides of March**	81
1981	**No Room for the Soviet Union**	88
1982	**Samurai Conservationist**	99
1982	**Tree Spiking**	106
1982	**Paint-Bombing the Russians**	110
1983	**Monkey Business in Grenada**	116
1983	**Blockade**	120

1984–1985	Cry Wolf	130
1985–1986	Chocolate Pie Cannons versus Bullets	136
1985	Pints with the Unspeakables	144
1986	Raid on Reykjavík	148
1987–1992	Curtains of Death	159
1988	Rascally Rabbits	166
1990	Eco-Hawks	170
1991	Pigeon Purgatory	178
1992	Columbus, Make My Day	183
1992–1994	Battle in the Lofoten	191
1993	The Nazi Bear Hunter	200
1993–1995	Cod War	204
1996–1998	Standing Up to an Angry Mob	212
1997	Hotel Lelystad	220
1998–1999	A Whale for the Killing	227
2000	Surviving Hollywood	232
2002	Treasure Island	237
2003–2006	The Siesta Conversation Club	244
2005	Ice Charades	249
2008	A Sack of Doubloons	257
2010	Blue Rage	266
2011	Viking Shores	271
2012	Escape from Germany	275
2012–2013	Mobilizing Neptune's Navy	283
2013	The Iron Wedge	293
2013	Exile at Sea	302
2005–2017	The Whale Wars	309
1992 & 2008	The Ships That Wouldn't Sink	317
	Afterword	324
	About the Author	331
	Photo Credits	332
	Index	333

Introduction

Since 1961, I have been an activist for animals and the environment. That was the year I joined the Kindness Club.

The Kindness Club was founded in 1959 by Aida Flemming, the wife of Hugh John Flemming, who at the time was the Conservative premier of my home province of New Brunswick, Canada.

My mother gave me some leaflets from the Kindness Club. I wrote to Aida Flemming to tell her that I wished to join the club and how much I loved beavers because I had spent an entire summer swimming with a family of beavers near Saint Andrews, New Brunswick. She wrote back, encouraging me to be protective not only of beavers but all animals.

I corresponded with her many times over the next few years and in 1967, when I was sixteen, I stopped to visit her at her home in Fredericton, New Brunswick. In March 1981, upon returning from the anti-sealing campaign in Prince Edward Island, my friend Al Johnson and I stopped to visit her again in Fredericton. It was during that visit when, after saying how proud she was of me for fighting the sealers, she jokingly called me the "hitman" for the Kindness Club. Al and I both laughed, and I replied, "I'm honored. I like it."

I am still the hitman for the Kindness Club. Aida was very instrumental in laying the foundation for a long, adventurous, and meaningful life and for that, I will always be grateful.

These adventures took me from my childhood in Canada to situations on every ocean and on every continent of the planet to fight for the rights of animals, nature, and Indigenous peoples.

1961

Beaver Tales and BB Guns

NEW BRUNSWICK, CANADA

My mother and maternal grandfather gave me a good foundation for being kind to animals. My father was a member of the Canadian Army, and when I was four my sister and I lived with my mother's father in Toronto. My grandfather's residence was not far from the Riverdale Zoo, a place where he took me quite often. Although he was in his late sixties, he always carried me on his shoulders. He was a big man and in days past he had been a bare-knuckle boxer, which was evident by his damaged earlobes and a few scars hidden behind his full white beard.

In the early 1950s, it was not unusual to see horses in the city, and I remember my grandfather confronting a much younger man who was harshly whipping his horse.

My grandfather told the man to stop and when he refused, he grabbed the whip and pulled it out of the man's hand.

"You have no right to interfere," the man yelled.

"I have every right," my grandfather answered.

"This is my horse, my property. Who the hell do you think you are?"

3

"Someone who is bigger, stronger, and—quite frankly—not a little coward like you. Whip that horse again and I'll knock you flat on the pavement."

The man meekly led his horse away down the street.

Sadly, upon his return from Korea, my father moved the family a thousand miles away to his native New Brunswick and a town called Saint Andrews on the shores of Passamaquoddy Bay. Saint Andrews is a small fishing village situated on the border of Canada and the US state of Maine and is the ancestral home of the Passamaquoddy people who live on both sides of the border.

The move may have had something to do with the fact that my father had hit my mother and, unfortunately for him, my grandfather saw him strike her. My sixty-eight-year-old grandfather decked the twenty-five-year-old recently returned soldier with one punch. I was never to see my grandfather again. My home life was not very comfortable: my father was abusive and I was the eldest in a family that, by 1960, included three brothers and two sisters. As a result, I spent a great deal of time on the beach, on the pier, or in the forest.

While Saint Andrews was a fishing town, it was primarily a lobster town. I remember the long stacks of traps along the roadway. I remember the smells and the noise from Conley's Lobster Factory, and I felt helpless as I watched the lobsters struggle, trying to free themselves from the belt conveying them to the deadly steamer in the cannery.

I would often sit on the end of the dock in Saint Andrews and look over the waters of Passamaquoddy Bay, where I could see whales and seals. There were many seabirds, which swooped down when the fishing boats returned in the late afternoon to bicker over the scraps as the fishermen cleaned their catches.

My very first activism on behalf of animals was in late September, when I was walking home from the dock. Dozens of lobster traps, filled with the brownish-green creatures, had just been off-loaded. No one was around, so I cut open one of the traps, delicately removed two of the lobsters, and placed them in a burlap sack lying nearby.

When I returned home, I filled a small tub with seawater and seaweed and put the lobsters in the water. I named them Flounderface and Bug-Eye. My brother and I had fun watching them break small branches and even a pencil with their strong claws, until one of them grabbed my brother's little finger and almost broke it. Because of my brother's injury, my father announced that we were going to have lobster for dinner. But as he was boiling the water, I managed to wrestle both the lobsters back into the burlap sack and hustle them down to the bay, where I released them back into the sea.

Despite a severe scolding from my father, I felt good knowing that Flounderface and Bug-Eye had returned home. I hoped they would stay clear of the lobster traps in the future.

Because a lobster can live for more than a century, I like to imagine that Flounderface and Bug-Eye are still living at the bottom of Passamaquoddy Bay.

The next summer, my father took the family to a small cabin in the woods. The cabin was on the shores of a small lake, surrounded by evergreens and silver birch trees. It was a beautiful place, a quiet place. The air was fresh and the water was cool, blue, and very clean.

I spent most of my time in the water, swimming and exploring, especially scouting the small creeks that ran into the lake.

One morning as I was making my way up the shallow bed of a creek, I saw a beaver dam. It was a wall of branches and mud about three feet high. Behind it was a small pond and in the center of the pond was a domed beaver lodge.

As I watched, I could see a small family of beavers slowly moving through the water. Some were pulling small branches and two were sitting on the bank.

As I stepped over the dam, there was a sharp slap on the pond. One of the beavers had struck the water with his paddle-shaped tail, and at once the two young beavers on the shore scurried toward the water's edge and dove beneath the surface.

I decided to get into the water behind the dam amid a tangle of newly cut leafy branches. With just my eyes and nose above the surface, I stayed completely still. About twenty minutes later I saw one head and then another slowly poke above the surface of the pond. I counted seven beavers in all.

For nearly an hour I watched them swim and go about their business, not moving a muscle until one of them approached my hiding spot. He came closer and closer until his nose almost touched mine. Suddenly he turned, slapped the water's surface with his tail, and disappeared. The other six disappeared beneath the surface as well.

I did not move; I waited another twenty minutes, until they appeared again on the surface and began to swim about.

Slowly I submerged my head beneath the water and swam toward one of the beavers. He swam around me a couple of times and then ducked behind a rock.

I returned to the pond every day for another week. The beavers became used to my being there, and every day they swam a little closer.

By the second week, they were accustomed to my presence and went about their business like I was not there.

They were a hardworking family, cutting small trees and gnawing branches, shoring up dams and stripping bark to stow away for food for the winter.

The younger beavers, there were five of them, were playful and I found myself swimming with them as they ducked behind rocks or hid in the branches floating near the dam. They seemed to enjoy chasing me about and I was having a wonderful time, so much so that I arrived at the pond early in the morning and stayed until late afternoon.

When the beavers ate bark, I would chew on spruce gum, the thick sap on the sides of some of the trees. I think that it lent me the smell of spruce, which I was sure the beavers could detect.

And then one day I dove under the beavers' house and surfaced inside their cozy wooden dome. It was dark, but my eyes adjusted to the darkness and the slivers of light penetrating the few cracks in the roof.

The beavers did not seem agitated and let me visit them in their home a few more times during the remainder of the summer. I named the most playful beaver Bucky.

I had a joyful time during the summer of 1960 and as I returned home to the fishing village where I lived, I was already looking forward to the next summer.

When autumn came, I had to go to school, and this meant bidding farewell to my beaver friends until the next spring.

During the second week of school, while I was walking to class with a group of other kids, we encountered a small skunk in distress. Her head was firmly stuck in an empty strawberry jam bottle.

Everyone told me to stay away from the skunk as I approached her and removed the bottle from her head. The skunk sprayed me.

The smell did not bother me, but when I took my seat in class, Mrs. Cumberland, my grade-four teacher, told me I had to go home because I was stinking up the classroom.

When I got home, my mother was not mad—although she did make me remove all my clothes and take a bath. A few days later, she gave me some leaflets for the Kindness Club, a group for children who loved animals.

A few of the boys made fun of me for the skunk incident and for speaking out against hunting in a county where hunting was entrenched in the local culture. It did not worry me; I was confident in my desire to help animals and, like my grandfather in his interaction with the younger man whipping his horse, I was bigger than most of them and not easily bullied.

I got in trouble that autumn when my father took me fishing in northern New Brunswick, close to his father's potato farm. He was not happy with me because I did not want to fish, and he told me to place the fish in a bag as he caught them. When he was ready to go home, he discovered that the bag was empty. I told him that the fish were drowning, and I had put them back into the stream.

He smacked me across the back of the head, called me an idiot, and screamed that "fish don't drown, you moron."

When we returned to my grandfather's farm, my dad gave me a beating with his belt and sent me to bed without supper. Later he told my mother that she was not to talk about this Kindness Club nonsense with me.

I could not wait for spring, for the snow to melt so that I could return to the beaver pond. The first day that I returned I noticed that the beaver dam was broken, and I could not see any beavers anywhere.

When I returned to the cabin, I was very upset and told my father that my beavers were gone.

He shrugged and said, "Most likely the trappers got them."

"What?" I cried.

"Trappers have to make a living, and beaver pelts fetch good money," he said.

I was devastated. These were my friends. I knew them.

I did not see another beaver that summer. While the year before I had returned from the woods happy, this time I returned home sad and angry.

And I remained angry. In November, I decided to do something about it while visiting my uncle's farm along the Saint Croix River. I put on snowshoes and walked through the woods, because my cousin had told me that a local trapper had set a trapline with rabbit snares and leghold traps. The trapper had marked his territory with yellow ribbons around tree trunks near the frozen streams.

As I walked along the trapper's trail, I removed the ribbons and the snares and located two leghold traps, which I stuffed in my bag.

Suddenly I saw something thrashing about in the snow. As I approached, the thrashing increased. I saw a snow-white weasel looking up at me with a snarl. I could see the blood on his leg and paw and drops of blood on the snow around him.

I took off my coat and slowly draped it over the weasel to hold him down until I could spring the trap to release him. He immediately ran into the woods, leaving me with my third trap of the day.

I tossed all three traps into the Saint Croix River.

I felt elated. I had saved another life.

For the next two months, I destroyed even more traps. One day in December, close to Christmastime, I found a young beaver caught in a leghold trap in the water, her head just above the surface. She was still alive.

I covered her with my coat, sprung the trap, and with great satisfaction watched as she swam away and ducked beneath the ice of the pond. I could see the snow-covered beaver house in the middle of the pond, and I hoped that she had returned home and that her wound would heal.

I tossed that trap into the middle of the pond and walked back through the woods in my wet coat. Although it was cold, I felt warm inside knowing that I had saved the life of a beaver.

It wasn't long before the locals were complaining that someone was raiding traplines and stealing the traps. They were also saying that they would shoot the guy doing it if they caught him.

So I stopped my anti-trapping efforts, but for only a few months. I eventually struck again, carefully and meticulously. I read about how an Indian had escaped the Mounties by putting his snowshoes on backward, and I made sure that my tracks never led to anywhere specifically.

The next summer, I got in trouble because I saw some boys shooting birds with BB rifles. I grabbed one boy's rifle and shot another in the ass before he could kill the bird he was aiming at. This of course led to the boy's parents calling the police, which led the police to visit my father, which led to another beating.

Many years later, in 1990, Washington State governor Dixy Lee Ray cited this incident in her book *Trashing the Planet* as "evidence of Watson's insanity." My response to her was that when I was young, in my hometown every boy shot every other boy with a BB gun. I just had a practical reason for doing so.

Over the next few years, I took delight in disrupting duck hunts with kites and horns and destroying leghold traps and snares at every opportunity. But when I was twelve, my father ran off with another woman, leaving my mother to raise and support six kids while working as a waitress. I helped the family finances with my paper route, and I also became quite good at smuggling margarine.

Back then, margarine in Canada was a white substance that came with a packet of yellow dye that had to be mixed into the margarine by hand. People hated it, especially because right across the border in Maine it came in four yellow sticks to a package and it was cheaper.

American-made margarine was illegal in Canada. In the late '50s and early '60s, children crossed the US border numerous times each day without papers and without being questioned. I smuggled a few pounds of American margarine into Canada each day. The modest profits were helpful to my mother.

Sadly, shortly after I turned thirteen, my mother died. My father took us kids to Toronto only days after the funeral.

On top of the profound sadness and disbelief I felt at my mother's death, I experienced a significant culture shock: no more forest or seashores, farms or fishing boats. Just tall buildings, streetcars, and noisy traffic—as well as the stockyards and the Canada Packers slaughterhouse just a few blocks from our house.

My work was just beginning.

1964-1965

My First Rodeo

TORONTO, ONTARIO, CANADA

After the death of my mother, my father moved my three brothers, my two sisters, and me from rural New Brunswick to the big city of Toronto.

Although I was born in Toronto, I found it to be an intimidating place—too big, too loud, and too chaotic compared to small-town New Brunswick. I attended grade seven in the neighborhood of Parkdale, where I joined the chess club and wrote my very first article for the school newspaper: an interview with a caretaker at Riverdale Zoo. This interview gave me the opportunity to see behind the scenes at the zoo, such as how the animals were treated and how they were fed.

The zoo staff seemed to care for the animals, but I found it depressing to see so many animals behind bars, like they had been sentenced to prison, which of course they had been—they were innocent, self-aware, sentient beings imprisoned against their will.

The most satisfying moment of the visit was when the zoo staff let me participate in the release of a large snapping turtle into the Don River. The turtle had spent the past few months recuperating from injuries, and it was nice to know that the zoo was helping injured wild animals and returning them to the wild when possible. The experience not only helped motivate my concern for animals but also sparked my love of writing.

In 1965, my father moved us to North York, part of the city, where I started grade eight. This move was an improvement, because back then North York was far from being developed. There was still farmland, and Black Creek ran through a small valley that was relatively wild and home to birds, frogs, snakes, raccoons, and foxes.

That was the year the Canadian Red Ensign was retired, and I stood in the courtyard of my school as the adults raised the red-and-white flag bearing a maple leaf, a symbol that years later would stand for so many things that disgusted me about Canada: whaling, the slaughter of baby seals, the trapping of beavers, the shooting of bears, the destruction of forests, the horror of the Indigenous residential schools, and the history of abuse and genocide of the people of the First Nations.

The Black Creek Valley was a beautiful wilderness oasis in the ever-expanding metropolis of Greater Toronto. Unfortunately, I also discovered a place of absolute horror within walking distance from where I went to school—the Canada Packer slaughterhouses at Keele and Saint Clair.

Some friends took me there one day to watch the Judas cow.

We watched from the sidewalk as some slaughterhouse workers led a single black-and-white cow across the street from the abattoir to the stockyard where hundreds of cows were held in pens. The workers entered the stockyard with the single cow and returned about ten minutes later with that same one cow leading some thirty other cows.

One of the boys explained to me that the one cow was called the Judas cow. They did not kill her; she lived in a special pen where she slept and ate.

"Her job is to lead the other cows to slaughter. My uncle who works here says it calms the other cows down and they peacefully follow her across the street and into the building."

"That's horrible," I said.

"Yeah, well, that's what they do," he said.

The boys then led me into the stockyard (back then, security at a place like that just did not exist). We walked down long aisles with holding pens for cows and pigs.

Apparently, most of the boys had been here quite often, and they came here to ride the cows.

"All you have to do is climb up on the fence and get on a cow's back and you can ride it around the pen," said the nephew of the man who worked there.

I watched as some of the boys mounted cows. The cows did not seem to mind, so I tried it myself. Unfortunately, one of the stockyard workers saw us and began yelling. We tried to flee, but I slipped and fell to the dirt floor of the pen and under the cow I was riding.

It was a frightening experience. All around me were the hooves of cows. Standing outside of the pen was the man trying to catch us, and I couldn't stand up because the cows' bodies were above me. All the other boys had run off.

I began to crawl under the cows toward the opposite side of the pen, and although the cattle were moving around, not one of them stepped on me. When I reached the other side of the pen, I squeezed under the bottom rail of the fence and ran back down the aisle toward the street with the man yelling at me from the other side of the pen.

A few days later it bothered me to think that those cows were awaiting their execution. Not one of them harmed me when I was on the dirt floor of the stockyard.

One Sunday afternoon I went back to the stockyard by myself. The abattoir was closed for the day, and the cows and pigs were in the stockyard unattended.

I went from pen to pen, unlatching the gates. I must have unlatched twenty gates before leaving.

The next day at school, my friend whose uncle worked at the packing plant told me that dozens of cows and pigs had escaped and had been running down the streets and that it was a big emergency. I had thought that they could get away; of course, it was impossible for cows and pigs to escape from the city. But at least they had a few hours of freedom before being caught and returned to their death-row prison cells.

My experiences at the stockyards left a lasting impression on me. Today more than seventy billion domestic animals are slaughtered annually by the global meat industry. This industry is not only cruel but also the leading cause of dead zones in the sea, the primary source for groundwater pollution, and the leading source of greenhouse gas emissions—even more than the transportation industry. These are all reasons I made all my ships vegetarian in 1979 and vegan beginning in 1999.

As my relationship with my father became more strained, I began to run away every summer, each time heading toward New Brunswick by hitching or riding the rails. At fourteen, I made it to my uncle's place, only to have him turn me over to child welfare. The child welfare authorities put me on a plane back to Ontario—my first-ever flight—and I was thrilled. It was worth the beating I received on my return.

I immediately ran away again, this time hitching to Windsor, where I tried to cross the border into Detroit by telling the authorities that I was heading to California to be a surfer. That did not work, and I was sent back home again.

When I was sixteen, my father decided that the only solution to my constantly running away was to commit me to the psychiatric hospital in London, Ontario, as unmanageable. The place was terrifying. I was locked up and forced to take medications without any explanation from the staff. I knew I had to escape from the place and, after studying the facility's layout for a week and collecting food, I made my break when the staff took a small group of patients to the library. It was winter and we had to cross the courtyard, so we were given coats to put over our pajamas.

About a quarter of a mile from the rear of the hospital were railway tracks. I had been keeping track of the trains' timetables. On the excuse of going to the bathroom, I slipped out of a side door and made a run for it across a snowy field in just slippers. I was too stressed to realize how cold it was until I reached a boxcar. I jumped in, rubbed my feet for an hour, and then shivered all the way from London to Toronto.

I went to my Aunt Jean's home, hoping to get help. But as I was speaking with her in the kitchen, I saw the police lights arrive outside, so I sprinted out the back door and spent the night under the heating vent of an apartment building.

The next day, I hitched to Montreal to the home of my Aunt Celine. She welcomed me in and allowed me to stay. I got a job at Expo 67 as a tour guide.

Working at Expo 67 was an amazing experience. I was captivated by all the national pavilions. I met Haile Selassie at the Ethiopian pavilion—although I was more impressed by his pet leopard, which he was walking on a leash. On July 1, 1967, I slipped by security at the Canadian pavilion to join the centennial celebration of the founding of Canada. I also danced with a hostess from the French pavilion, which went quite well until I confessed that I was only sixteen.

Those six months at Expo 67 opened up the world to me and was my alternative to attending high school that year.

1968-1969

A Boy Goes to Sea

VANCOUVER AND THE NORTH PACIFIC

At seventeen, I left my aunt's place in Montreal and hopped freight trains to the Canada's West Coast to finish my last year of high school.

It was a breathtaking trip. I had jumped a car carrier, which meant that I could ride the rails in absolute comfort. The cars all had their keys in them so they could be driven off the train on arrival. All I had to do was start the car. I had heat, radio, and a place to sleep.

Sitting in a car on the top deck of a Canadian National freight train as it traveled through the Rockies and down the Fraser Canyon was an amazing adventure for a seventeen-year-old boy.

I arrived in Vancouver without any money and camped out in the abandoned gun towers on Wreck Beach below the campus of the University of British Columbia (UBC).

I was able to get enough social-welfare assistance to cover taking classes at Vancouver City College (now Vancouver Community College). I also took on extracurricular activities to make money, like being a DJ for CKED college radio and working at Denton's Jungle Land, a pet store on Granville Street downtown. For two months in the summer, I was able to make good money planting trees along the coast.

I became involved with school politics and was elected as the only Students for a Democratic University (SDU) candidate for the VCC student council. The SDU was the Canadian version of Students for a Democratic Society in the United States.

When I heard that Jerry Rubin would be speaking at UBC, I arranged to have him speak at VCC. After Rubin's speaking engagement, hundreds of radical students invaded the UBC faculty lounge, where a party raged throughout the night. Police surrounded the place but were reluctant to enter for fear of causing damage to the interior of the building. They played it smart and just allowed everyone to depart peacefully the next morning.

The UBC protest later evolved into the student occupation of the administration buildings of Simon Fraser University. Students from both universities and my college were all involved in both occupations. The occupation at Simon Fraser had a very different outcome, the consequences of which I was lucky to avoid: 114 students were arrested when the Royal Canadian Mounted Police stormed the campus in November 1968. It would have been 118 arrested, except four of us had been delegated to go buy pizzas. While we were gone, the police raids happened—we ended up delivering pizzas to the jail in Burnaby.

Somehow through all this chaos and turmoil, I managed to pass my classes and complete the credits I needed to enroll at Simon Fraser University.

I decided not to go to college right away, primarily because of lack of funds. Instead, I decided to go to sea. I went down to the docks to see about getting a job on a ship, and after a few weeks, to my surprise and relief, I was hired as a deck boy on a Norwegian merchant vessel bound for the Persian Gulf and southern Africa.

My first night on the open sea, under the stars, I reveled in the moonlight dancing across the waves, the smell of the salt air, the vastness of the dark ocean all around me.

Every day there were whales and dolphins to glimpse as they surfaced and albatross to watch as they glided over the water, the tips of their wings so close yet never touching the moving swells.

I marveled at the schools of flying fish, scattered before the ship's bow, as they tried to escape from a predator below and were often snatched by a bird in the air above.

My greatest thrill was to take the wheel of the thirty-thousand-ton ship and keep her on course under the stern watch of Captain Johansson, who reprimanded me if I drifted more than a degree off course.

A month later, after a short stopover in Singapore, we pulled up to a dock in Bandar Shahpur, Iran. It was an old wooden dock in a very bad state of repair, surfaced with rotting planks that contained gaping holes.

Iran was such a different place from anywhere I had ever been before. It was uncomfortably hot and the landscape monotone: the water was beige, the land was beige and devoid of vegetation, and the sky was beige from the dust of the land.

Our ship was transporting a cargo of Canadian wheat, which took a few weeks to unload by hand with shovels and buckets. During that time I saw many ships come and go.

One day, a ship that carried an awful stink docked behind us. She was a livestock ship coming from Australia. We watched thousands of sheep being herded off the vessel and onto the dock to be run ashore.

I was appalled. A few of the sheep fell through the dock and broke their legs, and some had their eyes poked out from close contact with the horns of the rams. When the flock had passed, it had left a dozen bleeding and broken bodies lying in its wake, convulsing in pain. I watched as the Iranians walked down the dock, striking the wounded sheep with clubs, and then hauled off the bodies.

I found that this was a common shipment, and at least once a week a ship unloaded their cargo of live animals.

Because I was a seaman, I was able to visit one of the livestock ships. I saw firsthand the appalling conditions in which the sheep were kept—they were herded into tiny spaces to endure a long voyage standing or lying in their own filth. The stench was nauseating.

When I asked why the sheep were being transported live, other seamen told me that the Iranians demanded live animals so they could be ritually slaughtered. It was called halal. When I researched it, I found that the halal laws had been instituted in the Muslim religion for the purpose of alleviating the suffering of animals. And yet the suffering of the transport was horrific. It reminded me of a slave ship that I had read about in the history books. And like the slave ships, I discovered that the livestock ships left a trail of bodies in the sea from the percentage of animals that died being transported. The ship's crew told me that the losses, up to 10 percent of the animals loaded, was considered acceptable and normal.

The images of those terrified animals covered in blood and filth never left me.

Our ship carried on to Africa, where we loaded iron ore from South Africa and Mozambique bound for Japan.

In South Africa, I took the opportunity to visit Kruger National Park, where I was able to see elephants, rhinos, water buffalo, baboons, and other animals for the first time in the wild. I was fascinated yet sad that these animals, which once roamed all over the continent of Africa, were now confined to parks.

I was also a witness to apartheid. I remember returning to my ship in Durban around midnight, just as the warehouse workers were changing shifts. I was alone on a dark street as some fifty African men left the warehouse and began walking down the street toward me. Admittedly, I was concerned. These men had a legitimate reason to be angry with white people. But what they did truly astounded me. They all crossed the street without a word and without making eye contact with me. The realization struck me that they were fearful of me—not of me as a person, of course, but of offending me. Over the next few days, I saw many instances of this fear.

While in Durban I became aware of the imprisonment of Nelson Mandela. I was writing articles about my travels for the *Georgia Straight*, the alternative underground Vancouver weekly. I wrote an article about Mandela that was met with anger, as people assumed I was supporting a terrorist. Mandela was much hated in South Africa for opposing apartheid, and back then the idea that this man could one day be the president of South Africa was unthinkable and quite impossible.

Yet the impossible became possible, and years later this seeming dichotomy would be an inspiration for me: the answer to an impossible situation is to visualize and work toward an impossible solution.

In Beira, Mozambique, I was with other crewmembers in a seaman's bar called Moulin Rouge, where I was appalled to see barstools made from the feet of elephants and the walls lined with the heads of many animals, including elephants, lions, and giraffes.

As some of us were leaving the bar, a fight broke out and my group was caught in the middle trying to get out the door. One seaman used a knife to stab me in my right hand, forcing me to grab a bottle and strike him on the head to make my escape. This is the only time in my life when I've been forced to violently assault someone, but that knife was sufficient motivation and justification.

After loading up with iron ore, we set a course across the Indian Ocean and up the Pacific coast of Asia, bound for Japan. As we entered the South China Sea in mid-September, we ran straight into the teeth of Elsie, a super typhoon. It was my first major storm at sea, and I loved it. The power of the ocean was spectacular.

I took the storm as an opportunity to read the novel *Typhoon* by Joseph Conrad, and it was exhilarating to read about a typhoon while in the midst of one. It was as if I had willed the book to come to life as the ship rolled and bucked violently through a sea whipped up into a fury of froth and spray.

One of our lifeboats was torn away by the wind, and walls of water would surge over the bow and down the deck to viciously slam against the superstructure. There was an aura of real fear among some of the crew, including a few officers.

To my astonishment, I was not afraid. Instead, I was excited. The ocean was this wild and violently savage element, yet I felt strangely content to be rolling in our ship at the mercy of the wind and heaving swells. I was also lucky to be among the few crew to not suffer from seasickness. As such I was called upon to do double time at the wheel, but I did not mind. With the wheel in my hand, I felt like I was in total control of all thirty thousand tons of the ship, that I was responsible for the lives of all on board—and most importantly, I felt that I was dancing with the sea, stepping and leaning with the movements of the swells. It was exciting to see the heavy rain splash across the windows as the bow of the ship disappeared repeatedly into exploding bursts of foamy white water and salty spray.

The storm punched a hole into our bow and flooded the forward bosun's stores. I volunteered to join the crewmembers working their way forward on safety lines along the flooding deck to assess the damage. We made our way steadily, sometimes knocked to our feet by the waves of seawater surging down the decks.

When we arrived and opened the hatch, we saw dark water below as if we were looking down a well. The water rose and fell, mixed with paint from shattered paint cans and splinters of wood from the lumber stored down below. The steel ladder going down into the hatch was bent and twisted. We quickly sealed up the hatch and made our way back through the wind and the flood along the deck to deliver a damage report to the captain.

The next day, the storm was gone, and the sea was like a lake. The damage was extensive, but we discovered how lucky we had been. Apparently, another merchant ship had broken in two and was lost. Elsie killed 102 people, sent 24 individuals missing, and injured another 227. On our ship, one of the cooks had broken a finger.

We arrived in Niigata, Japan, a few days later. It was there that I got my first glimpse of Japanese whaling boats, the haunting emblems of an industry that I would battle years later.

In 1969, I returned to Vancouver after a year of serving with the Norwegian merchant marine. I arrived in Vancouver aboard the bulk carrier *Bris* in October, just in time to attend a rally on the US-Canadian border organized by the Sierra Club and the Quakers. The demonstration had been called to protest the underground testing of nuclear weapons beneath Amchitka Island in the Aleutian Islands. Thousands of people were protesting, and someone said, "Yes, but what are we going to *do* about it?"

What indeed?

People's Park

VANCOUVER, BRITISH COLUMBIA

At the beginning of 1970, I returned to school to take classes in communications at Simon Fraser University. It was there I became aware of Marshall McLuhan, whose philosophy regarding media had a great deal of influence on me. I was also getting a good media education by writing for the *Georgia Straight* and the *Yellow Journal*, both underground publications.

What I learned from McLuhan was that we live in a media culture, the media is more important than the message, the camera is the most powerful weapon on the planet, and there are just four important elements to a mainstream media story: sex, scandal, violence, and celebrity. The media, motivated by profit, manipulates every one of us every day, so surviving in a media culture requires understanding the nature of media and strategizing how to manipulate the media to serve a cause. In other words, corporations manipulate the media to sell products for profit, and politicians manipulate the media to gain power; therefore, activists need to manipulate the media to further causes.

In 1971, Bob Hunter published his book *The Storming of the Mind*, in which he described the need for "mind bombs." Today this would be referred to as going viral. Hunter was a columnist with the *Vancouver Sun*, and we met in 1971. He was the only person in Vancouver's mainstream media I had respect for—the only other media guy I respected was Walter Cronkite.

Vancouver in 1970 was a hotbed of radical activism with demonstrations, sit-ins, street theater, and a few riots. There was also a big drug scene, which did not affect me. I had never smoked anything, gotten drunk, or used drugs. If I was inclined to be addicted to anything, it was adventure and danger.

I was arrested for the first time in 1970, after I and a group of like-minded protestors organized to occupy a construction site near Stanley Park. We were opposing a plan to construct a Four Seasons hotel, which had a proposed cost of $40 million. We felt it had no place at the entrance to the city's large and beautiful park; I was also concerned that the location was a nesting area for birds. As occupiers, we renamed the site All Seasons Park, although it was being called People's Park by the media mainly because of the People's Park occupation in Berkeley, California.

I was part of the group tasked with tearing down the construction fence around the park. I was the only one in the group working as a journalist and the only one arrested and charged with willful damage to private property.

I opted for a jury trial, and well-known lawyer Peter Leask offered his services pro bono to defend me. The Four Seasons' lawyer talked about how much money it was costing the company, while I focused on the destruction of Canada geese nests and building an eyesore near the beloved park. I could see that the jury was sympathetic to my testimony while the hotel's lawyers talk about facts and figures, profits and losses was putting them to sleep.

I was acquitted.

My friend Rod Marining had taken charge of the occupation of All Seasons Park, which, because of incessant rain, came to be called Mud City. It was occupied for a year until the Vancouver government decided to have the property made into a park. It was named Devonian Harbor Park, and the government placed a plaque on the site praising the foresight of Vancouver's city council to make the park possible, neglecting to mention that without the occupation the development would have gone ahead.

For two months that summer, I was able to make good money planting trees up the coast. When I returned to the city, I was asked to attend a meeting. As a result of the 1969 border protest against nuclear testing, a group of us had started meeting at the Unitarian church on Oak Street in Vancouver to discuss ideas.

At the very first meeting, one of the Quakers remembered that in 1958 a protest boat, the thirty-foot sailing yacht *Golden Rule*, had sailed to oppose the nuclear test at Bikini Atoll in the Marshall Islands. Having just returned from sea a year earlier, I suggested we do the same. After much discussion, everyone decided that taking a boat to Amchitka to protest nuclear testing was the way to go.

But where to get the boat? And under what banner should we sail? The Sierra Club? The Quakers?

We all remembered the March 1964 earthquake in Alaska that sent a tsunami to devastate the shores of both Hawaii and British Columbia. On Vancouver Island, the town of Port Alberni was greatly damaged. So what we needed was a name that would inspire real concern about the possible consequences of the bomb.

We had named our little group the Don't Make a Wave Committee. The name was meant to invoke images of the tsunami, because the shock wave from the underground tests could cause another earthquake.

My primary concern for getting involved was the fact that the island of Amchitka was a wildlife reserve, and I felt it was ridiculous that a person could not legally bring a rifle onto the island yet the government could detonate a five-megaton bomb beneath it. A previous test had killed thousands of seals and otters from the shock waves in the sea surrounding the island.

We had a name, but now we needed a boat. Someone knew a fisherman named John Cormack, who was willing to charter his eighty-five-foot halibut seiner, the *Phyllis Cormack*, to the group. We would have to raise the money for the charter, fuel, and provisions.

All through 1970 and 1971 we worked at raising money. We organized a fundraising concert with Phil Ochs, James Taylor, and

Joni Mitchell, and I was one of many volunteers standing on the street asking for donations.

At one of our meetings, someone left the meeting early, flashed a peace sign, and said, "Peace."

Bill Darnell smiled and said, "Make it a green peace."

To which Bob Hunter responded, "Man, that's a great name for the boat."

And thus was born the name Greenpeace.

I continued to attend classes at Simon Fraser University, and I continued to attend meetings of the Don't Make a Wave Committee. Finally, in October 1971, the date was rapidly approaching for the scheduled underground nuclear test in Amchitka.

Thirteen crewmembers boarded the *Phyllis Cormack*, now known as the *Greenpeace*.

As the youngest member of the group, I was not chosen to go, to which John Cormack muttered, "So what am I going to do with a boatload of journalists, not a seaman among them?"

The group sailed north toward Amchitka, and they made it to the Aleutians where they were met and harassed by the United States Coast Guard. The US government just waited the protestors out, and after a month of bad weather the first Greenpeace mission decided to come home. However, the public was slowly getting the message that there was a protest boat trying to stop the bomb.

Meanwhile, back in Vancouver, we had organized a second boat and raised the funds thanks to the publicity the first crew had generated. This boat was not some slow-moving fishing boat. She was a recently retired Royal Canadian Navy minesweeper called the *Edgewater Fortune*.

This time I was on the crew.

We renamed the ship the *Greenpeace Too*. With the *Greenpeace* returning, the *Greenpeace Too* departed and headed north toward the Aleutian Islands. We passed the *Greenpeace*, and the two crews greeted each other briefly before we pushed on across the Gulf of Alaska toward the test site.

The publicity was growing. The US government had delayed the test to avoid a confrontation with the *Greenpeace* crew, and officials moved the test forward a few days to detonate the bomb before we could arrive. They did so when we were still a few hundred miles away from Amchitka.

We thought we had failed and sadly returned to Vancouver only to be surprised by a large crowd welcoming us home. As it turned out, that was the last test at Amchitka. We had created so much publicity that the US government decided to cancel further testing.

In 1972, we changed the name of the Don't Make a Wave Committee to the Greenpeace Foundation. We were on the crest of the emerging global environmental movement. I covered the first United Nations Conference on the Human Environment held in Stockholm that year, and I could see that ecological and animal activism would become a growing part of my future.

Eighty Days, Eighty Dollars

VANCOUVER TO VANCOUVER

Although the United States had agreed to cancel further under-ground atomic tests in Alaska, the French government continued to conduct atmospheric nuclear tests in the South Pacific.

My first task as a Greenpeace captain came in 1972, when I was twenty-one years old. I was asked to skipper the *Astral*, Bob Hunter's thirty-foot boat. Our target was the *Jeanne D'Arc*, the ten-thousand-ton French helicopter carrier that was visiting Vancouver and outfitted with six Exocet missiles and four one-hundred-millimeter guns. Our task was to protest the atmospheric nuclear tests in the South Pacific, specifically in Mururoa Atoll in French Polynesia.

"What do you want me to do, Bob?" I asked.

"We need to stop that ship," he answered.

"Well, okay, this should be a challenge," I said.

The *Jeanne D'Arc* was huge. I could see her approaching the Lions Gate Bridge as I positioned the *Astral* in the bay to block her path.

As the *Jeanne D'Arc* passed under the Lions Gate Bridge, Rod Marining was waiting on the bridge with a group of volunteers. Suddenly he dropped a long white banner, made up of dozens of bedsheets sewn together, from the bridge. On the banner, in large bold letters, were the words *Mururoa Mon Amour*.

With the banner almost touching the French warship, Rod and his team began dumping buckets of mushrooms and marshmallows, symbolizing atomic and hydrogen bombs, onto the French naval crew standing at attention on the aft helicopter deck. The sailors did not move as mushrooms and marshmallows rained softly down on their heads.

No sooner had the *Jeanne D'Arc* cleared the bridge when the crew suddenly saw a very tiny boat on a collision course with their ship. The *Astral* and the *Jeanne D'Arc* were bow to bow, with the distance closing. There were six of us aboard the *Astral*.

The *Astral* was like a mouse standing in the way of a *T. rex*.

Bob came into the wheelhouse to ask what I was doing.

"Trying to give them a scare," I said.

"Well, I don't know about them," Bob said, "but it looks pretty damn scary from here."

"Don't worry, Bob, they'll move."

The two vessels came closer toward each other, both moving slowly through the water. I had to admit, facing the huge *Jeanne D'Arc* was like facing a gray steel tsunami.

Suddenly the big warship turned a few degrees to port. I turned with her, keeping our bow directly on her bow. The *Jeanne D'Arc* turned a few degrees more to port and I followed. The two vessels edged closer until we were looking almost straight up at the anchors above us, each larger than our little boat.

We were lifted up on the bow wave and tossed aside, sliding down along the port side of the warship and trailing off into the wake. To our surprise, a few of the sailors broke rank and cheered. We had survived our game of chicken with the French navy, and they had blinked. We had kept our course and not faltered.

After that confrontation, when I was working at the *Georgia Straight*, someone made me an interesting challenge: I had just read *Around the World in Eighty Days* by Jules Verne when the *Straight*'s publisher, Dan McLeod, joked that I should do an article about it and reenact the trip.

"That's pretty easy to do today," I replied. "In 1872, it was indeed a challenge, but it's hardly a challenge today. However, I could try a new approach. How about around the world in eighty days on a dollar a day?"

So we made a bet. Dan advanced me the eighty dollars for the trip, and I would not have to pay him back if I succeeded.

I took a backpack, a sleeping bag, my passport, my seaman's book, a notebook and a pen, a Swiss Army knife, and a flashlight.

On the first day of my journey, I hitched a ride to the US border, walked across the line, and began to hitchhike south. It took me two days to reach San Francisco. Once in the Bay Area, I spent three nights sleeping on the beach near Fisherman's Wharf, going early each morning to the Scandinavian shipping offices to stand by for a position on a ship.

On the sixth day of my adventure, I was offered a job as an able seaman on the thirty-five-thousand-ton Swedish Bulk carrier *Jarl R. Trapp*. I had already spent fifty dollars on food and local transportation. Fortunately, that same day I was flown north to Portland, Oregon, to join the crew. Having to backtrack halfway to Vancouver wasn't helpful to my plans. To make matters worse, three days later—after loading grain and lumber—we sailed north to Vancouver, arriving twelve days after I had departed the same city on my quest to circle the globe.

It was another five days before we were able to depart from Vancouver. Finally, on day seventeen, the *Jarl R. Trapp* left the Strait of Juan de Fuca and made a course toward Singapore, a voyage of nine thousand nautical miles that took twenty-four days. We spent only a day in Singapore before heading out toward a port I had docked at in 1969, the Iranian port of Bandar Shahpur.

We reached Bandar Shahpur in seventeen days, which was day fifty-eight for me. I noticed that the regular shipments of sheep from Australia were still occurring, and once again I was forced to witness the misery of trampled, crippled, and blinded sheep on their way to a halal dinner. That left me with just twenty-two days to complete my quest. I collected my wages and signed off the ship two days later, and then I took a bus to Khorramshahr, Iran, where I was promptly arrested on suspicion of espionage.

With nineteen days left, I was tossed into a cell and interrogated.

Apparently, there was a disagreement between Great Britain and Iran over oil issues. The British were not welcome in the area where I had been observed taking pictures of the refineries. I said that yes, I did take pictures, but I was not British. The Iranian authorities had my passport, and one of the officers opened it, and pointed his finger at the image of a British crown and the words *British subject*.

"No, no, no," I said. I then tried to explain that I was Canadian.

In very broken English, the officer asked, "What is Canadian?" Striking the page with his index finger, he said again, more loudly, "You is British!"

I noticed that some of the officers were drinking ginger ale, which, for some reason, was quite popular in Iran at the time. It was Canada Dry brand, boasting a map of Canada on the bottle.

I pointed at the bottle and put my finger on the word *Canada* and then the map. I said, "Canada," pointing at myself to indicate that was where I was from.

Mystified, they all looked at me like I had confessed to being a genie in a bottle.

I was held for two days in an unpleasant cell, pending investigation into the question of whether Canada was a separate nation from Great Britain and to determine if I was involved with espionage. I was then deported—but not to Canada, unfortunately. Instead, I was sent to Kuwait.

I arrived in Kuwait with only sixteen days to complete my quest and just enough money to pay for a flight to Rome. With just two weeks left, my chances of success were looking very grim. I had some friends in Bari in southern Italy, so I hitched my way down south. There, I got a weeklong job in a boatyard, which paid for my train fare to London. I arrived in London with little money and only five days to get to Vancouver.

I went to Heathrow Airport, where I saw a group of American tennis players waiting to board a flight to Boston. Fortunately, this was many years before air travel was encumbered with draconian security measures. I did not even have to show a ticket to get stamped out of the country. I stood in line with the dozens of tennis players and simply walked onto the plane with them.

From Boston, I began the long hitchhiking journey up to Montreal and across Canada to Vancouver. I arrived on the eighty-third day.

I had failed to complete the challenge, but I wrote about it anyway. I did not have to pay back the eighty dollars and Dan paid me for the article.

1973

Hoka Hey

WOUNDED KNEE, SOUTH DAKOTA

In 1868, the Treaty of Fort Laramie, between the US government and the Sioux Nation, was signed. Ostensibly, the purpose of the treaty was to create peace between whites and the Sioux Nation. The treaty required the Sioux to relocate to a reservation in the Paha Sapa, the Black Hills of western South Dakota and northeastern Wyoming.

Just eight years later, the treaty was broken when gold was discovered in the Paha Sapa. In June 1876, General George Armstrong Custer invaded the sacred lands. He and his entire army of genocidal thugs were slain. I have heard this battle, in which the Indians were victorious, referred to as the *Massacre* of the Little Bighorn.

The US government's lust for both gold and revenge sealed the fate of the Sioux Nation, and they were confined to reservations under the control of the federal government. Then, in 1890, the United States Army slaughtered a band of Oglala in a place called Wounded Knee. Men, women, and children were executed with Hotchkiss guns. Historical sources refer to this mass execution as the *Battle* of Wounded Knee.

Fewer than a hundred years since Little Bighorn, the American Indian Movement (AIM) occupied the small village of Wounded Knee, South Dakota, in protest of continued injustice. The United States government responded by surrounding the village with some twenty-five hundred armed FBI agents, US Marshals, and soldiers.

My good friend David Garrick and I were in British Columbia when we read about this protest. We were longtime supporters of the First Nations and we decided right then and there to drive down to South Dakota to stand with AIM.

It was not easy. When we arrived, there was a wide circle of armed government men surrounding the village. It was March and the snow was still thick on the ground, but David and I were determined. We trudged through the snow from sixteen miles away until we reached the government lines. We tied branches in our clothing and crawled on hands and knees through the snow in the dark of a moonless night toward the flickering light of campfires in Wounded Knee.

We were afraid that we would be seen and shot. We could see a couple of large armored personnel carriers moving through the snow around us. We could hear the voices of the government men around their campfires. We could also hear and see the tracer bullets as they were fired into the darkness toward the Indians in Wounded Knee.

It took David and me more than two hours to crawl through the lines. The cold seeped through our boots and clothing, but we shivered and carried on until finally we were through the federal government's lines and able to walk into the village. We introduced ourselves to the leaders and said we had come to support them.

I spent the next three weeks as a medic, working in the makeshift hospital that Wounded Knee resistance had set up in a small log cabin.

I was also given access to the one phone line available in the village on the condition that I not mention anyone's name without permission. AIM security leader Stan Holder agreed to let me file reports to Bob Hunter at the *Vancouver Sun*.

I mentioned to Stan that it was strange that the FBI was allowing a working phone line.

"Well, of course they are listening to every word we say," he replied. With a laugh he added, "And of course they are paying the phone bill."

Food was scarce, the nights were cold and filled with rifle fire, and it was obvious that we had no chance of winning a fight against the United States government.

I spoke with Russell Means, one of the leaders in Wounded Knee, and asked him if we could win this battle. There were so many of them and so few of us.

He laughed. "Of course not. We have no hope of winning. We are here because it is the right thing to do, the just thing to do—in fact, the only thing to do. We can't worry about the odds, nor can we worry about winning or losing. We stand in the present to protest the injustices of the past for the benefit of future generations."

"But we could be killed here," I said.

Again, he smiled. "Yes, that is entirely possible, but the alternative is to do nothing."

Later, I heard Dennis Banks, one of AIM's leaders, say, "*Hoka hey.*" I asked someone nearby, "What does that mean?"

"It means 'It is a good day to die.' A warrior is always ready to die for what he believes in."

Learning the meaning of the phrase *hoka hey* was an incredible lesson for me—it led me to a deeper understanding that to fight for a cause meant having the courage to sacrifice for that cause, even one's life.

One night as I was walking down the hill in the dark from the Catholic church, I heard a bullet whistle past my ear. It was a cloudy, coal-black night, and I had felt confident that it was safe to be out walking. Later I found out that the US Marshals had star scopes. I also realized that they were deliberately shooting at anyone, with thousands of rounds being fired into the village every night.

On another night our makeshift hospital got a call on the walkie-talkies that someone had been hit. My fellow medics and I ran down the road with a stretcher. Some warriors guided us to the spot where Rocque Madrid was lying. As we ran back with him on the stretcher, bullets were striking the ground close to us.

When we got him to our hospital, Chief Crow Dog removed the bullet that had lodged between two of Rocque's ribs. Fortunately, the bullet was almost spent when it hit Rocque. I was amazed to see

Chief Crow Dog chewing on sage root as he removed the bullet. He then spat the sage root into his hand and plugged the wound with it. Over the next few days, Rocque's wound healed quite well and without any infection.

David and I participated in a sweat lodge ceremony with Wallace Black Elk. There were only a half dozen white men in Wounded Knee, and we were received with a mixture of gratitude and distrust. I do have to admit that for the Indigenous protestors, Wounded Knee represented survival while for us it was an education.

With food running low, more than forty people injured, and two Indian men killed, it was time for noncombatants like David and me to leave. There were enough provisions for only a small group to remain. AIM leader Pedro Bissonette signed our passports and designated us as citizens of the Oglala Nation of Wounded Knee. We left the way we entered, crawling on our hands and knees in the dark through enemy lines. It was more dangerous leaving because the soldiers were frustrated and angry; at one point, we buried ourselves in the snow as an armored personnel carrier rumbled by only a few yards away from us with a soldier sitting atop the vehicle, manning a machine gun.

David and I made it across some fifteen miles of grassland to the home of Dewey Brave Heart. He drove us to the border of the reservation, and from there David and I hitchhiked to Rapid City to catch a bus back home to Vancouver.

1973-1975

No Tanks, I'm Heading to Turkey

ATHENS, GREECE

After the experience at Wounded Knee, I worked for a few months for the Vancouver Park Board helping build the seawall bicycle path, after which I felt the need to take a vacation and decided to fly to Greece to visit some friends in Rhodes.

As it turned out, my timing was not so great. I landed in Athens on November 13, 1973, and decided to stay a few days at the Pensione Diana, which was only a few blocks away from the National Technical University of Athens (also known as Athens Polytechnic).

I spent a few days touring Athens, attending a student demonstration against the government, and going to the theater one night to watch *Dr. Strangelove* with Greek subtitles. I found it paradoxical that I was watching that particular movie in Athens, since at the time Greece was a dictatorship and the Stanley Kubrick film was quite political and controversial. I had seen another film a year before: the Costa-Gravas film *Z* about the rise of fascism in Greece. That film was indeed banned in Greece; but fortunately, since I'd seen it before arriving in Greece, it gave me some idea about what to expect.

What I did not expect was a tank smashing its way down the street in front of the pensione where I was staying, crushing parked cars and pointing a machine gun at anyone who stepped out on the street. A few blocks away, another tank was crashing through the gates of Athens Polytechnic.

Not one to shun a confrontation, I ran over to the university to see hundreds of students protesting. I saw Molotov cocktails being thrown and heard gunshots. Some of the students were ripping down large posters that depicted a Greek soldier on his knees praying to a bleeding Jesus Christ on the cross while long-haired hippy students threw rocks at Jesus. As they did so, club-wielding soldiers moved in and began bashing heads mercilessly. Jesus was obviously on the side of the fascists in the birthplace of democracy—at least that was the point of view of the military. While I did not see anyone being shot at the time, it was later determined that people died as a result of the conflict, including a five-year-old boy.

Later that evening, I went to the blood donor clinic. The technicians took a liter of blood, and, after identifying my blood type, asked if I could donate another liter. I said no. Apparently, my blood type—A negative—was not common. They offered to pay for the extra liter, but I was not about to let them drain me of blood for any price.

I wrote an article about the student uprising and then caught a ferry for Rhodes. Inspired by Leonard Cohen, I intended to sit on a beach and write poetry.

I spent several weeks living in an abandoned stone house on a beach outside a small town called Lindos. I made a trip into town once a week to buy bread, biscuits, ouzo, and retsina—retsina for me and ouzo to trade with shepherds in exchange for feta cheese. I also found lots of oranges to pick. I made a campfire every night and the whole arrangement was pleasant—but I was not writing poetry, despite reading plenty of Byron and Coleridge.

I spent many hours each day snorkeling in the Aegean Sea, and that pastime showed me that the mysteries beneath the water were even more tantalizing and seductive than the excitement on land.

Sitting on the beach one moonlit evening, I came to the realization that I simply did not have enough life experience to be a poet. I was also getting more and more intolerant of the political situation in Greece, where a military dictatorship was posing as a democracy.

I caught a ferry to Marmaris in Turkey and a bus to Istanbul, where I met up with fellow travelers. In my ensuing conversations with them, I discovered how difficult it was for women to travel in Turkey. So I came up with the idea to be a tour guide. I posted a sign in a popular tourist spot called the Pudding Shop and offered my services, even though my experience as a tour guide was a decidedly missing qualification. Also, I spoke only a few words of Turkish.

I did have a bus schedule and convinced a group of eight women to sign on: young women from Canada, the United States, Japan, and Norway. My role was as a protective escort—I knew that if the women were seen with me, no one would harass them. I was even able to take them into places women just did not go, like the coffee-houses (although that did raise a few macho eyebrows).

I took the women on a circuit: south down to Izmir, across into Aleppo, Syria, and back to Istanbul via Ankara in the span of two weeks. It was a nice job for about two months, with my being only twenty-two and in the constant company of many young women. But despite the obvious temptations, I kept things strictly professional.

There was not much money to be made as a tour guide, so I returned to Canada and took a job as a deckhand on the Canadian Coast Guard buoy tender CCGS *Camsell* out of Victoria. A few months later, I was transferred to the hovercraft search and rescue unit at Vancouver International Airport. It was while working in Vancouver that I got a call from my friend Robert Hunter. He asked me to meet him at the Alcazar Pub downtown—he had an idea he wanted to run by me.

Bob told me he had been approached by Paul Spong, PhD, a somewhat unconventional whale scientist who had asked him if anything could be done to save the whales.

Over a couple pints of beer, Bob and I decided to organize a Greenpeace campaign to save the whales. And that was the question he had for me.

"Well, we could intervene with small boats to block the harpooners," I suggested.

"Do you think it would work?" Bob asked.

"Hell, I don't know. Nobody has ever tried it before," I replied.

So Bob recruited John Cormack and the *Phyllis Cormack* (a.k.a. the *Greenpeace*), the same fishing boat the Don't Make a Wave Committee had taken to Amchitka in 1971. I went about organizing fundraising efforts to purchase a couple of Zodiac inflatable boats.

Not everyone was in favor of the idea. The Quaker faction wanted nothing to do with it, which was not surprising considering that historically the Quakers were notorious whale killers. This was the first schism within Greenpeace, and the Quaker "peace" contingent departed, leaving the playing field to us "green" people and allowing us to intervene—albeit nonviolently—with the industrial Goliaths of doom intent on the violent destruction of the planet.

It took a year of planning to raise the funds, secure the boats, and recruit a crew of thirteen. By March 1975, we were ready to sail. But we had one very big problem. Where on the North Pacific Ocean was the Russian whaling fleet and how were we going to find them?

We started in Vancouver, sailed up to the Queen Charlotte Islands (also known as Haida Gwaii), and then traveled down the coast until we reached Mendocino Ridge some sixty-five miles off the coast of Northern California. This was before the two-hundred-mile territorial limit was imposed by most nations, and because the Soviet whaling fleet was operating so close to the US mainland, we received some important intelligence that enabled us to locate the Russians: the coordinates were passed to us from a congressman's aide using a North Vancouver phone book as our code manual.

There has been a lot of talk over the years of our finding the fleet by consulting the *I Ching*, taking guidance from celestial bodies or the whales, or praying. The reality, however, was that we'd used precise coordinates from the US government.

Eye of the Cachalot

NORTH PACIFIC OCEAN

When we pull back the dark blue shroud of the sea and peer into the inky blackness of the mysterious world below, we cannot see, but we most certainly can hear the voice and the songs of the cachalot, or sperm whale.

There is no other living thing on this planet that can compare with this leviathan of the depths. The cachalot has the largest and one of the most complex brains of any animal—this whale is an explorer of the deep ocean, navigating at crushing depths guided by sonar and the ability to use sound as a weapon in the hunt for squid. The cachalot is without a doubt the greatest mind in the sea and, in my opinion, the greatest and most beautiful mind to have ever existed on this planet.

The cachalot was my greatest teacher, and my encounter with a dying sperm whale radically shifted my paradigm on the nature of life and intelligence, in addition to every other aspect of my life.

I am what I am and I do what I do in large part because of one fateful day in June 1975.

I was the youngest cofounder of Greenpeace, and in May 1975, I served as the first mate on the first Greenpeace voyage to protect whales. Our target was the Soviet whaling fleet. A month after our departure, we found and engaged the Russian whalers some sixty-five miles off the coast near Mendocino, California.

It was the ultimate David and Goliath encounter. Our crew of thirteen on a very slow eighty-five-foot fishing boat was sailing straight into the midst of a large, industrialized whaling fleet: the *Dalniy Vostok*, the factory ship, and four hunter-killer harpoon vessels. We were armed with only our cameras and our passion to defend the whales.

As we approached the factory ship, we came upon the floating lifeless body of a young whale marked with a flag. I scrambled onto the floating carcass to measure the body. The dark skin was warm to the touch, and I could see a harpoon shaft buried deep into the side of the whale, blood oozing out in a steady stream. My hand touched the hot blood and I felt both rising anger and helplessness.

With a harpoon vessel rapidly approaching and a high-powered hose being directed at me, I jumped back into our inflatable boat and returned to our vessel, where the crewmembers were unloading two more Zodiacs.

Without hesitation, all three boats raced toward a harpoon vessel that was in hot pursuit of a pod of eight sperm whales. Our only tactic was a page torn from Mahatma Gandhi—we would simply place our bodies between the whales and the harpoon, naively believing that the whalers would not risk killing humans to kill a whale.

Within minutes, we were in position. I was piloting a small boat with expedition leader Robert Hunter. We were flanked on each side by an inflatable boat, one with photographer Rex Weyler and the other with cameraman Fred Easton.

I had my hand on the throttle and my eyes on Bob, and we were both amazed at what we were doing. Behind us a steel-hulled harpoon vessel more than a hundred feet long was bearing down on us at full speed in very rough water, with the harpooner swiveling his cannon, trying to get a shot. In front of us, eight magnificent cachalot were fleeing for their lives. We were so close we could smell their breath, so close we could feel the spray from their blowholes on our faces, and so close that we were looking through the shimmering rainbows that the sun created each time they blew.

Stopping a Russian whaler and saving sperm whales in the North Pacific.

Each time the harpooner tried to take a shot, I would maneuver our small boat to block him. For twenty minutes we prevented him from firing. Despite our efforts, the whales could not escape; they were unable to dive because they had no time to take in enough air for a descent, and they were clearly fatigued.

I heard yelling. I turned to see the Soviet captain running forward on the catwalk. He approached the harpooner crouching behind his gun and yelled into his ear. The captain then stood up, smiled as he looked down on us, and slashed his index finger across his throat—a very clear signal that Gandhi's teaching was not going to work for us that day.

The harpoon cannon roared, the harpoon flew over our heads, and the cable slashed the water beside us as it struck. Horrified, we saw the harpoon slam into the backside of a female whale in the pod. She screamed, rolling onto her side, scarlet blood fountaining into the salty air.

Suddenly the largest whale in the pod thunderously slapped the water with his tail and dove. He turned and swam directly under us.

With a roar, he hurled himself from the surface of the sea toward the harpooner on the bow.

But the harpooner was ready—he had loaded an unattached harpoon into the cannon and as the whale rose out of the water, the gun spat that explosive-tipped arrow point-blank into the head of the whale. He screamed and fell back into the sea.

We sat there shocked in our tiny boat, dwarfed by whaling ship and whale as the cachalot rolled in agony on the surface, a scarlet stain spreading rapidly outward from his body.

And then it happened. I saw the eye of the cachalot. He saw me. I watched as a trail of bloody bubbles approached us rapidly until his head rose high out of the water, towering over us at such an angle that he merely had to descend to crush us.

As he rose from the water, a shower of brine and blood rained down on us. His head was so close I could have encircled one of his teeth in his lower jaw with my fingers. I saw my reflection in his eye, and I caught a glimmer of understanding. I felt that the whale sensed what we had tried to do.

Instead of falling forward, the dying whale forced himself back as he began to sink into the sea. I saw his eye slip beneath the surface, still looking straight at me until he disappeared into the darkening depths. He was gone.

The sun was low on the western horizon, the light was getting dim, and our little boat bobbed on the sea like an insignificant cork surrounded by the entire Russian whaling fleet.

I was in shock, horrified, angry, sad, and also relieved that I was still alive. That whale could easily have killed us but chose not to do so, and I realized that I was in debt to that amazing being for sparing my life.

But I was wrestling with more than my emotions. As the sun sank and the lights of the fleet began to sparkle over the gray water, I asked myself why. Why were the Russians killing these magnificent, beautiful, intelligent, self-aware, socially complex, sentient beings? No one hunted the cachalot for food. They were killed for the highly prized spermaceti and sperm oil in their bodies. Sperm oil is highly resistant to heat, and one of its most valued uses was for lubricating heat-producing machinery. It also provided the lubrication for inter-continental ballistic missiles. These wonderful animals were being killed for the purpose of manufacturing weapons meant for the mass extermination of human beings!

At that moment my entire perspective shifted with the realiza-tion that the human species—my species—was clearly, murderously insane. From that moment on, I said to myself that I would do every-thing I could to save whales, dolphins, and other species in the sea. I was done with the crazy concerns of humanity, with the politics, religion, economics, and trivialities of hominid primates.

And my allegiance ever since has been to the whales and to the citizens of the sea. I serve them, and I will always do so in recogni-tion that my life was spared by a cachalot. We humans are not the superior, most intelligent species that we delude ourselves into think-ing we are.

That experience was nearly fifty years ago, and I have spent nearly five decades hunting down whalers, sealers, shark-finners, and fish poachers. My greatest satisfaction is knowing that my interventions have saved the lives of thousands of whales.

When I close my eyes, I see the whales that are alive because we intervened. I see them swimming with newborn calves, I see them diving into the depths and breaching from the sea because on that day in June 1975, I looked into the eye of a being more intelligent, more compassionate, and more beautiful than any I had ever seen before and have not seen since.

I caught a glimpse of an intelligent mind in the sea that exposed humanity's anthropocentric delusions of superiority, a mind that humbled me and made me recognize that the life of a whale is equal in value to the life of a human. A life worth fighting for and worth dying for.

1976

Urban Warfare

VANCOUVER, CANADA

n the mid-1970s, I saw a help-wanted ad in a Vancouver community newsletter. Pappas Bros. Furs was having a fur auction, with fur buyers coming from around the world to purchase Canadian pelts.

I remember saying to Marilyn Kaga, my girlfriend at the time, "Wow, now this is an opportunity, a chance to sabotage the furriers and have them pay me to do it."

"What are you talking about?" she asked.

"Pappas Bros. is looking for part-time workers."

"You want to work for a fur company?"

"Absolutely. This is an opportunity I can't pass up."

So I headed downtown to Pappas Bros. I'd never set foot in the place before, so I was quite disgusted with the racks and racks of animal skins. Bears, wolves, coyotes, wolverines, beavers, muskrats, otters, raccoons, and even skunks had been killed for their pelts.

I filled out the application and sat outside an office with some other guys waiting for the interview. When my name was called, I got up, entered the office, and sat down before a small man with a mustache who looked somewhat bored with the whole process.

He looked at me and asked if I had any experience with the fur business.

I looked him in the eye and with a straight face said, "When I was a kid, I had a trapline in New Brunswick."

"What were you catching?" he asked.

"Primarily beaver. Caught them, skinned them, and sold them to support my family. My mother was a single mother with six kids, so it helped quite a lot."

He smiled. "Well, we don't need your services as a trapper. This job is primarily carrying furs from the warehouse to the tables where the buyers can look them over. Are you good at identifying pelts?"

"Absolutely, I can certainly do that."

He showed me some pictures of assorted pelts and was satisfied that I was able to identify each one.

"Great, you're hired. We will need you here on Monday at seven o'clock."

We shook hands and I left with a smile. I was not sure what I would do, but I intended to do something to sabotage this disgusting company.

As I was leaving, I pointed to two small holes in the window behind the man. "Are those bullet holes?"

"No, protestors did that with slingshots."

"Wow!" I exclaimed. "That's intense. Who would do that?"

"Animal rights fanatics—forced us to install surveillance cameras."

As I left, I thought, *Hmm, cameras. That's good to know.*

With the help of my friend Al Johnson, I had been at war with the fur industry for some time. Al was a pilot for American Airlines and a former Canadian fighter pilot, so what we were doing was much riskier for him than for me, but we were confident we would not get caught: the fur industry had plastered the city with billboards promoting fur for the whole family. In one night, driving around in Al's VW van, we took out every single one of these billboards with paint grenades, lightbulbs filled with red paint mixed with paint thinner to create runny splatters. The next morning, we drove around the city to survey our handiwork with great satisfaction—huge bloodred blotches completely defaced every one of the vile billboards.

I called the billboard company posing as a reporter to ask why all their fur billboards were covered in red paint.

"It appears some people don't like the fur industry," the man on the other end of the line said.

"Will you be replacing the damaged signs?" I asked.

"Probably not," he said.

Well, that emboldened us, and the next night we set out again: Al drove and I positioned myself in the back seat, armed with a wrist rocket and some marbles. A wrist rocket is a slingshot with a brace on the wrist, giving it more power and greater accuracy. The marbles were the perfect projectile for the mission because they shattered on impact and made a small hole in their targets and yet the shots were barely noticeable to anyone walking close by. The shattered projectile destroyed the evidence, making the damage look like a bullet hole without a bullet to be found.

The object was not to break the large windows of fur stores but to damage them enough that the stores were forced to replace them. The neat little holes did not even trigger the alarms, and we freely hit most of the stores in town until we passed one store with a stuffed lynx on display. I fired, but this time the entire large window shattered on impact, setting off the alarm.

We were out of there before the police arrived, but as we headed east on Hastings Street, cop cars passing us with their lights and sirens running, I let off a couple of shots at one more target for the night—the windows of Pappas Bros. Furs.

And now I was about to go to work for the place.

I arrived on Monday morning along with a dozen other temporary workers. The showroom was bustling with buyers from around the world. I was assigned to help two furriers from New York City. They were extremely impolite. To them I was just a gofer, and they had me fetching bales of fur from the warehouse to be brought to their table for examination.

"Bring us wolf," barked one of the men.

I spent the morning running back and forth at their bidding. If any of the pelts were not to their liking, they rudely made comments that it was my fault for not bringing them the best. They sent back a dozen bales for every one they selected. I was told to place the selected lots on a cart and return the rejects. All the wolf pelts looked quite perfect to me. It was a mystery: What were they looking for? However, I did as I was told, although when I could, I took their chosen bales back and replaced them with ones they'd rejected.

Toward the end of the first day, my big chance came. I was pushing a cart full of pelts at the back of the warehouse when I noticed a large blue dumpster half-filled with empty cardboard boxes. I quickly removed some of the boxes, tossed a couple of dozen pelts in the dumpster, and covered them back up with the boxes.

That night I went home feeling like I had accomplished a few things that would impact the profits of Pappas Bros.

The next morning was my second day at work, and I was relieved to see that the dumpster had been emptied. That morning I brought in a sharp box cutter, and each time the buyers selected a bale and asked me to place it on their cart, I made cuts on the inside of the pelts, cuts that I hoped the buyers would not notice until they returned to New York with their purchases.

I was expecting to be fired at some point. The moment came on the second day following a conversation with the buyers who were examining farm-raised fox pelts.

One of the buyers smiled and said that the advantage of the farm-raised animals was that they did not have any cuts or damage from traps or bullets.

"Really?" I asked. "How are they killed?"

One of the buyers proudly replied, "They gas them, clean and efficient."

I then asked, "You guys are Jewish, right?"

They nodded, so I said, "Well, I think you guys would sympathize with the suffering these animals are forced to endure in the gas chambers. That is how the Nazis killed six million Jews, is it not?"

I could see them becoming visibly angry. One of them said, "You can't compare the murder of human beings to animals."

I should have ended the conversation right there, but I said, "I don't think that the Nazis saw the difference. What they did was evil and immoral, and what you're doing is also evil and immoral."

That job lasted a day and a half. Pappas Bros. Furs paid me for my hours and told me to never come back.

1976

Shepherds on the Labrador Front

NEWFOUNDLAND

I n 1976, I took the position of first officer on the *Greenpeace VII* during the campaign to confront the Soviet whaling fleet a second time in the North Pacific waters north of Hawaii. I was getting increasingly frustrated that despite our protests and attempts to block the harpoons, we were not having much success in stopping the whalers.

In the summer of 1975, my colleagues and I had returned from the confrontation with the Russian whalers to San Francisco. The film of the harpoon flying over our heads was aired coast-to-coast on CBS. Americans were shocked to see Russians killing whales off the coast of California. People the world over were shocked to see that the Russian whalers were quite prepared to risk killing human beings in their efforts to kill whales. Unfortunately, our return from confronting the Soviet whalers in 1976 did not get as much attention. The media was always looking for something new, and blocking harpoons was so last year. We needed new strategies and tactics.

I returned to Vancouver with a fierce conviction to defend not only whales but also seals, sharks, turtles, and fish. Toward that end

I met with up David Garrick, my comrade during the occupation of Wounded Knee. David had served as cook on the two previous whale campaign voyages and, like me, he was a writer for the *Georgia Straight*. I approached him with the idea to defend the newborn harp seals, called whitecoats, killed every spring off the eastern coast of Canada, the very place where I was raised. When I was eight years old, I witnessed the killing of a whitecoat seal. That act of violence had troubled me for years.

David agreed with me when I asked, "How can we oppose the killing of animals by others in the world without addressing the slaughter of defenseless animals in our very own home?"

The plan I came up with to protect the seals was unusual. We would cross the country to Newfoundland and then take helicopters out a hundred miles offshore to the ice. When we reached the seals' location, we would paint them green.

Painting seals might seem peculiar. However, the idea came to me because Canadian government biologists were putting indelible dye on seal pups for their population studies. The seal pups remain helpless on the ice and are fed by their mothers for about three weeks, and during that time they have snowy white fur. The dye had no negative effects on the baby seals nor did their mothers reject them. And because the baby seals have white coats for only three weeks, the dye came off when the seals grew a new coat of hair.

The dye had another advantage: it would make the seal fur commercially worthless. Consumers wanted snow-white fur, not fur spoiled with green dye.

When the sealers found out about our plan, they were furious. Of course, that made the politicians concerned.

Joining David and me was a small group of volunteers, including American Airlines captain Al Johnson; my girlfriend, Marilyn Kaga; cameraman Ron Precious; Bob Hunter; and Patrick Moore. We traveled across Canada by train, drove through heavy snow up to northern Newfoundland, and confronted a group of sealers trying to block our way into Saint Anthony, Newfoundland. They were very hostile, banging on the sides of our van, blocking the roads, dangling nooses in front of us, and cursing and screaming nonstop. The Mounties stood by and watched.

Robert Hunter and me blocking a Norwegian sealing ship on the ice floes 200 mile off the coast of Labrador.

We ignored the sealers' threats and made it to our hotel, a boardinghouse called Decker's. Ma Decker was as nice to us as the sealers were hostile.

That night, Bob Hunter and I went to the local pub. The others were either too tired or too scared to join us. The patrons were not friendly yet not overly hostile, and we had a few cordial debates before calling it a night. When we opened the pub door, however, we were met with a raging blizzard and a complete whiteout. It took us nearly an hour to cover the quarter mile back to Decker's. We could find our way only by walking from one telephone pole to the next. When we finally opened the door to the boardinghouse, our hair and beards were dripping with icicles and our clothing was white with frost.

Our two helicopters, flying from Quebec, joined us the next day. From Saint Anthony, we traveled to deserted Belle Isle, set up a winter camp, and made ready to fly to the ice.

Unfortunately, we never got to paint the seals. The Greenpeace board of directors outvoted me. They had caved in to pressure from the politicians and ordered me not to use the green dye. All we could do was fly to the ice and block the sealers every time they tried to kill a seal.

The change of plans was frustrating, but our group came up with another idea. We could see a big Norwegian sealing ship moving through the ice, collecting the piles of pelts left by the sealers after they killed the seal pups. In the path of the red-hulled sealing ship, the *Arctic Explorer*, was a baby harp seal. Bob Hunter and I ran to him and then turned our backs on the approaching ship. The ice beneath our feet was very solid, but we could see the ship making steady progress as she broke her way through the ice toward us.

The sealing ship stopped but then began to move toward us again. I looked at Bob and we both agreed that we would not move, no matter what.

One of the sealers on the ice yelled up to the bridge. "The bastards aren't moving."

The captain on the sealing ship intended to scare us off so he kept pushing forward. He finally stopped again only about ten yards behind us, or so we thought. Our cameraman was filming, and our crewmembers were standing on one side with a couple of sealers standing on the other.

Suddenly the large ship began to move slowly forward. The ice began cracking beneath our feet. The baby seal looked up at us. Now the ice was beginning to bulge beneath us.

One of the sealers on the ice yelled toward the bridge. "Captain, they're not moving."

I felt the ice heave under my feet. I almost lost my balance. Just then the ship stopped again only three yards behind us. I picked up the baby seal and took him to safety.

We made numerous flights to the ice some one hundred miles offshore to block individual sealers. The most dangerous day of the mission was when another blizzard occurred and prevented the helicopters from reaching us on Belle Isle in order to take us back to the mainland.

We were low on supplies, especially fuel for the little stoves we used for cooking and keeping warm. The crewmembers were divided among three small tents. Fortunately, my tentmate was my girlfriend and we kept relatively warm. Patrick Moore and his wife, Eileen, were in the second tent. In the third tent, Al Johnson, Ron Precious, and David Garrick did not have the luxury of female companions, and Al decided to use jet fuel in the little stoves. We had three barrels of jet fuel outside that we were saving for the helicopters. The problem was that burning jet fuel required constant pumping and created thick soot, which quickly covered the interior walls of the tent. All three men spent the next few days coughing, and both Al Johnson and Ron Precious acquired their nicknames of Jet Johnson and Black Lung Precious.

The blizzard lasted four days, but there were a few hours when it died down, and the helicopters took the opportunity to remove us from Belle Isle. We had to leave the tents and the supplies behind and made it back to Saint Anthony just before the storm renewed with greater intensity.

When we returned to Belle Isle two days later, we discovered that our tents and supplies had been ripped away by the wind and blown out to sea. It was a close escape.

1977

Brigitte Bardot and the Media Circus

THE COAST OF LABRADOR

In the spring of 1977, I returned to defend the baby seals—this time with the intention to be more aggressive and more effective. I organized six helicopters, and we had an unexpected secret weapon.

We based our operations out of a town called Blanc-Sablon, Quebec, near the border of Labrador. Once again, we set up a forward base camp on Belle Isle.

A new law had been passed forbidding our helicopters to land within half a nautical mile of a sealing ship or a seal hunt, which meant that the helicopters had to drop us off at quite a distance from the sealing operations. Normally this would not have been a problem, but when we arrived, we could see large ocean swells moving through the ice pack. The floes were broken up and moving up, down, and sideways. It was a very daunting surprise. A reporter for *Time* magazine who had come with us refused to get out of the helicopter. "You're crazy if you think you can cross that," he said.

"We are crazy indeed," I replied, "because we intend to do exactly that."

We headed out at a run, jumping from ice floe to ice floe, watching the pans of ice smash against one another and realizing the consequences should one of us slip and fall between the heavy, grinding ice.

It was a strange experience to be running across heaving and bucking ice floes two hundred miles out to sea toward a sealing ship and a group of sealers on the ice in the distance. We passed numerous mother seals with their babies and stayed focused on reaching our goal.

The first sealer we came across was standing over a helpless seal pup, blood dripping from his gloves and smeared on his jacket. He was about to club the pup, so I rushed toward him, grabbed the club from his hand, and tossed it into the sea to be swallowed up by the moving ice.

As we moved closer to the sealing ship, we passed the skinned bodies of hundreds of seal pups and eventually came across a large pile of bloody pelts waiting to be picked up by the ship. I handcuffed myself to the bound pile of pelts to protest the slaughter and to slow down the operations. I felt safe in doing so; a helicopter carrying two Royal Canadian Mounted Police officers had just landed, and I felt confident that there would no danger of violence from the sealers while the police were present.

I was wrong.

An order came from the ship to haul in the pile of pelts. The winch line tightened, and the pile began to move across the ice. I was knocked off my feet and dragged along behind it as the handcuffs dug into my wrist. The bloody pile was hauled across the ice and into the sea, pulling me into the freezing water. The sealers dragged me through the slush alongside the ship and began to pull the pile of pelts up the side of the hull. To avoid having my arm broken, I grabbed the pelts with my other hand. Suddenly, they dropped the pile and once again I was plunged into the frigid sea. I turned and looked toward the police helicopter only to see the three police officers inside. They were simply spectators, watching this crisis play out through their sunglasses and doing nothing. They reminded me of the character Boss Godfrey in the movie *Cool Hand Luke*—cold and uncaring. They made me ashamed to be a Canadian.

I was losing sensation in my legs; the water was incredibly cold. The sealers kept me partially submerged for more than a minute, then hauled me back up into the air. The handcuffs broke, and I fell back into the sea, unable to move. Peter Ballem, one of my crew, jumped into the sea to pull me onto the ice, and that is when the Mounties stepped out of the helicopter to tell me I was under arrest for breaking the law, as I had interfered with a sealing operation. The Mounties ordered the sealing crew to strap me to a medical stretcher, and once again I was tied to the winch and hauled up the side of the ship to the deck. The crew dragged me across the bloody deck, sealers kicking me and spitting on me, before taking me below and locking me in a cabin.

Peter Ballem convinced the Mounties to let him board the ship with me. In addition to being a volunteer, he was also our lawyer.

It was a painful night. I had been exposed to subzero sea temperatures for more than ten minutes, and for hours my body felt like it was on fire as spasms of pain shot through my arms and legs.

During the night the Norwegian captain angrily entered my cabin, cursing and berating me for what I did.

"You bastards ruined our whaling, and now you want to ruin the seal fishery."

I managed to smile and say, "Seals are not fish."

This made him angrier. "My men should have killed you today."

Peter Ballem interrupted. "I would be very careful—I'm his lawyer."

His face turning red, the captain screamed, "I don't fucking care who you are. These are our seals and none of your goddamn business!"

As he turned to leave, I said, "Well, we are making it our business."

He slammed the door.

Finally, the next morning, the Mounties gave permission for one of our helicopters to land by the ship to retrieve Peter and me. Painfully I climbed into the helicopter for the two-hundred-mile flight back to Blanc-Sablon.

When we arrived, the snow was blowing in a chilly light wind. As I stepped out of the helicopter, a woman suddenly ran up to greet me with a hug and kisses. She was speaking in French, and she called me her hero. It was all quite brief and unexpected, and I had no idea who she was.

As Peter and I walked toward our car so that I could go to the hospital, I asked Bob Cummings, our media director, who that woman was.

"Brigitte Bardot."

"Really? I would love an instant replay on that."

Brigitte Bardot had flown in on a private jet to personally oppose the slaughter of the baby seals. Her presence in Canada would bring much-needed publicity to the plight of baby seals and our efforts to help them.

The Canadian government and the sealers were furious. With Bardot's arrival, our campaign instantly became international and extremely popular. The next day, I took her out to the ice where she was photographed embracing a baby seal. Within a week that photograph was gracing the cover of *Paris Match*, a widely read French news magazine. That issue brought international attention to the atrocities committed during the seal hunt. At that point, this was the most successful and largest Greenpeace campaign ever mounted.

What really impressed me about Bardot was how utterly fearless she was. We flew through a whiteout and landed on moving ice floes, and she never demonstrated a trace of concern. She underscored my view that every story needed one or more of the four basic elements of media. With her we had sex and celebrity, the violence and the danger of the campaign, and the scandal of Canadian taxpayers subsidizing this horrific mass slaughter of newborn baby harp seals.

When I returned to Vancouver after the campaign, it was not to any congratulations from the board of Greenpeace. Bob Hunter was no longer president of the board. He had been replaced by Patrick Moore, PhD, and I was criticized for using violence during the campaign.

"What violence?" I demanded.

I felt that Moore had been wanting to remove me from Greenpeace for a few years. As president he had the power, and now he had the excuse.

Bringing Brigitte Bardot to the ice floes off Labrador to help save baby seals.

"You threw a sealing club into the sea. That is a violation of our policy on nonviolence. Our job is to bear witness and not to physically interfere."

I was astounded. "That was an act of nonviolence," I said. "I saved the life of a seal by destroying a weapon meant to inflict a violent death on a sentient being. I don't respect this thing called bearing witness. It translates as cowardice to me."

Moore smiled. "No, that was the man's property, and you maliciously destroyed his property."

"Indeed I did," I replied angrily. "Violence is causing pain and death to a sentient being. You can't commit violence against an object, especially an object used to injure and kill. Destroying a weapon of destruction is to me a very nonviolent thing to do—and damn, if I am ever in the position where I must do it again, I'll do it again without hesitation."

"Not under Greenpeace's name you won't," Moore shot back.

The board voted on Moore's motion to remove me from the Greenpeace board. In response, I resigned from Greenpeace completely.

I'd gone from being a prominent Greenpeace activist to being an outcast from an organization I cofounded. I found myself alienated, disrespected, and ignored by my former comrades. Yet what I had done on the ice, complete with pictures of my being immersed in the frigid sea by the sealers, was featured in the next Greenpeace fundraising appeal letter focusing on the baby seals we saved.

I decided to start a new organization with a different strategy. I did not wish to bear witness or to protest. To me, protesting was submissive and bearing witness was cowardly. Instead I wanted to intervene to stop the killing, the destruction, and the cruelty.

I called the strategy aggressive nonviolence.

Butcher of Uganda

KENYA AND UGANDA

In 1978, I led a campaign to East Africa to investigate the ivory trade. I set up the short-lived organization Earthforce!, and this became its first mission. I was also representing *Defenders*, the magazine of the organization Defenders of Wildlife, as a contributing editor.

Accompanying me to Africa were my friends Al "Jet" Johnson, veterinarian Bruce Bunting, and veteran explorer Cliff Ward, who had recently hiked the length of the Great Rift Valley. Our objective was to collect evidence to support a bill sponsored by Democratic congressman Anthony Beilenson of California to ban the importing of ivory into the United States. This bill, eventually called the African Elephant Conservation Act, became law in 1988, a decade after our investigation. I believe some of the evidence we collected contributed to the passing of that act.

Arriving in Nairobi, Kenya, we were greeted by our old friend Gary Gallon from Vancouver, who was now heading up the United Nations Environmental Liaison Center. Gary introduced us to elephant conservationist Iain Douglas-Hamilton, DPhil, one of the world's leading authorities on African elephants. I had read all his papers, and it was an honor to meet with him. We spent a few hours jumping on his trampoline, and the next day he took us out to meet the elephants. They were awesome, beautiful, and majestic—I was awed to see them up close. We toured Tsavo East National Park and Meru National Park, met with wardens and rangers, and, when we returned to Nairobi, decided to gather evidence on the illegal ivory trade.

I got into trouble trying to learn Swahili. Sitting in the bar of a hotel near Tsavo East National Park, I noticed a picture of an elderly baboon behind the bartender. I pointed at it and innocently said, "Mzee gani mheshimiwa."

The bartender gasped and replied, "You can't say that—you can't call our president a baboon."

"What are you talking about? All I said was that guy"—I pointed at the picture of the baboon—"looks like a very honorable gentleman."

The bartender leaned in and whispered like he was afraid to be overheard, even though we were the only two people in the bar. "*Mzee* is the title for Jomo Kenyatta."

Just then Jet came into the bar. "What's up?"

"Not much," I said, "except that I linguistically stepped into some embarrassing shit. I mistakenly called the president a baboon."

"Why did you do that?"

"Well, I did not do it intentionally. I think I'll give up trying to learn Swahili."

We headed back to Nairobi the next day. We learned there was a curio shop in the middle of Nairobi. Jet, Bruce, Cliff, and I decided to go see what the shop was selling.

It was a horror show. Stools made of elephants' feet, lion and leopard pelts, ivory tusks, warthog teeth, a gorilla's hand made into an ashtray—the shop was comprised of two floors of atrocities. When we began taking pictures, all hell broke loose.

"No pictures, no pictures!" screamed a salesclerk. Three security guards came running toward us, so we complied and proceeded to walk out of the store. But one of the guards ordered us to surrender our cameras.

"Not a chance," Cliff said to them. Because he was well over six feet tall, they backed off. As I followed Cliff, another guard went into a dramatic kung fu stance to block me. He kicked at me, and I countered with a swift boot to his crotch. We then jumped into our rented Land Rover and took off down the street, feeling relieved to get away with our pictures.

Cliff, who was driving, suddenly said, "We're being followed."

I looked back at what initially seemed like a comical sight: in the car quickly catching up to us were four men brandishing clubs out of the rear windows. I recognized two as guards we'd seen at the curio shop.

Their car was faster than the Land Rover, and they rammed us from behind. They rammed a second time, causing the Land Rover to swerve off the road, through a flock of frightened chickens and into some bushes. Suddenly the four men were out of the car and banging on the Land Rover with their clubs while screaming obscenities. Things were getting out of control, and we were relieved to hear an approaching siren.

The police arrived and our assailants backed off with wild gestures, finger-pointing, and hateful stares as they made their complaint to the police.

The cops then escorted us back to the shop, where Cliff and I were taken to separate rooms to be questioned by the police along with the owner of the shop. The owner accused us of stealing, trespassing, and assault.

I listened for a while and then had to interrupt. "Wait a minute. That is not what happened."

One of the officers, a corporal, turned and snapped. "This businessman is a taxpayer. You are a nobody. You will shut your mouth."

I fell silent while the shop's owner went on with more accusations, describing us as hooligans out to ruin his business.

Again, I interrupted. "Come on now, that's a lie. We were only taking pictures."

This time the corporal glared at me; he was not amused. Cliff and I were escorted back to the street, where Jet and Bruce were waiting. We were told to get back into the Land Rover and follow the police car. We assumed we were going to the police station, but the police car turned into an alley and drove to a secluded parking lot. One of the police officers and told us to stay in our car and wait. The entire situation felt somewhat strange and ominous.

A few minutes later, a black car drove into the parking lot. Jet was instructed to walk over to the car. An officer rolled down the left rear window. The officer did not get out, so Jet leaned over to speak with him.

The officer smiled and said, "We don't want to ruin your vacation—if you make us happy, we'll make you happy."

Jet caught on quickly. "Oh, you would like some money."

"If you insist," the officer replied.

Jet asked, "Would two hundred dollars American make you happy?"

With a big grin, the officer replied, "Oh yes, that would make us very happy indeed."

And just like that, we were free to go.

After that, we were more careful and discreet. We eventually discovered warehouses where ivory was kept, and we saw trucks transporting the ivory. When we found out who owned the warehouses and the trucks, we realized that we could be in a great deal of trouble. The warehouses were owned by Margaret Kenyatta and the trucks were owned by Mama Ngina Kenyatta, the daughter and wife of Kenya president Jomo Kenyatta.

Realizing there was little we could do to halt the ivory operations if they were being run by the president's family, Jet and I decided to visit Uganda. We both had visas from the Ugandan embassy in Washington, DC, although we were concerned about the numbers on the visas. Mine was 001 and Jet's was 002. It did not appear that there were many requests for visas to visit Uganda, which was hardly surprising considering that the president was the murderous Idi Amin. We were very familiar with the horror stories arising from his dictatorship.

Jet and I boarded the Lunatic Express in Nairobi bound for Kampala. I had received permission to interview Idi Amin and, armed with the visas and the letter of permission, Jet and I found ourselves on our way westward through Kenya.

I was lost in thought about what questions to ask Amin when Jet interrupted my train of thought by pulling a .22-caliber pistol from his bag.

"Where did you get that?" I asked.

"Bought it through the black market in Nairobi," he answered rather calmly.

"And?" I asked. "Why? What for?"

"Here's the plan," he answered. "When you interview him, I'll shoot the bastard."

"What the hell?" I exclaimed. "Are you insane? We can't shoot the president of Uganda."

"Why the hell not? It's the perfect opportunity. I'll be filming you, and the gun will be in the camera case."

"Absolutely not, Jet. No way. Ain't going to happen," I said nervously. Just talking about it was crazy. "You're kidding me, right?"

"No, I'm dead serious. If you had a chance to shoot Hitler, would you not have done it? We came here to save elephants, and killing Amin may end elephant killing in Uganda, but it will also save Ugandans from this monster."

I sighed. "You just had to play the Hitler card to guilt me, didn't you?"

Jet's eyes lit up. "So you'll do it?"

"Well, aside from smuggling a gun into the presence of a fucking dictator, there is one important little detail we need to figure out," I countered.

"Which is?" Jet asked.

"Okay, we shoot him. How do we escape?"

Jet looked surprised that I would even ask the question and gave me a very serious look. "Escape? There's no escape. They will either shoot us or hang us or worse, I'm sure."

"Wonderful. I mean, that's not an attractive outcome."

"Well, no," Jet interjected, "but we can change the world. We save thousands of lives and we rid the planet of a very violent and toxic piece of crap."

"Okay, okay. I get it," I said without a great deal of enthusiasm.

We stayed quiet for the rest of the trip. I'd been reading *The Roots of Heaven* by Romain Gary prior to our conversation, but I read the same page a dozen times without reading it afterward. My mind kept rambling through the numerous possibilities of the outcome of the decision we had agreed on. There certainly was no way out that I could imagine.

Thus it was with a great deal of trepidation that we came to the border, but Idi Amin's superstitious and paranoid mind saved the day for us. The Israeli raid on Entebbe had occurred less than two years before, and I'm sure that was a factor in Uganda denying us entry because Amin was reported to be highly paranoid and suspicious of outsiders. I attempted—without an abundance of zeal, I confess—to argue that we had visas and a letter granting an audience with Amin for an interview. The border guards could not have cared less. They did not even bother to search us—thankfully. Their orders were to deny entry to foreigners, and that left us on the platform waiting for a train to take us back to Nairobi.

I had mixed feelings during the return trip, but sitting in the bar in Nairobi that evening, I felt very much relieved. Yes, Idi Amin was still alive—but so were we.

But it was not to be. The dictator eventually orchestrated his own overthrow: in 1979, Idi Amin fled Uganda when Kampala fell to enemy troops after he made the rather stupid decision to invade Tanzania in 1978, a few months after we left Africa.

Painting Baby Seals

THE GULF OF SAINT LAWRENCE

Leaving Greenpeace in 1977 meant leaving the seal campaign that I had organized and led. I needed to continue protecting the seals, but without Greenpeace resources I simply did not have the means to organize a campaign. I needed a way to get back to the ice to disrupt the sealing ships, which meant I needed a ship, but I did not have a penny to my name.

I sent off letters to various animal organizations, and one organization replied. Cleveland Amory of New York City–based Fund for Animals asked me to meet him in Los Angeles.

I borrowed five hundred dollars from my girlfriend, Starlet, flew into LA, took a bus to Beverly Hills, and met Cleveland in the coffee shop of the Beverly Hills Hotel. He did not beat around the bush.

"What can you do for the seals?" he asked.

"We must continue to hold the attention of the media and the public to keep the pressure on Canada. My plan is to go to the ice off the eastern coast of Canada and spray indelible organic dye on the baby seals. It won't hurt them, but it will destroy the commercial value of their pelts."

He looked at me very seriously and asked, "How will you get there?"

"I need a ship."

"Do you know where to get a ship?" he asked.

"I do."

"Good. Go find a ship and I'll send you the money to buy it."

I smiled. "And I will need airfare to get to Europe."

"I'll get you airfare and expenses," he said, smiling.

And with that I was off to England, where I found my first ship, a recently retired side trawler named the *Westella*. I negotiated the price down to $120,000, and Cleveland followed through and wired the money for the purchase. On December 5, 1978, I took command of the ship and renamed the vessel *Sea Shepherd*.

We were only three months away from the opening of the seal hunt. I had the ship but not the funds for outfitting and fueling the vessel for the North Atlantic crossing. For those funds, Cleveland introduced me to zoologist and veterinary surgeon Bill Jordan of the Royal Society for the Prevention of Cruelty to Animals (RSPCA).

The RSPCA donated £50 thousand to outfit and fuel the ship, and I departed from Yorkshire with a handful of volunteers and a couple of hired local Hull fishermen. We headed to Boston for final preparations, weathering the winter storms of the North Atlantic.

The drama started as soon as we reached Boston when I caught two of the hired fishermen attempting to sabotage my ship. I called the port police, they called the Boston police, the Boston police called the state police, the state police called the Coast Guard, and they all came to the old army dock in South Boston, sirens blaring and vehicles discharging dozens of officers—all because somewhere in the chain of command someone had mentioned mutiny.

That kind of attention aroused the curiosity of the local media as well, so our plans to quietly prepare the ship were scuttled. Canada would now be aware of what we were intending to do.

The lead detective for the Boston police was excited. The two crewmembers were taken away for questioning and he told me, "I'm retiring next week, and I've investigated practically every crime in the book, but this is my first mutiny case."

"Well, I don't know if it's mutiny—I caught them trying to sabotage the steering gear on the ship."

He laughed. "Oh well. Sounds like mutiny to me."

An hour later, after questioning the pair, the detective said, "The choice is yours: I can charge them and that will mean going to trial—who knows when—or I can just escort them to the airport and put them on a plane back to England."

"Probably best to take them to the airport," I said. "We have a campaign, and I can't be delayed by a trial."

Finally, with the troublemakers gone, we set to work to ready the ship. The *Sea Shepherd* would be the very first anti-sealing ship to go to the seal hunt.

On March 1, we departed Boston with a crew of thirty-two, including an RSPCA representative, Cleveland Amory, and a dozen reporters. I set a course for the Cabot Strait, the entrance to the Gulf of Saint Lawrence, where we began to push through the thick ice into the gulf.

The next evening, we had reached a three-ship sealing fleet that was being escorted by a large Canadian Coast Guard icebreaker. I wedged my ship into the pack ice and, with a crew of eight volunteers, I headed across the ice in the dark of night armed with spray cans of dye. We were determined to place a dark blue X on the backside of every white-coated baby seal we could find.

With the light of dawn, we were spotted, and two helicopters were dispatched by the Canadian Coast Guard to apprehend us under Canada's Seal Protection Regulations, a set of strange Orwellian laws that made it illegal to take photos of or film the seal hunt or to even witness a seal being killed by a sealer. Mounties and officers from the government department called Fisheries and Oceans lighted from the helicopters.

I caught the blow of a fisheries officer's club with the edge of my staff and felt a sharp pain jolt through my arms. A Mountie jabbed a pole toward my ribs, and I deflected that attack just in time to spin around and face a third officer coming at me from behind. I swung at him so hard his pole splintered and broke in two.

They had me—it was simply a matter of time. I was precariously balanced on a small pan of slope ice floating in the middle of a

ten-foot-wide lead of frigid water. On both sides, along the more
solid ice pack, stood a dozen or more Mounties and fisheries officers, armed with seal clubs and long poles, not to mention sidearms.

They were yelling angrily at me.

"Big goddamn fucking hero!" shouted Stanley Dudka, the head
fisheries officer responsible for policing the Gulf of Saint Lawrence.
"Standing in the middle of the lead! You want a medal, hero?"

"Are you going to give me one, Dudka?"

"We're going to send you away for the rest of your worthless
fucking life!" Dudka screamed. He then lunged at me with his pole,
but I brought mine down hard, dislodging the weapon from his
hands. It clattered onto the ice and rolled into the inky black water.

"You make me sick, Dudka—you and these Dudley Do-Right
types. You should be ashamed of yourselves, defending this bloody
perversion."

"You're the criminal here, asshole," he snarled back. "We're the
law."

"If you're the law, I ain't interested in the law. Take your baby-
killing laws and shove them up your ass, Dudka."

Out of the corner of my eye, I saw a flash of something dark.
Instinctively I stepped aside. A fisheries officer went hurtling by me,
only to plunge headfirst into the freezing water. He surfaced, sput-
tering and panicked, as other officers moved to pull him out and onto
the ice.

Thankfully, the lead opened and my small pan of ice moved out
of reach of the officers. In the water around my little surfboard-size
island of ice, dozens of mother seals popped their heads quizzically
out of the sea, their coal-black eyes frightened yet curious. On the
ice, a few seal pups cried and scuttled about, seeking their mothers.
Around them were bloody corpses, glaringly and obscenely scarlet
on the bluish-white ice, their sightless eyes bulging.

All of my crew had already been arrested and were sitting on the ice,
hands cuffed behind their backs. Half a mile away to the north loomed
the Canadian Coast Guard icebreaker *Wolfe*. Beyond the icebreaker,
three dark sealing ships moved freely among the seals, methodically
dispatching their club-wielding agents of cruelty and death.

The first Sea Shepherd campaign—marking baby seals with harmless organic indelible dye in the Gulf of Saint Lawrence to damage the commercial value of their pelts.

I felt overwhelmingly frustrated. Compared to the government, we had so little power. It had taken all my energy just to reach the ice, only to fall into the clutches of the Mounties and the fish cops.

On the other hand, we had accomplished our mission and embarrassed the Canadian government. We had painted baby seals—more than a thousand of them.

Only a day earlier, as the *Sea Shepherd*'s hull pushed through the ice of the Cabot Strait, it had likely seemed impossible to the Canadian government and the sealers that we could even reach the whitecoats, much less spray them with dye to render their fur commercially useless. But we had arrived. We had barged, rammed, heaved, and forced our way through the thick ice for 150 miles to reach the sealing fleet. We knew they would pounce on us in the morning. They had not expected us to cross the treacherous ice floes in the dark of night.

I thought of the first whitecoat I encountered just hours before. The pup lay calmly, looking up at me with that wide-eyed innocence that I had grown used to but always managed to melt my heart. I knelt and laid my hand on her back. The pup cried weakly, her eyes as trusting as only the eyes of a newborn can be. I sprayed indelible red dye on the snow-white backside of the baby seal. I then picked her up and gently moved her to an area between two mounds of ice, where she would not be easily seen by the sealers the next morning.

Now it was daylight, and the forces of Canadian law were trying to take me down. A Coast Guard helicopter came in closer and attempted to push me off the ice pan. I raised my pole as if to throw it like a spear into the chopper's blades. The pilot got the message and backed off.

For twenty more minutes my opponents tried to get me off the floating pan of ice. Finally, they found a way. They threw a rope across the lead, and then officers on each side of the lead simply walked forward with the rope between them to force me into the water.

The icy water sent a stinging sensation down my backside. It momentarily paralyzed me, and the officers were able to pull me alongside and onto the ice where several other officers were waiting.

As I was being pulled onto the ice, Dudka came over and kicked me hard in the groin. Grinding his boot into my hand, he growled, "Resist me, you fucking son of a bitch. Come on, resist me, and I'll kill you!"

He was still kicking me as the Mounties struggled to handcuff me. They tied my feet together; with my hands manacled behind my back, I was entirely at their mercy.

They tossed me in the back seat of the helicopter and flew me to the *Wolfe*. Once we were all on the deck, they untied my feet, and I was able to stand up. My crewmembers were all there in handcuffs, but before I could say a word a Mountie grabbed me by my hair. "You come with me."

The officers dragged me out onto the deck, where the Arctic air hit my soaked body like a knife. They threw me down on the deck and told me not to move.

Shivering and aching all over, with my hands and feet growing numb, I knew I had to get up and move. As I struggled to my feet, an officer placed his boot on my rear and shoved me back onto my knees. Each time I tried to stand, an officer would kick or push me back down. They kept me lying on that deck for more two hours, laughing and joking in French.

Finally, barely conscious, I began to bang my head on the steel deck. It hurt, but I did it again. I began to bleed.

One of the officers shook me. "What the hell do you think you're doing? Are you crazy?"

"You bastards, I know what you're doing. I intend to have some bruises for the coroner. You've killed Indians like this, you fucking thugs."

They pulled me to my feet. "Have you had enough?" a Mountie taunted, leaning over me. "Do you think you will return to the ice next year? Do you speak English?"

"No," I managed to groan. I was lying.

"Good," he said. "If you return next time, we'll kill you."

They brought me back inside, and a few hours later flew us all by helicopter to the jail on the Magdalen Islands.

For the first time, I realized that I was the enemy of my own country, a traitor to my own people. And sitting there in that bleak jail on that godforsaken windswept island, I came to a disturbing realization: I was a political prisoner.

Sinking the *Sierra*

PORTUGAL

I n 1979, of all the illegal whaling ships operating in defiance of the International Whaling Commission, the most notorious was the *Sierra*.

The *Sierra* was a catcher-factory vessel and had been slaughtering whales with no repercussions for more than ten years. She'd also been sailing under flags of convenience. Built in 1960 in the Netherlands as a fast catcher boat for a Dutch whaling fleet, she had worked with the Dutch factory ship *Willem Barendsz* in the Antarctic for four years, until the blue whale population bottomed out and the Dutch whaling industry went bankrupt. In 1967, the *Sierra* was converted at a Dutch shipyard into both a harpoon vessel and processor and was refitted with a stern slipway for hauling in whales. A huge freezing plant was installed below deck, and she became a one-ship whaling fleet registered in the Bahamas with the intent of supplying whale meat to Japan.

From 1968 to 1971, this one ship slaughtered 1,676 whales, including Bryde's whales, humpbacks, and even the rare southern right whales. In 1971, the Bahamian government revoked the ship's registration and levied a heavy fine against the owners for various violations, a fine that was never paid. In liquidation proceedings in South Africa, the ship was seized by the mortgage holder, a Norwegian bank called Forretningsbanken of Trondheim. The ship found a new owner, a company called Sierra Fishing and Trading Company that was registered in the Canary Islands and run by an entrepreneur named Andrew Behr.

In 1973, Behr reregistered his company as the Sierra Agency in South Africa and had the ship reflagged under the Somali flag. In June of that year, Behr signed a contract with Taiyo Canada Ltd., the Canadian subsidiary of Japan's Taiyo Fishery Company. The three-year agreement called for the delivery of three thousand tons of sei and Bryde's whale meat to be delivered to ports in Africa each year. Taiyo placed six Japanese experts on the ship to supervise the selection of whale meat. The *Sierra* slaughtered between four and five hundred whales each year along the coast of Angola.

The *Sierra* specialized in hunting legally protected whales, meaning critically endangered species, nursing infants, and mothers, the whales that were the easiest to find and to kill. Even among the world's outlaw whalers at the time, the *Sierra* was notorious for ruthlessness. Once, a Nigerian coastal patrol boat surprised the whalers after they had just wiped out an entire pod of whales in a bay well inside Nigerian waters. The *Sierra* aimed its harpoon gun at the patrol boat and escaped out to sea.

The *Sierra* had a clear objective: Kill the whales. Kill them all, down to the last surviving infant, and make as much profit as possible. Andrew Behr defended this policy in 1975 when he said, "There can be no doubt about the fact that whales are doomed to extinction."

In 1976, I desperately wanted to track down the *Sierra* to end her bloody campaign of violence. Greenpeace had wanted no part of it, but in 1978, with the assistance of Cleveland Amory and the Fund for Animals, I was able to purchase the British side trawler *Westella*, the ship that I renamed *Sea Shepherd*.

In June 1979, after refitting the ship in Bermuda, I took the *Sea Shepherd* to Boston to recruit a crew of volunteers. On July 1, 1979, we set off on a voyage across the North Atlantic toward Portugal.

I had very little intelligence on the location of the *Sierra*. All that I knew was that the whaler was working in an area as far north as northern Portugal and as far south as Angola. I was told it was a fool's errand, that it was impossible to find the ship in an area that large. Nonetheless, I set off with the objective of heading toward northern Portugal and then moving south.

We stopped briefly in the Azores, where I fired two crewmembers for getting drunk at a sports bar and shooting their mouths off about hunting for the *Sierra*. When they refused to leave the ship after threatening me, I marched them down the gangway at the point of a sword.

After departing the Portuguese islands, I saw a wonderful sight: a large migration of leatherback sea turtles. I made the decision to stop so that we could swim in the sea with the turtles. We swam with the leatherbacks for over an hour and then proceeded eastward toward the northern coast of Portugal.

Around noon the next day, I saw a ship on the horizon on a southerly course and decided to intercept her. As we got closer, I saw that she had the shape of a whaler. My heart raced. As we got even closer, I could see a huge *S* painted on the funnel. As we got closer still, I could read the name on the stern in bold letters: *Sierra*.

We had her. As impossible as it was, we had her. If not for the hour we had stopped to swim with the turtles, we would have missed her completely. And fortunately, we were faster.

One of my crew, Alex Pacheco, urged me to act immediately. "Let's ram the bastards now before they get away."

"I can't," I replied. "The sea is too rough, and I can't control the situation. We could get people killed. We'll chase them until we get the opportunity to disable them."

The whaler changed course due east and we chased the *Sierra* for some twenty-four hours straight into the Portuguese port of Oporto. As the *Sierra* drifted in the middle of the harbor, I decided to clear customs, always keeping an eye on the whaler.

With customs cleared, I noticed that the *Sierra* was getting ready to depart. I quickly called customs to request a clearance to leave. My request was denied. I was told I would have to wait for four hours for a clearance. It was obvious that Captain Arvid Nordengen had helpful contacts within the port authority.

I had nineteen crewmembers aboard, and I quickly called a meeting with them. "The *Sierra* is preparing to get underway. I will not let that ship escape," I declared.

I asked my chief engineer, Peter Woof, to start the main engine and then addressed the crew. "In ten minutes, I intend to cast off the lines. We will cross the harbor toward the *Sierra* with the intention of ramming full speed into the side of the ship. I can't guarantee you won't be hurt, but I'm quite certain we'll all be arrested and sent to a Portuguese jail. You are welcome to come along; if you don't want to, you have exactly ten minutes to pack your bags and get to the dock."

Most of the crewmembers just stared, not moving.

"I said, make up your mind—stay or go, but do it now."

Eighteen of the crewmembers hurried below to pack their things, leaving a lone Jerry Doran standing on the bridge. I knew Peter Woof in the engine room would be staying.

"Jerry, can you get on deck and pull in the lines?" I asked.

A few minutes later, the rest of the crew was standing on the dock. They helped let go of the lines and Jerry hauled them in. We were underway.

I telegraphed down to Peter to go full speed ahead as we moved quickly across the bay toward the *Sierra*. I needed to give them a warning.

Picking up the VHF transceiver, I said, "*Sierra, Sierra*, this is the whale protection ship *Sea Shepherd*. I intend to ram you. I repeat, I intend to ram you."

I aimed the bow toward the *Sierra*'s bow. I would deliver a warning blow with the intent to damage the harpoon.

I saw crewmembers on the deck, some staring, some laughing as we approached.

We struck. I could hear the grinding and buckling of steel plates as we shot across the bow of the whaler. As soon as the stern was clear, I made a hard turn to starboard to circle behind the *Sierra* in a wide arc that would set me up for a second impact.

I heard shots and saw Captain Nordengen standing on the bridge-wing, aiming a rifle at my ship. He was firing directly at my wheelhouse. A bullet shattered the green starboard running light.

I focused on where I wanted to strike. I knew that below deck in the area just aft of the forepeak was a refrigerated cargo space. That meant there would be no crewmembers on the other side of the portside hull.

When we struck, the *Sierra* leaned heavily to starboard. Because I had struck at a slight angle, the *Sea Shepherd* left a huge slice in the *Sierra*'s hull—six feet across and eight feet down toward the waterline—exposing the cargo of frozen whale meat within. My engines pushed us into the whaler. We were dug in at an angle.

The whaling ship fired her engine from a dead stop to full speed ahead. Thick black smoke spurted from her funnel as she moved to escape us by heading toward some Portuguese naval ships across the bay. I decided to depart from the port and headed for the harbor entrance, which would take us out to sea.

It was not long before we were being pursued by a Portuguese naval vessel. I was ordered to stop. They threatened to fire. I made the error of complying. (Later a navy officer said they would not have fired if we had not complied. It was a lesson learned from a miscalculation that I would never make again.)

Returning to the port, we passed by the *Sierra*. I was able to see the extent of the damage we had inflicted. The whalers yelled and cursed at us as we passed. Jerry, Peter, and I were escorted into an inner harbor behind a drawbridge that would prevent us from escaping. Our passports were confiscated, although we were not arrested.

The next morning, I was escorted to the port captain's office. The captain suggested that I might be charged with gross criminal negligence.

"Negligence?" I replied. "Captain, there was nothing negligent about what we did. We hit that ship precisely where we intended to hit her. It can't be negligent if it was deliberate."

The port captain laughed and said, "That may be true, but the real issue for us is that we don't know who owns the *Sierra*, and no one representing that ship has lodged a complaint."

The hunting down and ramming of the pirate whaler *Sierra* on July 16, 1979, and after repairs, sinking it in Lisbon Harbor on February 6, 1980.

Our passports were returned, and Jerry, Peter, and I made our way back to the *Sea Shepherd*, where my former crewmembers were waiting.

One of my crew approached and said, "If I'd known we would get away with it, I would have been there with you."

I smiled. "Sometimes you have to do what you have to do without fear of the consequences."

A few months later, a Portuguese judge ordered the *Sea Shepherd* turned over to the Sierra Agency. There were no charges and no trial, just a judgment that we were not allowed to appeal. I suspected the judge took a bribe to set this legal process in motion.

During the Christmas holiday, Peter Woof and I returned to Oporto, where we found that our ship had been looted while under the "care" of the Portuguese authorities.

I was not going to have my ship turned into a pirate whaler. On New Year's Eve 1979, Peter Woof and I boarded the *Sea Shepherd* and scuttled her in the harbor. We then made our escape from Portugal.

Meanwhile, the *Sierra* had been towed to Lisbon and repaired at a cost of roughly a million dollars. I heard rumors that the *Sierra* would be ready to resume whaling by the end of February.

In the dead of night on February 6, 1980, anonymous volunteers entered the black waters of the Tagus River near Lisbon to place a limpet mine under the hull of the pirate whaler. It detonated underneath the *Sierra* while the ship was alongside the dock. No one was aboard the *Sierra* as the vessel quickly sank into the mud of the riverbed. The career of the most notorious pirate whaler in the history of whaling was over.

Also in 1980, two of Spain's four whaling ships, the *Isba I* and *Isba II*, were sunk in a Spanish harbor. The sinking of these ships meant fewer whales killed, although there were still pirate whalers on the oceans that needed to be stopped.

In April of the same year the pirate whaler *Cape Fisher*, which had had its name changed name to the *Astrid*, was in the Canary Islands. My friend Al Johnson flew to Las Palmas and posted hundreds of leaflets offering $25,000 to anyone that would sink the ship. As a result, the ship's leaders could not trust their crew, and the owner made the decision to sell it to a fishing company.

And shortly after, in response to the publicity, Andrew Behr's other whaling ships—the *Susan I* and the *Theresa III*—were seized and impounded by the South African government.

In less than a year, my comrades and I had managed to shut down every single pirate whaling operation in the Atlantic Ocean— and we did so without injuring a single person.

1981

The Ides of March

PRINCE EDWARD ISLAND

Early in 1981, I managed to find and purchase a second British side trawler, the *St. Giles*, and renamed her the *Sea Shepherd II*. I moved her from Hull in Yorkshire to Greenock, Scotland, to refit and prepare her for sea. In the meantime, on the other side of the North Atlantic, the annual slaughter of baby harp seals was about to get underway, and I needed a boat to reach them.

I had just read Kenneth Brower's book *The Starship and the Canoe* about famed physicist Freeman Dyson and his son, George Dyson. Freeman had drawn up plans for a nuclear-powered space-ship, and George was a brilliant designer of kayaks. As it happened, George lived in a tree house near Vancouver and was a friend of my fellow Greenpeace cofounder Robert Hunter.

I approached George Dyson with an offer to rent one of his three-person kayaks, complete with sails. I told him I wanted to venture out from the beach of Prince Edward Island into the Gulf of Saint Lawrence to disrupt the commercial seal slaughter. He agreed to let me have one of his boats.

So, in late February, my friend Al Johnson took a month off from his job as a commercial pilot for American Airlines to accompany me on a trans-Canada road trip from Vancouver to Charlottetown with the eighteen-foot-long kayak strapped to the roof of my station wagon.

I did have one small problem. My conviction for disrupting the 1979 seal hunt was still before the highest court in Quebec, the Court of Appeal. One of the conditions placed on me by Judge Yvon Mercier was that I was banned from the six eastern Canadian provinces for three years.

My Acadian grandfather, great-grandfather, and great-great grandfather had all been born in Prince Edward Island and my own mother was buried in the province of New Brunswick, which meant I had zero respect for the judge's orders. He had also ordered me not to communicate with any journalist anywhere in the world on any subject whatsoever. I had broken that order the very day I was released from prison in Quebec and had defied the judge to charge me. He had not.

As soon as Al and I drove across the Ottawa River into Quebec, I was in contempt of the judge's order. We drove on through Quebec, through New Brunswick, and across the bridge onto Prince Edward Island, where we were met by Fund for Animals vice president Lewis (Lew) Regenstein.

The three of us drove straight to the beach to unload the kayak, but a white station wagon with British Columbia plates hauling a very large kayak in the month of March attracted attention. As we began to unload the boat, we saw two Royal Canadian Mounted Police cars approaching.

I quickly left my friends and ran down the beach and into a wooded area before the Mounties could notice me. Lying in the snow, I saw them approach Al and Lew to question them.

The police asked where I was. Both Al and Lew said they had no idea. The officers asked what they were doing with the kayak, and they replied, "Kayaking."

"In the winter with this ice?" asked an incredulous Mountie, pointing to the water that was filled with broken pans of thick ice.

Kayaking from Prince Edward Island to disrupt a commercial seal hunt.

Al smiled. "Kayaking is a winter sport—I mean, the Inuit do it all the time."

The Mounties waited for two hours, hoping I would show up. Lew and Al took the kayak out for a short trip through the open leads. When the Mounties finally left, I walked back to the beach.

There were still a couple of days before the seal hunt would begin, so Al, Lew, and I drove back to Charlottetown and booked hotel rooms for the next two days. Of course, the Mounties tracked me down, ordered me to leave the province, and told me to take the kayak with me. Lew stayed behind and Al decided to drive with me to ensure that the Mounties would not harm me, since in 1979, they had threatened to kill me if I returned.

To make sure we left town, a police escort followed us out of the province and continued to follow us into New Brunswick. We drove north to Chatham (Miramichi), and they were still on our tail.

"It looks like they intend to follow us all the way back to Ontario. We need to lose them," I said to Al.

As we left Chatham, a snowstorm broke out. I was studying the road map and saw that there was a dirt road cutting through the heart of the province toward Plaster Rock, about one hundred miles away.

"How are we on gas?" I asked Al, who was driving.

"Three-quarters full."

"Great, in three miles there is a side road just beyond a turn in the road; we can take that road. There is a good chance that in this heavy snow they won't see us turn."

There was one car in front of us, and the Mounties were trailing a quarter of a mile behind us. We saw the turnoff. Al quickly veered and shut off the headlights. After a few hundred yards, he turned off the engine to kill the brake lights. We saw the Mounties drive past the turnoff.

We then headed down a very dark and deserted road that was quickly being covered in snow. We kept to the middle of the road as we drove through the forest and falling snow. We didn't pass a single gas station or dwelling all the way to Plaster Rock.

Upon reaching Plaster Rock, we drove down to Fredericton to make a brief stop to visit Aida Flemming, the founder of the Kindness Club. Aida was eighty-five that year, but she remembered me from when I wrote to her in the early '60s. She gave us a hot meal and we continued to Toronto with another plan and another approach.

In Toronto we met up with Wayne and Madeleine Millard. Wayne and Madeleine were working on a film about the harp seals called *Hunt Without Pity*. Wayne was also a pilot and the owner of Millardair, an airplane maintenance company. Wayne and Madeleine were planning to fly back to Charlottetown in their Cessna 187 taildragger, and Al and I took them up on their offer to let us fly with them.

We flew back in the small plane to Charlottetown airport and, while Wayne and Madeleine went into the terminal to report in, Al and I slipped quietly through the terminal. Once I was outside, Al returned to the terminal to rent a car, and Wayne met up with us to transfer our bags containing Mustang Survival suits, dye sprayers, walking sticks, and a rubber raft. With that, we drove to Cavendish Beach.

The seal pups were just a few hundred yards off the beach. We took the bags to the edge of a cliff overlooking the beach and tossed them to the sand below. It was so dark I could not see the actual beach below, but our idea was to toss the gear down first and then find a way to climb down.

I waited at the top of the cliff while Al went to park the car in a safe place. As I was waiting, three cars came down the road and appeared to be searching, shining lights across the flat area between the road and the cliffs. They were going to see me if I didn't move—I had no choice. I looked down over the cliff. I could not see the bottom, but I recalled that it was about a fifteen-foot drop.

As the cars' lights swept closer, I jumped into the darkness and—although the sand was frozen solid—I managed not to injure myself as I fell.

I waited at the base of the cliff for half an hour before Al was able to join me.

"I don't know what those guys were looking for, but they're gone now," he told me when he reappeared.

We put on the Mustang Survival suits, fastened crampons on our boots, and, towing the raft, headed out across the ice toward the sound of seal pups barking for their mothers.

And there they were: beautiful, innocent, dark-eyed, two-week-old seal pups with creamy white fur, lying helpless on the ice. They were not afraid of Al or me as we sprayed red Xs on their backs with the indelible organic dye. The dye would not harm them, but it would damage the commercial value of their pelts.

We spent hours on the ice painting seal pups, jumping from ice floe to ice floe. At one point, a seal pup began to suck on the toe of my boot. I gave him a pat on the head and moved on.

We came across one pup that seemed to be marked with a bluish dye. On closer inspection, I discovered that it was a blueback, a baby hooded seal. Suddenly there was a loud roar, and a gigantic seal burst out of the water and slid onto the ice nearby. It was a male hooded seal. Unlike the timid female harp seals, male hooded seals aggressively defend their territory when females are present.

The male chased us across the ice for about a hundred yards. Then, seeing that we were no longer a threat, he halted and returned to the pup.

We had been on the ice for hours when we saw that it was slowly being pushed out to sea. We sprayed huge red letters on the ice to form the same phrase in both English and French: *Save the seals.*

We were about two miles offshore and the ice was slowly breaking up, so we spent some time paddling through slush and broken ice; occasionally we took turns getting into the frigid water to push in areas where the ice was thick.

At one point, as Al was in the water pushing, he laughed and said, "In the air force, we called this minimal thrust and strong drag."

After three hours we finally made it to the beach, still under the cover of darkness. We returned to the car and drove back to Charlottetown. Al got a room and I snuck in before anyone could identify me.

The next morning, in a provincial park, the sealers were down on the beach looking for seals to club. Wayne Millard was also there to capture some of the sealers' horrifically sadistic behavior; that is, until the Mounties arrived and arrested him for breaking the Seal Protection Regulations by filming the killing of seals without the government's permission.

The surprise of the day for the authorities happened when a fisheries helicopter spotted our message on the ice some thirteen miles offshore. The ice had retreated from the beach by about ten miles outward from the place we had been. The local TV network flew out to film our floating message and then contacted me.

The reporters asked where I was, and I said, "An undisclosed location."

"Are you on the island?"

"No comment," I replied.

"How did you get out that far to leave that message?" they asked.

I laughed and said, "We swam."

That evening after Wayne had posted bail, he contacted us to say he was flying back to Toronto and asked if we would like a lift. Al and I drove back to the airport to return the car. I slipped through a service entrance onto the runway and made my way to the plane.

Back in Toronto, I held a press conference with Wayne and Madeleine Millard to expose the atrocities Wayne had filmed on the ice. I then drove to Vancouver to return the kayak to George Dyson. After that, I flew to the Washington, DC, area where the *Sea*

Shepherd II was waiting to begin the long voyage to Soviet Siberia via the Panama Canal.

With very little funding, my crew and I were stuck in Alexandria, Virginia, until I could find a way to fuel the ship. A local yacht club near the *Sea Shepherd II*'s berth had an old tank full of diesel that we could have, although procuring it involved transporting the fuel with a bucket brigade of crew and volunteers. I also asked every crewmember to donate one thousand dollars to help pay for fuel.

When we reached the Panama Canal, I realized that we did not have funds for the canal fee. All I had was $200 and the canal fee was $2,500.

Desperate times called for desperate measures, so I took the $200 to a hotel casino in Cristóbal.

As the roulette wheel began to turn, I slapped all my cash down on black twenty-two.

As some of my crew watched the spinning wheel, the little white ball bounced into red thirty-six. Before I could even groan at the loss, the ball bounced out of red thirty-six and jumped up the side and, five spaces onward, dropped into black twenty-two for a win of $4,400.

Marc Busch cheered and said, "We gotta try that again."

"Absolutely not," I said. "We have what we need and I'm not going to risk it. But I do think we have enough for a couple of drinks at the bar."

1981

No Room for the Soviet Union

SOVIET SIBERIA

My crew and I had made it to the Bering Sea coast of Siberia. I dropped anchor two miles off the beach near the small Soviet town Lorino. What we were about to do had not been done since the days of World War II: we were going to invade the Soviet Union.

Once anchored, we lowered the Zodiac. I jumped into the boat with photographer Eric Schwartz and engineer Robert Osborn, leaving my first officer, Neil Sanderson, in command of the ship.

With my left hand on the throttle of the Mercury Marine outboard motor, I made a beeline for the shore. As we approached, I felt as if our little boat were a time machine. The buildings on the beach looked like the century-old, desolate, and remote whaling station on South Georgia Island in the South Atlantic Ocean.

As the forbidding shore loomed larger, I could make out a few people walking about; it became obvious that two of the figures on the beach were Soviet soldiers in dark green uniforms with rifles slung over their shoulders. I looked at my two shipmates.

"Well, guys, this is it. Just act like we belong here, like we do this sort of thing every day."

We reached the backwash of the gentle surf, white crushed sea-shells sluicing around us. I hit the stop button on the outboard motor and yanked up the prop so it wouldn't smash against the gritty bottom. We rode in on a small wave and skidded smoothly onto the beach.

We had landed almost four hundred feet from the whaling station. Chunks of fresh whale meat were being hacked at by distinctly Caucasian-looking women, some with blue eyes and blond hair. This discovery was our first piece of evidence: the whaling operation was, according to the Soviet Union's report to the International Whaling Commission (IWC), an Indigenous activity. We became suspicious when the kill quota had recently risen, and my hunch was that the whales were being slaughtered not for Indigenous human consumption but instead as a source of cheap meat for fur farms. The Russians had denied the IWC's requests to inspect the place.

And there they were up on the ridge: long lines of cages housing animals. I counted fifty sheds. Neither Eric, Robert, nor I could see what kind of animals were imprisoned in the cages, but we suspected fox and sable. We were well aware that not only was sable fur a monopoly of the Soviet Union but also that it was a capital offense to smuggle the animals out of the Soviet Union.

On the beach, the women were piling up dark-reddish slabs of meat and whitish blubber. I could smell the stench of slaughter. Gulls circled everywhere, dropping down frequently to pick off pieces of meat from the bloodstained concrete surface that the women were working on.

Amazingly, the women ignored us completely—they acted like we were not even there. Even more amazing was the fact that the two soldiers did not approach us or pay any attention to us. We were dressed in bright orange Mustang Survival suits and carrying cameras, yet the attitude around us was nonchalant.

Eric began snapping pictures. He captured the operations happening around the conveyor belt and secured the evidence we needed to prove that Lorino was a major commercial fur-farming facility and not an aboriginal whaling community.

As Eric took pictures, I looked up toward the town. The only thing Russian about it was a baroque Russian Orthodox church with its

Invading Soviet Siberia in August 1981 to document illegal Russian whaling operations.

broken cross and onion-shaped steeple. I was beginning to think that we could just stroll into town when Bob suddenly spoke up: "Paul, I think we're about to have some trouble. Look over there."

The two soldiers, rifles still slung over their shoulders, were walking along the beach toward us, but they still did not seem interested in us at all. They were a few hundred feet away, taking their time as they walked toward us.

Robert stepped back into the boat while Eric kept taking pictures. I noticed some children running down to the shore to see us. Out of the corner of my eye, I watched as the soldiers approached. When they were about a hundred yards away, I quietly told Eric to slowly return to the boat.

Eric waded into the water. I followed him and began to push the boat toward deeper water. Waist-deep in the water, my hands on the bow of the Zodiac, I heard a voice speaking Russian behind me. As I turned I could clearly see the red stars on their hats. They were both very young—just boys, really—and one of them had been issued a uniform at least two sizes too big. His skinny neck stuck out from the rim of his collar.

I jumped into the boat, and we motored a few hundred feet down the beach. The two soldier boys leisurely followed.

The children on the shore were loudly calling to us and we smiled back at them. The women continued to ignore us. Looking across the water, I could see my ship, the *Sea Shepherd II*, and the red flag at the stern, and it dawned on me. From a distance, our British Red Ensign looked very much like the Soviet flag. The women and the soldiers most likely thought that we were Soviet scientists.

We did not wish to suddenly flee, fearing that would arouse suspicion. More and more children were arriving. I tossed some chocolate bars onto the beach. The kids just stared at them suspiciously, as if they did not know what they were. I opened one of the bars, peeled back the packaging, and took a bite. They got the idea and eagerly snatched up the candy.

The soldiers had caught up with us. The taller one asked me something. The semester of Russian I had taken at Simon Fraser University years before now finally paid off—sort of.

The soldier called out. "Choto eta?" (What is this?)

I turned, smiled, and said, "Dosvidaniya." (Goodbye.)

The soldier did not smile. He repeated himself, this time much louder: "Choto eta?"

Still smiling, I shrugged my shoulders, noticing that he was looking at our boat. Then I answered, "Eto Zodiac." (This is the Zodiac.)

He was staring at the boat, puzzled. Then he turned toward me with wide eyes. "Nyet!" he yelled. "Eto Mercury! Eto Amerikan!" (No! It's Mercury! This is American!)

Again, I gave him a smile, which caused him to step hurriedly back and fumble for his rifle. The other soldier jerked away at once and unslung his weapon fearfully. It was easy to read their minds.

Lights had gone off and bells were ringing inside their heads as they realized that standing before them was . . . the enemy.

Their boots crushed the seashells and gravel on the beach as these two slack-jawed Russian soldiers backed up behind the nearest abandoned longboat. Intuitively they were seeking cover, almost as if they expected us to whip out six-shooters and gun them down cowboy-style. Perhaps they thought we were about to start the shoot-out at the Siberian corral.

One of the soldiers yelled at me. I couldn't understand what he was saying. He yelled again and this time I heard him more clearly: "Vy kto?" (Who are you?) He was asking who we were, which confirmed to me that they were still uncertain about us. I smiled and pointed at my ship.

Stepping into the boat, I pulled the starter for the outboard motor. The engine roared and we were about to get underway when the soldier who had been speaking quickly unslung his rifle. I turned my back on him and quietly asked Eric and Robert what he was doing.

"He's aiming his rifle at us," Eric said.

I was counting on the soldiers' being young and confused. And I reasoned that they would hesitate to shoot someone in the back when they really did not know who they were shooting at. I was also counting on the fact that they could not be superefficient soldiers if they had been relegated to patrolling a very remote beach like this.

With our boat moving slowly away from the beach, Robert, who was trying to simultaneously smile and talk through clenched teeth, said, "The first soldier has his gun pointed at us and the second soldier is unslinging his. Both soldiers now have their guns pointed at us, but they appear to be puzzled."

"Good," I said. "Keep waving, keep smiling."

Robert said nervously, "I think we should turn back and let them take us in. These guys are going to shoot any second."

"No way," I replied. "If we go back, we go to prison. We lose the evidence, and everything we've risked will be for nothing. If they shoot us, they will have an international incident on their hands."

"Do you think that'll worry the Russians?" Eric, ever the pragmatic journalist, demanded.

"No, but it's a possibility that it might worry these two guys with the guns. They don't strike me as the killing type."

"I sure as hell hope not," Robert replied. We moved farther away from the beach. When I felt sure we were out of range, I gunned the motor and sped back to our ship. I felt strangely confident that the soldiers would not fire, but a small measure of doubt sent a brief shiver up my back.

Robert was looking back with the binoculars and reported that the two soldiers were running toward the town.

"Probably to report us," said Eric.

Once back aboard, I reported to the rest of the crew that we had gotten what we came for. I had Neil send the news over the ham radio that we had secured the evidence.

The two young soldiers on the beach had not been idle. Within fifteen minutes of our return to the ship, we were overflown by two Soviet helicopter gunships. They flew in circles around us. Each green machine sported a large red star on its side, and two machine gunners were poised in the doorways on each side with their fingers on the triggers of their weapons.

My Australian second mate, Marc Busch, said, "What do we do now, mate?"

"Ignore them," I said.

A few minutes later the helicopters dropped flares on our decks. The crew scrambled to retrieve them and toss them over the side of the ship.

"Now what?" Marc asked.

"Ignore them," I repeated.

The two helicopters fired their guns across the bow of the *Sea Shepherd II*.

Again, I ignored them.

Marc reported, "There is a ship on the radar approaching us very fast."

I ran to the bridgewing, and through the binoculars it was plain to see that the ship approaching us was military. She was doing thirty knots. We were doing fifteen, and the Soviet ship was just over eight miles away.

"How far to the line, Marc? To US waters?" I asked.

"Just over twenty miles, mate. What do we do?"

"Nothing. We'll keep running, but ask Neil to relay every movement to Roy Harrison in Los Angeles." Roy was a retired policeman who had become our regular amateur radio contact.

I put the crew to work greasing the gunwales, preparing the water hoses, distributing gas masks, and raising the flags. In addition to the British Red Ensign on the stern, we were flying the Soviet courtesy flag, the United Nations flag, and the flags representing all the nationalities of the crew aboard, which included Canada, Australia, West Germany, Scotland, England, and the United States.

Eric Schwartz entered the wheelhouse. "These choppers sure look nasty," he said.

I looked at him and with a laugh asked, "Worried?"

"What, me worry?" he answered. And with a laugh and his camera, he was out the door.

It did not take long for our pursuer to catch up to us. The ship was a Soviet frigate. She was big—and she carried a big gun on her forward deck. Smaller guns protruded from her sides. Her name was Айсберг, meaning iceberg.

We could plainly see the Soviet sailors on the ships, some of them carrying automatic rifles. The frigate pulled up alongside us at a distance of approximately a hundred feet. Her captain looked down on us from his four-story-high bridge deck. I was beginning to have a few nagging doubts about whether we were going to get out of this.

The comparison between the huge frigate, the two helicopter gunships, and our old trawler was surreal. It felt like machines from two different ages were meeting in some kind of time warp. Technically we were the aliens, but the Soviet ship and those choppers looked like something out of *Star Wars*.

The Soviets raised some signal flags, ordering us to stop.

Once again Marc asked, "What do we do now?"

"How far are we from the line?"

"Just over eleven miles."

"Ignore them. Keep the present course and speed."

Marc took the wheel. Neil was in the radio room, and I declared the wheelhouse off-limits to the rest of the crew.

For ten more minutes, our two ships moved alongside each other as the two helicopter gunships continued to circle above us. The warship was ominous with her big gray bow cleaving the sea and sending showers of spray across the decks of the *Sea Shepherd II*. It was as if a daunting sea monster had surfaced and was now eyeing us hungrily.

The Soviets lowered the flags and ran up another set of flags, this time demanding that we identify ourselves.

"Ignore it," I said. "They can read."

"He's flashing a signal to us now," Marc reported. "Same message. He wants us to stop the ship."

"Really, who uses Aldis lamps these days?"

"I don't know, Captain—I think we should stop," Marc said nervously.

"Marc, if we stop this ship and let these characters aboard, this ship will be theirs, and you, me, and the rest of the crew will be on pick-and-shovel detail in the Siberian salt mines. We are not stopping."

Suddenly, the VHF radio erupted and a deep, heavily accented voice said, "*Sea Shepherd*, *Sea Shepherd*, stop your engines immediately!"

I picked up the handset reluctantly and said, "Stop killing whales."

There was a slight pause on the other end, but then the voice returned: "*Sea Shepherd*, stop your engines. Prepare to be boarded by the Soviet Union."

I answered with a chuckle. "Sorry, we do not have room for the Soviet Union."

The Soviet captain responded, sounding quite irritated. "Stop your engines now. You are in violation of the laws of the Soviet Union. You are under arrest! This is an order."

March looked at me. "Well, mate, that's that, isn't it? We have to stop now."

"Marc, the one absolute thing we are not going to do is to stop our engines. I lost one ship to the Portuguese when I stopped for them two years ago—I'm not about to lose a second."

Marc looked alarmed. "But what if he threatens to fire?"

"Then we call his bluff."

"Then what do we do if they fire?"

"Then they will have an international incident on their hands and that will surely publicize this illegal whale slaughter. They won't fire—not without higher authority. They won't fire, I'm pretty sure of that."

The Russian voice interrupted us. "*Sea Shepherd*, you are under arrest."

I answered the Russians. "You are in violation of the regulations of the International Whaling Commission. Your nation is involved in illegal whaling operations. We have already radioed this information to the United States. I do not intend to stop this ship, nor will I allow your men to board us. We do not recognize the authority of a pirate whaling nation."

The Soviet captain did not answer. Instead, he sped up and crossed our bow, playing out a thick cable with the intention of fouling our prop. We passed over it without harm.

I radioed the Soviet commander. "Captain, we have a protected prop, that tactic will not work."

The captain did not answer. He circled behind us and once again sped ahead, this time stopping his ship in front of us. If I did not stop, I would slam into his port side.

"Captain!" I yelled into the VHF radio. "Your ship is worth tens of millions of dollars. My ship, not so much. Please get out of the way or I will run into you. I have no intention of stopping. I repeat, I will not stop."

With the distance between the two ships closing, Marc did not waver—he held the wheel steady. "Jesus, Captain. We can't hit him. There will be hell to pay if we do, and I'm sure I'll never see Melbourne again."

"Marc, don't change course, not even a degree. We cannot be seen as weak. I'm not bluffing. He moves or we hit him."

I spoke into the ship's intercom system. "Stand by for a ramming. Hold tight and make sure you have your life jacket."

Things were unfolding quickly. Everything rested with that Soviet captain. He had to assume I was crazy. He had to weigh the cost of explaining a damaged ship to his superiors. He had to be aware of the responsibility he had to his crew and to the property of the Soviet government.

From the bridge I could see that there was very little water separating us from the other vessel. Finally, to our immense relief, the frigate lurched forward, allowing us to pass aft of her stern by only fifty-five yards.

I could sense that the Soviet commander was angry now. The warship circled behind us and approached our starboard side once again. With a mere sixty feet between the two ships, the Soviet sailors were whipping off the tarps of the deck guns on their port bridgewing.

I yelled down to some of my crew on the main deck. "Stand fast, keep smiling, and keep waving."

I could hear Neil communicating with Roy from the radio room. I left the wheelhouse and stepped outside onto the starboard bridgewing, where I could look across at the Russians. I could see the sailors loading an ammunition belt and then waiting for orders. This was the moment of reckoning. It appeared that they were preparing to rake our decks with .50-caliber machine-gun fire and then board us. I could see other sailors on their main deck preparing two launches. The silence over the radio was ominous. There would be no more talking.

And then a miracle occurred.

If there had been no witnesses, I would never have dared to report what happened. I'd be in the position of someone who had seen a flying saucer. Who would believe me?

There was a sudden cheer from the deck. It seemed senseless. I thought my crewmembers were flipping out. But it wasn't just my crew. The Russians had stopped their preparations. And they were pointing wildly to the water between our ships; for suddenly, without warning, the space between the two ships erupted in a shower of water. The spray obscured our view of the other ship for a moment, and then the mist dispersed in rainbow-tinted droplets. My crew continued to cheer. The Soviets looked surprised.

A large California gray whale had surfaced between the two ships and spouted. It remained for a few moments on the surface and then dove. The space between the two ships opened as the Soviets veered to starboard and Marc instinctively turned to port.

A whale—a glorious, beloved whale! Like a hand coming up from the sea between the Russians and us. I shuddered. Nobody who experienced this moment could help but feel that something mystical had just happened.

For the second time in my life, a whale had saved me.

Eric Schwartz came onto the bridge. "Christ, did you see that? It was incredible."

I didn't answer. The Russians had fallen behind. One of the helicopters turned around, and a few moments later the second one turned and followed.

Looking into the radar, Marc said, "We have land up ahead. It's Saint Lawrence Island."

I dashed into the chart room and quickly calculated our position. The Russians had stopped pursuing us when we crossed into American waters.

We who would shepherd the whales had been shepherded by a whale through the valley of the shadow of death.

1982

Samurai Conservationist

IKI ISLAND, JAPAN

After returning from my invasion of the Soviet Union, I decided to take on the horrific dolphin slaughter at Iki Island, Japan.

In late February 1978, fishermen in Nagasaki Prefecture had rounded up and cold-bloodedly massacred more than a thousand dolphins. The unsuspecting dolphins were clubbed and speared on the beaches and in the shallows. The Japanese fishermen were careless about where they thrust the spears. The gentle dolphins were wounded repeatedly by spear thrusts to their tails, heads, and other body parts. This was no display of "humane" killing. The fishermen appeared to derive sadistic pleasure from inflicting such dreadful torment on the dolphins. They were in a festive mood and unconcerned about public opinion. The spearing was accompanied by laughter and smiles directed toward the cameras of Japanese television crews. The killers displayed their barbarity to the world with all the satisfaction of a trench-coated pervert flashing his genitals. The mutilated bodies of the dolphins were finally towed out of the blood-filled bay and dumped for the sharks to feed on.

The fishermen boasted before the cameras that they had dealt with these "gangsters of the sea." They said they had slaughtered the dolphins to protect their livelihoods—in their view, the fish belonged to people, not thieving dolphin bandits.

A month later, seventy-six dolphins were clubbed to death on Tsushima Island, also located within Nagasaki Prefecture. With the fish populations drastically reduced because of overfishing and pollution, the fishermen were doing what fishermen the world over were inclined to do. They chose an innocent scapegoat to take the brunt of their anger. They denied their own culpability, and the prefecture government condoned and encouraged the butchery by offering a bounty for every dolphin slain. The bounty was described as a subsidy for countermeasures against harmful maritime mammals.

By 1980, the bounty was increased, and the dolphins' bodies were being disposed of in a huge meat grinder financed by the government. The dolphins were rendered into pig food and fertilizer. In the spring of 1980, the world outside of Japan was horrified by films and photographs illustrating the wholesale slaughter.

Bloodred waves lapped along the sandy shore. Dolphins thrashed about in pain, attempting to avoid the spears of the fishermen. Hundreds of the terrified sentient beings screamed in a language we do not understand as the killing continued, relentlessly and without pity. By late afternoon, the bay was boiling with blood and the beach was a hellish scarlet canvas splattered with obscenely mutilated bodies.

Outside of Japan, the world was enraged. But nothing was done. That changed on the last day of February 1980, when my friend Dexter Cate of Hawaii paddled a small kayak across the bay under cover of darkness to Tsushima Island. He beached his boat and quickly ran to the holding nets keeping the dolphins captive. He cut the ropes binding the nets.

The dolphins did not move; they did not swim away. The healthy and strong dolphins refused to leave the injured and weak members of their pod.

Dexter jumped into the holding pen and began to push and shove the dolphins out of the enclosure. Three hundred captive dolphins escaped and swam out to sea.

The next morning, the fishermen found Dexter sitting on the beach near the broken holding pens. He had made no attempt to escape. The angry fishermen took him to Katsumoto and turned him over to the police, who placed him under arrest.

Dexter's name became a legend on Iki Island. A year later, schoolchildren were acting out a play in which Dexter was discovered releasing the dolphins. They dramatically played out the role of indignant and morally correct fishermen beating this criminal senseless as just retribution for his interference in Japanese affairs.

Dexter spent almost three months in jail awaiting trial. At the trial he was given a six-month suspended sentence and deported back to Hawaii.

In 1981, Patrick Wall of Canada was arrested for releasing dolphins at Iki Island. He was jailed for two months and then deported. Upon his release, he joined my crew on the *Sea Shepherd II* voyage to defend the whales in Siberia.

Despite the arrests, the publicity, and the pressure from the US government, the dolphin killing mercilessly continued. In November 1981, with our mission to Soviet Siberia completed, the situation in Japan screamed out for my attention.

I officially opened my campaign to protect dolphins in Japan before the Japanese consulate in Los Angeles on December 7, the anniversary of the attack on Pearl Harbor. I wanted to address the members of the consulate when they were most sensitive. When the Japanese consul refused to meet with me, I responded by slicing the Japanese flag in half with a katana, a Japanese sword. I publicly pledged that the two pieces would be sewn back together when the dolphin massacres were over.

This action elicited a response from Mr. Watanabe of the consulate, who accused me of gross disrespect toward Japan. I replied that Japan's disrespect for the lives of the dolphins was far more egregious. I informed the consulate that I intended to sail the *Sea Shepherd II* to Japan to intervene in the dolphin slaughter at Iki Island.

My crew and I departed from Los Angeles for Honolulu in December, and by February 23, we were ready to depart from Hawaii for Iki Island, Japan. That same day, the Japanese consul in Honolulu requested that I delay my departure because he wished to give me a message from the Japanese government.

The next day, the consul contacted me to say that the Japanese government had extended an invitation to me to meet with the fishermen on Iki Island. I agreed to do so.

I flew to Japan, where I was very surprised to be met at the airport in Osaka by scores of Japanese journalists. I then took a short flight from Osaka to Fukuoka, where I met with BBC reporter Robert Friend and American filmmaker Peter Brown, who had flown in from Los Angeles to do a story for NBC's *Real People.*

The next morning turned out to be quite amusing. Peter Brown and I were both bumped from the short flight to Iki Island, the reason being that the flight had been sold out to Japanese journalists. When the reporters realized that without me on the flight they would not have story, two reporters drew the short straws and got off the plane, freeing up seats for Peter and me.

We were met at the Iki Island airport by Mr. Urase, the representative for the Nagasaki Prefecture government. Peter and I then drove in a convoy of journalists, police, and government officials to a town hall for a meeting.

As we were walking to the town hall, surrounded by police, I was approached by a man who described himself as an employee of Greenpeace from Tokyo. In broken English, he said, "Captain Watson, I am Japanese, and I think I understand the Japanese people better than you do. You should go home now and let me solve this problem. The Japanese people will stop killing dolphins only through their own efforts. You must understand this and leave this to us. You do not understand the people."

I looked at him and his Greenpeace button and replied, "I agree with you that you most probably understand the Japanese people better than I do; but then again, I don't pretend to understand them. I do, however, believe that I understand the dolphins better than you and that is the reason I am here—to save the dolphins. I am not here to argue with any Japanese person. I am here to say that killing dolphins is murder. There is no cultural excuse for murder."

Traveling to Iki Island, Japan, in 1982 to negotiate ending the dolphin slaughter.

He began to yell at me when suddenly two police officers grabbed him and escorted him to a police car and placed him in the back seat. "Our apologies, sir," the police said. "You are a guest of the government, and this man cannot be allowed to harass you."

The meeting with the fishermen began with their lecturing me on how bad dolphins were and that preserving their lives could not be justified on moral or ecological grounds.

One fisherman stood up and asked, "What is more important, the life of a dolphin or the life of a human being?"

I answered that both lives were equally important.

The fisherman scoffed and asked, "If you had to choose between saving the life of a dolphin or saving the life of an Iki Island fisherman, what choice would you make?"

Without hesitation, I answered, "I did not come here to save Japanese fishermen—I came here to save dolphins."

My answer caught them off guard. They seemed to be expecting an indication of liberal hypocrisy. I was finding that the more I stood on my principles, the more respect they gave me.

The next day, my friend Al Johnson arrived with Mina Fukuda, a Japanese flight attendant from Air France who he was dating.

She volunteered to be my interpreter. Her assistance would make my discussions with the fishermen much easier.

Some of the fishermen and police officers were both mystified and angry that Mina, a native of Nagasaki Prefecture, supported us. They tried to talk her out of her involvement.

"I love dolphins," she said, and then she walked away.

The meeting began with Mr. Urase saying, "Iki Island has already been the victim of violence as perpetuated by Mr. Dexter Cate, and we understand that Sea Shepherd is even more extreme than Mr. Cate. If we do not agree, will you also commit acts of violence against us?"

"Mr. Urase, we are indeed more extreme than Mr. Cate—very much so. I know Mr. Cate. He is a very gentle person. And he is extreme—extremely nonviolent. I am also nonviolent, but I have not hesitated to destroy violent machines. Call me whatever you wish, but we intend to disrupt your violent and murderous campaign of massacring defenseless dolphins. We will cut nets to save the lives of dolphins."

"Then it is true—you admit to being a pirate."

"Mr. Urase, if you wish to call me a pirate, then I will be a pirate. All I want is for you to understand our position on this matter."

After a few hours of debate, one thing was quite clear. The fishermen realized that we would call for a boycott of Japanese products and that we intended to sail to Japan to physically disrupt the killing.

The local mayor was clearly concerned about both a boycott and the threat of confrontations outside of his harbor. He said that it was unfortunate that the blood in the water and the screaming dolphins made it appear that the people of Iki Island were cruel. He said that there would be no killing this year and he would work to see that there would be no killing in the future.

Mina Fukuda said that the fishermen were impressed that I was straightforward about our intentions. She told me, "They understand duty, and you are defending the rights of the dolphins and are prepared to take the risks to stop the killing. One of the fishermen called you a dolphin samurai."

No more dolphins were killed in the waters around Iki Island, and we did not need to return to Japan until October 2003, that time to oppose the dolphin-killing fishermen of Taiji, a village on the main island of Honshu.

Upon my return from Iki Island, I organized a crew in Ireland to camp out on the Inishkea Islands in the Irish Sea to interfere with the killing of gray seals by Irish fishermen. They slept among the seals in the rookery and successfully kept the fishermen away. In October 1982, the government of Ireland passed legislation to ban the gray seal hunt in the Irish Sea. It was a satisfying victory.

Emboldened by this success, I sent a Sea Shepherd crew to the Shetland Islands of Scotland to disrupt fishermen's plans to kill seals. My crew kept the fishermen from landing their boats on the seal rookeries. The publicity from the confrontations helped raise enough funds for Sea Shepherd to purchase the island of Little Green Holm in the Orkney Islands. We declared it to be a permanent sanctuary for the seals.

Tree Spiking

GROUSE MOUNTAIN, BRITISH COLUMBIA, CANADA

As a child I witnessed my father break a chainsaw on a horseshoe that had been nailed to a tree a century before. Over time, the horseshoe had become the internal armor protecting the heart of the elderly and noble living being. I was secretly delighted.

In 1982, the Grouse Mountain ski resort in North Vancouver, British Columbia, announced that it was selling the timber rights to the south slope of Grouse Mountain. The decision meant that loggers would clear-cut the mountain overlooking the cities of North Vancouver and Vancouver.

The public was outraged. Despite efforts by the North Vancouver city council, petitions from schoolchildren, and appeals from prominent citizens, the resort would not relent.

In response, I organized a small cadre of concerned ecoactivists, and we formed an action group that we called the North Vancouver Garden and Arbor Club. The team included my close friends Rod Marining, David Garrick, and Al Johnson. We started out early on a Sunday morning, each of us armed with a hammer and a backpack filled with six-inch nails.

The six of us spiked some two thousand trees and pulled out every survey stake we could find. We posted warning signs that the entire slope had been randomly spiked. We then drove back to Vancouver and dropped off a media release and photos at the *Vancouver Sun* and *Province* newspapers.

The next day, the shit hit the fan—both newspapers ran front-page stories about our tree-spiking efforts. We followed up with interviews on TV stations wearing animal masks, each of us identified ourselves as spokesperson Wally Cedarleaf.

Within a day the sawmills stated flatly that they would not buy timber from the spiked lot. The deal was off. The owners of Grouse Mountain resorts were furious. We were denounced as ecoterrorists by those we thought would be allies: the North Vancouver city council, Greenpeace, Western Canada Wilderness Society, and others. Not that we gave a damn—the trees were saved, and Grouse Mountain would remain intact. The tactic had worked.

The Royal Canadian Mounted Police investigated the case, and their sleuthing led them to my doorstep. My group was questioned; we did not respond, except to point out that there was actually no law against spiking trees and that the area was open to the public, so we had not trespassed. The people in the logging industry also did not push it—they realized that if they prosecuted us, the resulting publicity over such a simple tactic would do more harm than good to their image. Tree spiking was a tactic that worked and was not illegal (although, as a result of our actions, laws were soon passed that made it illegal).

I told the Mounties that the trees belonged to the citizens who lived in the forests. The forest was home to hundreds of species, and we had no right to destroy their homes. Needless to say, they were unimpressed.

"You have no right to break the law" was all they could say.

To which I replied, "Then arrest me. But do tell me, what law have I broken? There is no law against spiking a tree, at least not yet."

"We'll be watching you," one of them said as they left.

"I'm sure you will. Come see me when the logging industry manages to pay off the politicians to make it illegal. Until then we will continue to spike every damn tree under threat by termite-minded parasites."

Prior to spiking the trees, I had consulted an arborist. I asked how to spike a tree without harming it. I then made inquiries of the logging industry while pretending to be an insurance investigator. I asked if chainsaws had safety mechanisms that would prevent the chains from breaking and striking the operators. I was assured that such an accident could not happen because all the chainsaws used chain guards to prevent a broken chain from whipping back into the face of an operator. I was also told that the sawmills required safety shields between the mill saws and the operators.

I asked, "Is it possible for a logger or a sawmill worker to be injured if the saw should strike a metallic object like a nail or a spike embedded in a log?" The answer from three different industry representatives was a definitive no.

Therefore, I concluded that tree spiking was a perfect non-violent tactic. It would not hurt the trees. It would not hurt the loggers. It was simple. Materials were easy to obtain. It was not illegal. It could not be defined as damaging property, since trees—being living creatures—cannot in my opinion be considered human property. Recognition of trees as property is an anthropocentric concept.

The most hostile criticism of my efforts came from an unexpected group. I had been writing for some time for the *Earth First!*, the newsletter for the group of the same name. Earth First! had been established by Dave Foreman, Howie Wolke, and Mike Roselle in 1980. They had been inspired by Edward Abbey's book *The Monkey Wrench Gang*. Shortly after the work of the North Vancouver Garden and Arbor Club, I met up with Mike Roselle to pass on the tactic to Earth First!

A small group within Earth First! decided that the rights of workers to make a living should become a priority over the earth. I engaged in a few debates, but in the end I decided it was not worth debating. It was a tactic that worked and did not hurt anyone. I simply described it as the inoculation of trees against a disease called clear-cutting.

Tree spiking cost the logging industry a great deal because metal detectors were required to search for spikes. The metal detectors were countered with the use of ceramic spikes, which could not be detected. Plastic spikes were also used for trees destined for pulp mills. The plastic would melt during the pulping process, damaging the equipment. Both ceramic spikes and plastic spikes were inserted after drilling a hole in the tree, and the hole was then plugged, making the procedure undetectable.

I publicly denounced the need to destroy trees to make paper. There were alternatives. In 1975, I had visited Thomas Miwa, a chemist at the Northern Regional Research Laboratory in Peoria, Illinois, part of the United States Department of Agriculture. I was there to talk to him about jojoba oil being a viable alternative to sperm whale oil, but we also discussed alternatives for making paper. There were many alternatives, such as hemp and bamboo.

According to Miwa, these alternatives were not being used because the industry had invested hundreds of millions of dollars in the machinery needed for pulping wood. "I suppose when they wipe out the trees," he said, "they will get around to using alternatives."

Paint-Bombing the Russians

THE STRAIT OF JUAN DE FUCA

The year 1982 was extremely busy for me. In March I had flown to Iki Island in Japan to successfully negotiate the end of the dolphin slaughter. In addition, Warren Rogers's book *Sea Shepherd: My Fight for Whales and Seals* was published by W. W. Norton, and the book's publicity tour took me to New York and Washington, DC, and necessitated that I speak before the National Press Club.

In April, I brought the *Sea Shepherd II* back to Seattle from Honolulu to begin preparations for the seal campaign on Canada's East Coast in March 1983. This meant I also needed to raise funds to finance the campaign. Toward this end, I decided to spend the summer swimming the length of Lake Union every day to train for a fundraising marathon swim of the Georgia Strait from Nanaimo to Vancouver, something that had never successfully been done before.

At 6:00 a.m. on September 11, *Sea Shepherd II* crewmembers Tate Landis and John Miller joined me as I dove off the pier in Nanaimo. Our goal was to swim to Jericho Beach in Vancouver. With heavy rain and swells, it was not the most ideal day for the swim. On top of the challenging weather, we were almost hit by the ferry *Queen of Oak Bay* as we swam out of Nanaimo's harbor.

My friend Al Johnson escorted us in a small rental boat. When night came, we used light sticks so Al could see us; at one point, Al had to throw us a rope and tow us out of the way of a tug and log barge. Shortly after, John Miller dropped out because of leg cramps.

We had calculated that if we left Nanaimo on an incoming tide, it would push us north up the Georgia Strait, and the outgoing tide would pull us south right into Vancouver's harbor. That plan worked almost perfectly until the next morning when we reached the entrance to the bay. We were forced to battle the tide again, spending an entire hour without making any headway.

Twenty-nine hours after we left Nanaimo, we arrived on Jericho Beach. Every muscle in my body ached, and my tongue was so swollen from the salt water I could not speak properly to the members of the media who greeted us. We had covered more than thirty-four miles because of the push and pull of the tides.

That night I was so sore that I could not sleep. Al came to me with the idea that we should act against a Soviet spy ship in the Strait of Juan de Fuca. "Canadian and American planes and ships are shadowing a spy ship at the entrance of the Strait of Juan de Fuca," he said excitedly.

"And?" I replied.

"Let's take the ship out there and confront the Soviets about their illegal whaling operations in Siberia."

It sounded like a good idea, so we returned to Seattle to prepare the ship. I mistakenly thought it would be wise to have an "objective" journalist come with us. I called a columnist for the *Seattle Times* named Erik Lacitis, who had written a positive article about us in 1979 when we had hunted down the pirate whaling ship *Sierra* off of Portugal.

The next day, Lacitis called back and said that he felt confronting the Soviet ship was a reckless idea. Not only would he not go, he told me, but he had also reported our plans to the US Coast Guard. The Coast Guard came down to our ship and advised me not to take any action against the Soviet ship. They also informed me that they were not going to give me clearance to depart Seattle.

Al and I got together with my chief engineer, Carroll Vogel, to discuss an alternative approach. The Soviet ship was the twenty-six-hundred-ton *Gavril Sarychev*. She was thirty miles off the mouth of the Strait of Juan de Fuca, on the border between the United States and Canada. The ship and her fifty-man crew were being closely watched by the HMCS *Saskatchewan* and was also under observation by long-range Lockheed Aurora tracker planes out of the Royal Canadian Air Force base in Comox. The *Gavril Sarychev* was attempting to spy on the sea trials of the Ohio class nuclear-powered submarine out of Bangor Base, Washington. The Soviet ship was bristling with electronic listening devices, but she was in a position where neither Canada nor the United States could legally force her to leave.

Al came up with an idea. "We can charter a plane in Canada and fly out and over the ship in the Pacific."

"We could get pictures, but that's about it," I said.

Carroll, however, had an alternative idea. "Let's bomb it."

Al and I both laughed nervously. "Carroll, we can't bomb a ship," I said.

"Well, not with actual bombs. We can drop protest messages onto their deck, and we can do it dramatically—in a way the Russians will notice. You guys go back to Canada and arrange for the plane. I'll take care of what we need to deliver the messages."

Al and I returned to Vancouver. We located a plane, a blue-and-white Cessna 187 taildragger we could rent from Altair Aviation in Pitt Meadows. Al, being a professional American Airlines pilot, had no problem securing the rental.

The next morning, Carroll met us at the Pitt Meadows airport with a couple of boxes. In each box were sixteen large light bulbs. Fifteen of them were filled with red paint and one was filled with yellow paint.

"What I have here," explained Carroll, "are sixteen industrial-size light bulbs. Each is filled with paint, so that we can see where it hits. The yellow one is a marker. Each bulb is attached to a string, and the string is attached to a small envelope containing a message in Russian that says, 'Stop illegally killing whales in Siberia.'"

"So *these* are your bombs! Great idea," I said.

"Al will be the pilot and you and I will be the bombardiers," Carroll replied.

Carroll and I loaded the bulbs into the back seat of the aircraft, took our seats, put on the earphones so we could communicate, and waited for Al to finish his preflight checklist.

We took off and flew over the Fraser River, across the Georgia Strait, over Victoria, and down the Strait of Juan de Fuca.

"I have the ship in sight," Al said over the plane's intercom.

Ahead of us was the *Gavril Sarychev*. She was flanked by two Canadian naval vessels on one side and two American vessels on the other. I assumed that the navies had no idea what we were doing, but they certainly took notice as we circled low over the Soviet vessel.

Al's voice crackled through the headsets: "Let's get to it."

Al brought the plane into a position heading straight and low and aimed at the ship's bridge. We looked to be on a collision course. I trusted Al's aviation skills absolutely, but both Carroll and I were nervous as we prepared our paint bombs for the drop.

We opened the plane's side windows and readied ourselves as the plane flew only a few yards above the bow of the ship. As soon as we saw the deck below, we dropped the light bulbs. We watched the paint bombs fall and crash onto the ship's deck.

Within seconds, Al pulled up to avoid a collision with the bridge. We'd cleared the *Gavril Sarychev* beautifully, when suddenly there was a loud clank and the plane dove at an angle toward the water. I was sure we were going to crash. Carroll and I were helpless, but we could see Al looking quite calm as he recovered the plane and began to gain altitude from only a few yards above the water.

"What the hell was that?" I yelled.

"I have no idea," replied Al. "They might have shot at us."

Looking back, we could see sailors on the aft deck. To our delight, we also saw numerous red blotches and one yellow blotch on the ship's main deck.

"I think we scored all sixteen hits," Carroll said excitedly.

"Wonderful," said Al, "but now we have another problem. There are two fighter planes heading for us from the southeast, and they are coming fast."

Al pulled the plane into a steep ascent. Carroll and I could see the two US fighter planes in the distance, heading straight for us.

"What do you think they intend to do?" I asked Al nervously.

"My guess is that they intend to shoot us down for attacking the Soviet ship. They could take it as an act of war, I suppose," Al said calmly. "But don't worry—I've got this."

The Cessna climbed thousands of feet into the air and suddenly, with the fighter jets closing in, Al put the plane into a steep dive, angling to the north—a move that quickly brought us safely back into Canadian airspace.

"I doubt Canada has anything to shoot us down with. The Yanks came out of the Whidbey base in Washington State," he said.

Carroll and I watched the fighter planes, still at a safe distance, turn to overfly the Soviet ship and the Canadian and US escort vessels.

We were unsure if the Cessna's wheels had been damaged, so Al brought the plane in carefully, keeping the nose up as we touched down. We were relieved when the front wheels landed gently on the runway at Pitt Meadows.

We were expecting to be met by the police, but they did not show. A quick inspection of the plane revealed a four-inch gash in the right wing.

"What could have caused that?" I asked.

Al looked at it closely. "It appears that we may have struck a whip antenna on the top of the *Gavril Sarychev*'s wheelhouse."

"That could have sliced off the wing," said Carroll.

Al said, "That was a possibility, but we made it back safely."

As Carroll and I walked back to the small terminal, he asked me if Al was always so calm about things like that.

"I think so," I answered. "He once crashed a Sabre jet off the end of a runway in New Brunswick. Totaled the thing but got away with just a broken ankle. He once told me that the crash should have killed him, and he hasn't felt any fear of anything since."

We retrieved the car and picked up Al from the rental office.

"What did they say about the damage to the plane?" I asked.

"Nothing," he replied with a smile.

"Really?" I responded. "I'm amazed."

"Well, I didn't tell them."

Although Al was the pilot, I was the one arrested for organizing the paint-bombing venture. I was charged with vandalism and destruction of private property.

My lawyer argued that the lower court could not try the case because there were no witnesses, the crew of the Soviet ship was not able to testify, and the only evidence was that I had admitted to leading the campaign. Carroll was a US citizen, so he wasn't charged.

The judge said that the fact that I admitted to paint-bombing the ship, despite pleading not guilty, was enough for him to proceed. My lawyer decided to file a petition to the Supreme Court of Canada in Ottawa. After many months, the Supreme Court decided that the trial could proceed in the lower court.

On the day the trial was scheduled, I found myself before a new judge. She asked where the witnesses were. When she was told they were Soviet citizens and unable to attend the trial, she tossed out the case out. I was free to go.

1983

Monkey Business in Grenada

GRENADA, WEST INDIES

I n January 1983, my crew and I transited the Panama Canal for the second time, and I brought the *Sea Shepherd II* into Grenada. It was to be a brief stop enroute to disrupt the slaughter of seals in Canada's Gulf of Saint Lawrence. I had agreed to take a shipment of medical gear, books, and agricultural tools to Grenada on behalf of Oxfam.

I was not enthusiastic about doing humanitarian relief work. It often involved politics and bureaucracy, which were annoying to deal with. My second officer, Bobby David, had urged me to do it and I'd agreed.

The opposition began even before we could load the supplies. The fishermen's union in British Columbia was part of the coalition providing the supplies, and the group took exception to its items being transported by a ship that was involved in opposing the Canadian sealing industry.

At a meeting with the fishermen's union, I replied that the group's objection was fine with me. This was not my idea and I was not being paid. I told the group that I had thought our assistance would be appreciated, but apparently it wasn't. I got up and left the meeting.

The next day, an Oxfam representative called me to apologize and asked me to reconsider. I did, and we departed Vancouver with the supplies—only to encounter the bureaucrats at the Panama Canal, who wanted to know what was in our hold. I responded that we were carrying personal effects and ship supplies. Fortunately, they did not look, and we set off across the Caribbean for Grenada.

Reaching the Spice Isle, we entered Saint George's harbor and dropped the anchor. I went ashore to meet with the harbormaster to see about discharging our cargo of relief supplies. I was naively confident that the authorities would not give us a hard time. After all, we came bearing gifts.

"Who is your agent here in Grenada?" asked the harbormaster.

"We don't have an agent; our ship is registered as a yacht."

The harbormaster looked annoyed. "All cargo vessels are required by regulations to have an agent."

"We don't have cargo in a commercial sense; we have goods that have been donated to Grenada by Canadians sympathetic to your revolution. Your minister of agriculture is aware of these goods and has been waiting to receive them."

The harbormaster was not impressed. "The minister of agriculture is of little concern to me. I need to know how you will be paying the tonnage tax."

I looked at him angrily. "Tonnage tax! For Chrissakes, we are bringing in materials that have been contributed to Grenada and you want to tax us to unload the stuff we are bringing to you free of charge?"

"That is correct—the regulations say you must pay tonnage tax."

I looked at him for a moment and then said, "If you think I'm going to pay money to a petty, tight-assed bureaucrat like yourself, you are very much mistaken."

"Someone must pay it, or the cargo cannot be discharged," mumbled the harbormaster.

"Look," I said, "I'm going back to my ship, and I will wait there for an hour. If I am not given a berth to discharge this cargo and if the tonnage tax is not waived, I will unload the entire cargo into the middle of the harbor, and you can tell the minister of agriculture that he needs to swim out and get it. You can pick up that phone and call the minister—or the prime minister for all I care—but I want that damn cargo off my ship."

An hour later, I received a message from the harbormaster to bring my ship alongside the dock to discharge the cargo.

After that, the authorities gave us a grudging welcome. There was no official thanks. The local media and the people of Saint George's were much more appreciative and friendly, and we stayed a week to rest up before heading north.

At the time, the Reagan administration was claiming that Cuba was attempting to take over Grenada. I did see a couple of Cubans supervising some construction projects, but I myself never saw any Cuban soldiers.

According to reports in the American media and from the White House, the Cubans were building a military airport on the island that would allow Soviet aircraft to come and go. Warehouses were supposedly stockpiled with weapons, and Cuban soldiers were supposedly terrorizing the citizens and abusing the Americans attending medical school on the island.

My crew and I saw none of that. In fact, some of us had hiked over to where the supposed fighter base was being built. The workers there were friendly and made no attempt to restrict our access. They told us that the construction was for a new commercial airport, which, they said, was sorely needed.

My crew and I did pull off our own covert raid while we were in Grenada. Our task was a hostage-saving mission and our target was the Saint George's zoo. It was a deplorable place. During our daytime inspection, we noticed that the monkeys were being horribly mistreated. It was sickening to see people making fun of them as they threw stones and sticks at them. The cages were dirty, and monkeys' fur was matted.

Some of my crewmembers pleaded with me to do something about it.

"Not sure what we can do about it," I replied.

One of my crew suggested that maybe we could release them. There was a jungle nearby.

I thought about it and decided it was worth trying.

We traded some Canadian beer for some sedatives from a couple of American medical students. We did not tell them what the sedatives were for, just that we needed some on the ship.

That night, I sent four of my crew over the outside wall of the zoo. They then picked the locks on the monkeys' cages. I was monitoring their movements on the VHF radio on an obscure channel. Picking the locks was simple. Suddenly I heard loud screeching and screaming over the radio. I was surprised no one was alerted. Apparently, the zoo had zero security.

Despite the hysterics of the monkeys, my crew managed to inject each one of the little ingrates with the sedatives. The cacophony died down, scream by scream.

The sleeping monkeys were then loaded into the trunk of a car we had rented and driven into the jungle near the center of the island.

When the trunk was opened, the monkeys began to wake up. They blinked, staggered drunkenly into the surrounding greenery, and were soon out of sight.

The mission was a complete success. We quickly left the island the next morning, before the monkey caper could come back to haunt us.

We were pretty sure the monkeys would be able to cope in the jungle of Grenada, free from abuse and the deplorable conditions of the zoo. However, I was criticized by some conservation groups, who accused me of releasing an exotic species into an island ecosystem.

I responded by saying we had not brought the monkeys to Grenada, and we were not going to stand by and watch them suffer without intervening. Besides, I said, these primates could not possibly do more damage than the *Homo sapiens* had already done to the island's ecosystem.

1983

Blockade

VANCOUVER ISLAND TO NEWFOUNDLAND

Returning to Hawaii, I brought the *Sea Shepherd II* back to Vancouver to prepare the ship for another long voyage: this time from Vancouver, back through the Panama Canal with a stop in Grenada, and on to Portland, Maine, as the jumping-off point for a return to the ice floes off Newfoundland to defend baby seals.

My crew and I departed from Portland at the end of the first week of March and headed toward the harbor entrance of Saint John's, Newfoundland. Our objective was to blockade the Newfoundland sealing fleet inside the harbor.

It was an audaciously bold plan, and it took the sealers and the government completely by surprise. We prevented the entire fleet from departing for more than a week. I told the port that if anyone tried to force us away, we would scuttle the ship in the narrows to permanently close the port.

A large Canadian Coast Guard icebreaker arrived to demand that we remove ourselves from blocking the harbor entrance. Unfortunately, we had to move. A strong northeasterly was blowing and pushing heavy ice toward the shore. Such a wind with ice conditions could force our ship onto the rocks. I headed seaward with the ice-breaker in pursuit. We made it out fourteen nautical miles before the ice brought us to a halt. The Coast Guard ship stopped two miles to the west of our position.

Both ships became tightly frozen in the pressure of the surrounding concrete-hard ice. The *Sea Shepherd II* was lifted by the ice, and we keeled over at twenty-two degrees, making it very difficult to walk, sleep, or eat. We were locked into the ice for days, and we noticed that every day we were pushed a few more miles toward the shore of Newfoundland. The Coast Guard ship was only a half mile off the rocks when the pressure released, and she was able to escape the grip of the ice. A few hours later we were free, and we headed back to the harbor entrance of Saint John's to continue to prevent the sealing fleet from leaving.

We held the blockade for another week, but I had an agent onshore who informed me that two sealing ships had left for the Gulf of Saint Lawrence and were killing seals. That was some seven hundred miles away. We waited until dark; fortunately, a dense fog moved in and allowed us to slip away from the harbor entrance and the Coast Guard. We made our way around the bottom of Newfoundland and into the Gulf of Saint Lawrence.

There were two sealing ships in the ice, the *Techno Venture* and the *Chester*. We caught them by surprise early in the morning, before any of the sealers had been dispatched to the ice.

All around us were lovely white balls of fur—thousands of newborn baby seals. I had no intention of allowing any seals to die that day.

We moved closer to the *Chester* as the dawn arrived.

"*Chester, Chester*, this is the *Sea Shepherd II*," I radioed.

After a few minutes of silence, they responded. "*Sea Shepherd, Sea Shepherd*, this is the *Chester*. What do you want?"

I knew I had to be careful with my words. I did not wish to provide any evidence that I was threatening them.

"*Chester*, Captain, it's a great day. I'd like to go into port in the Magdalen Islands and buy your crew some drinks."

The captain did not answer, but we saw his engines start up and he turned and began moving slowly through the ice toward the Magdalen Islands. The *Techno Venture* followed.

We were surprised and delighted the sealers gave up so early. We were left in the midst of thousands of baby harp seals. I stepped off the ship onto the ice. The sun was warm, and pools of fresh water were forming in the white-blue ice. Little bundles of white fur with black noses and watery black eyes cried out as we passed them.

An hour later, a Canadian Coast Guard helicopter disturbed the tranquility of the seal nursery. The helicopter flew low over us and headed back to the Magdalen Islands.

The sun set over a quiet and peaceful patch of ice. Our ship was surrounded by the sounds of nursing seals.

That serenity was shattered around midnight when we saw a blinding searchlight approaching from a few miles away. Slowly I began to discern the outline of a huge Canadian Coast Guard ice-breaker, the *John A. MacDonald*. She was quickly crashing toward us through the ice, smashing ice floes like a huge, angry hammer. To our horror, the ship was heading toward a group of baby seals lying help-lessly on the ice. The government ship did not slow down—she ran over the seal pups, crushing them as they tried frantically to escape.

The massive ship came straight toward us until it was about 650 feet away. She then turned, displaying her length—more than 300 feet. She then moved away about half a mile and stopped. The ship did not radio us; she just silently stood off, waiting for morning.

When the sun rose again, the sealing ships had returned, feeling safe now with the giant red-and-white bodyguard protecting them. The sealing boats were beginning to send men with clubs onto the ice.

I had no intention of just sitting there and watching baby seals being clubbed.

Suddenly, to intimidate us, the icebreaker came full speed toward us once again. We moved quickly toward the *Chester*, about a mile away, with the icebreaker bearing down on us from behind.

I radioed the *Chester*. "*Chester, Chester*, this is the *Sea Shepherd*. Captain, get your men off the ice. I'm going to ram that floe, and I intend to break it in half."

The radio belched out the voice of the commanding officer on the *John A. MacDonald*. "*Sea Shepherd II*, you are under arrest. Stop your ship immediately."

I ignored the order and kept on course toward the sealers.

"Marc, turn on the speakers and let's play some Wagner," I said.

The speakers began to thunder out the apocalyptic strains of "Ride of the Valkyries." The black-clad sealers looked toward us and the startling red hull coming fast behind us. They began to run, some of them dropping their seal clubs on the ice.

The sealers were scurrying up the sides of the *Chester* as I swung the wheel hard to port. Behind us, the *John A. MacDonald*, because of her superior speed and size, could not turn as quickly. She slammed hard into the floe, splitting it sixteen hundred feet across and conveniently separating the sealers on the *Chester* from their innocent victims on the ice.

The icebreaker had hit the floe so hard that she was stuck fast into the ice. This gave us the chance to head after another sealing vessel that had entered the area seeking the protection of the Canadian Coast Guard.

When we approached close enough to read the name on the bow, I radioed the ship. "*Sadie Charles*, *Sadie Charles*, this is the seal conservation and protection ship *Sea Shepherd II*. Please call your men off the ice and return to the Magdalen Islands."

There was a long silence followed by an angry voice swearing in a thick Quebecois accent.

The sealers had been clubbing seals earlier, and about three hundred pelts lay in a pool of blood on the *Sadie Charles*'s deck. We headed toward her at full speed, hitting the ice and splitting it—the seals were on one side and the sealers were on the other. We passed so close that the *Sadie Charles* was pushed hard over.

Seeing that the Coast Guard was not able to stop us from intervening, the sealing boats got underway and left the area.

The *John A. MacDonald* continued following us, however. I decided that it was time to retreat to sea, so we began moving through the ice back toward the entrance of the Cabot Strait.

"I think we have made the Canadian government very angry," I said to the crew. "So it's probably time to go home."

Unfortunately, the weather was not our friend—a northerly was picking up and the wind was becoming increasingly strong. The pressure on the ice pack was getting intense. Within a few hours, we were locked in solid—trapped in the ice. We were thirteen miles off the coast of Cape Breton Island, Nova Scotia.

We were only thirty-one miles from the sea, but we could go no farther. The *John A. MacDonald* was joined by a second large Canadian Coast Guard icebreaker, the *Sir William Alexander*. We could see helicopters coming in and dropping off scores of Mounties and fisheries officers.

With the approaching darkness we could see the two large ice-breakers sitting and waiting. They were biding their time until morning to assault our ship. I called a crew meeting to say that there would be no preventing our arrest and the seizure of the ship in the morning.

Ben White spoke up. "I have an idea."

"Yes, Ben?" I answered.

"Why don't we walk out of here under cover of darkness?"

"What do you mean?"

"We know that they will take the ship in the morning. Imagine their surprise when they board this ship and find that you are not here. I suggest that you and I—because this is my dumb idea—and two engineers walk to shore tonight. If we arrive before dawn, we can hide out and travel by night. They will most likely take the ship to Sydney, Nova Scotia. My idea is for us to get to Sydney, board the ship, fire up the engine, and make a getaway to Maine."

I looked at Ben. It was a very dumb idea, but it was better than no idea at all. Besides, we'd always been good at attempting the impossible.

My chief engineer, Carroll Vogel, and my first mate, Cliff Rogers, thought the idea was crazy. Paul Pezwick, however, was up for it, as was Bernard Carlais, our carpenter from France.

I turned command of the ship over to Cliff Rogers and at midnight, with the wind howling and the snow stinging our faces, the four of us draped white sheets around our orange survival suits and stepped out onto the ice. We each carried long poles and a small pack with a canteen of water, a thermos of hot chocolate, some chocolate bars, extra wool socks, a compass, and a small map.

The icebreakers were routinely rotating searchlights, and at each approach of the light we lay down on the ice, covering ourselves with the white sheets. Under pressure from the north wind, the ice pack was hard, and we had the lighthouse at Chéticamp to guide us. If we could walk two to three miles an hour, we could make it to shore in five to six hours. Once on shore we could find a place to hide until the next evening.

For the first two hours we made excellent time. Then the wind began to die down and, with the release of pressure, the ice began to grind and groan.

"This is not good, boys," I said. "The pressure is letting up."

We quickened our pace but to no avail. The ice pack was moving away from land and up the coast toward the Cabot Strait.

I was the first to fall through the ice. As I stood watching Paul Pezwick and Ben White probe a lead with their poles in search of sure footing, the ice beneath me gave way and I plunged chest-deep into thick slush. Chilled to the bone, I clawed my way back onto a pan of ice as another pan moved toward me, threatening to crush me.

I got onto the ice just before the two pieces of ice collided. The bottom of the pan that was behind me rode up and over the floe I was on, and about three tons of ice came crashing down almost on top of me. The floe I was on broke into three pieces. I got up, stumbled, and then used my pole to vault across a wide lead of water to a more solid piece of ice.

The next three hours saw all of us immersed in the sea numerous times as the ice beneath our feet gave way. As the sun rose, we were devastated to discover the ice breaking into smaller and smaller pieces. Seals were popping their heads out of the water to watch as we struggled across the ice.

Meanwhile, the *Sea Shepherd II* was finally free to move, but she and the crew did not get far. The Mounties had launched their assault. The *Sir William Alexander* rammed into our ship's starboard stern and fired tear gas and smoke canisters across the decks. The Mounties turned on the *Sir William Alexander*'s water cannons and began to pour water down the funnel to kill the engine of the *Sea Shepherd II*. Cliff Rogers tried to maneuver away from the water

Defending baby seals on the ice floes off Newfoundland in 1983.

cannons, but the *John A. MacDonald*, with rifle-toting Mounties lining her rails, slammed into the *Sea Shepherd II* on her port side. They dropped boarding planks, and the Mounties—sporting gas masks, flak jackets, helmets, and cutting tools—assaulted the ship.

The bridge doors were smashed open, and the Mounties threw Cliff, Jet Johnson, and Josephine Mussomeli to the deck and aimed their rifles at them.

Carroll Vogel and his engine crew had barricaded the engine room, but the Mounties cut through the quarter-inch-thick steel bulkhead and quickly took them prisoners. In fewer than ten minutes, all sixteen crew were handcuffed and marched out to the deck.

The Mounties had done a quick head count and realized they were four people short, so they meticulously searched the ship. The crew did not say a word. At the same time, the four of us who were still trying to pick our way through the ice were exposed in the daylight to anyone on the shore. We were only a mile off, and we could see people watching as we slowly made our way toward land.

There were Mounties awaiting us on the beach. They were friendly but they took us into custody and locked us up.

Ben laughingly said, "I told you at the beginning this was a dumb idea. It was a *very* dumb idea—in fact, the dumbest idea ever."

I smiled. "You're right. It was a dumb idea, but damn it, it was like climbing Mount Everest or going over Niagara Falls in a barrel. We walked across thirteen miles of chaotic ice floes and survived. That was worth doing."

The next morning, the Mounties drove us to Sydney, Nova Scotia, where they had taken the rest of my crew. The *Sea Shepherd II* was towed to Prince Edward Island. The Crown prosecutor said there was insufficient evidence to charge us, which did not please the Mounties.

Each of us was handcuffed to two Mounties, and then all twenty of us were escorted to the airport. The forty Mounties flew with us to Percé, Quebec, where we were charged under Quebec law—specifically, to be arraigned before Judge Yvon Mercier, the same judge we had dealt with in 1979. He was known as the hanging judge for the seal hunters. He made no pretense of being objective.

The Percé jail, normally closed for the winter, was opened just for us. We spent the next two weeks there waiting to raise bail. We were treated very well by the guards, who were all grateful that we provided them with a few weeks' employment. They were so appreciative that they gave us the run of the place, allowed me to use the office to speak with journalists, and even allowed us to visit the pub across the street without being escorted. Granted, it did not make much sense to try to escape from a town where the roads were cut off due to a blizzard.

We had to return in the spring for the trial and our strategy was bizarre, but I did not see any other options. Mercier was going to severely punish us. I instructed the crew to be hostile to the judge. "We need to really piss him off," I said. My reasoning was that if he was going to convict—and we knew he would—he really had to throw the book at us.

And he did. Except he reacted with even more malice than we had anticipated.

After the trial, only Paul Pezwick and I were ordered to return to court, this time in Quebec City.

Pezwick lived in Boston, so I flew there and rented a car to drive us north across the border. We parked in the garage beneath the courthouse and reported to the reception desk.

Walking up to the desk, I asked the clerk, "Excuse me, can you tell me where Judge Mercier's courtroom is?"

The young man behind the desk looked at us with obvious distaste.

"Je ne parlez pas Anglais," he said. (I don't speak English.)

Patiently I repeated myself: "Quel salle pour Judge Mercier si'l vous plaît." (Which room for Judge Mercier, please.)

Impatiently he responded, "Je ne parlez pas Anglais." (I don't speak English.)

Now I was angry. I looked straight into his eyes and said, "Look here, asshole, where the fuck is Judge Mercier's courtroom?"

With a slightly frightened stammer, he blurted out, "Courtroom 205."

"Merci," I replied.

As we walked away, Pezwick said, "I guess he *does* understand English."

With a laugh I said, "Maybe, maybe not—but he sure as hell understands English curses."

We found the courtroom and waited for the judge to arrive. He looked at us with a sinister smile and proceeded to pronounce the sentence. It was a little hard to follow, because it was only in French—Quebec courts were not bilingual like the rest of Canada— but I got the gist of it.

Each crewmember was fined $3,000, except for engineer Paul Pezwick and me. Pezwick was a second offender from our 1979 campaign, and he was given three months in jail and a $7,000 fine. I was sentenced to fifteen months for conspiracy to break the Seal Protection Act, six months for breaking the act, a $75,000 fine, and the confiscation of my ship. I was also given a court order barring me from corresponding with any journalist anywhere in the world for three years, plus I was prohibited from entering the five eastern Canadian provinces for three years.

My first thought was the cost of the rental car in the basement of the courthouse and the cost of parking for at least three months until Paul was released.

Mercier stood up to leave, and just before he opened the door to his chambers I shouted out, "Hey, Judge Mercier!"

Surprised, he turned around and smiled. He was about to cite me with a contempt of court. But before he could do so, I shouted, "Merry Christmas, Your Honor!"

Clearly pissed, he turned his back and left the courtroom.

"Damn," I said to Pezwick, "I was hoping he would charge me with contempt for saying Merry Christmas. That would have helped our case."

We were immediately handcuffed and ordered into prison. It was December 20, 1984. After nine days we were released, pending appeal. A year later, the Quebec Court of Appeal overturned Mercier's ruling on the grounds that it was excessive. The convictions were quashed. My strategy had worked. I next initiated a lawsuit against the government for damages done to my ship and to secure the release of the ship.

That took another year before I won both the lawsuit and the release of the ship.

In the meantime, without a ship, I decided to launch a campaign to protect wolves in British Columbia.

Cry Wolf

PEACE RIVER VALLEY, BRITISH COLUMBIA

love wolves. During the occupation of Wounded Knee in 1973, I was given the Lakota name Gray Wolf Clear Water. So, in 1984, I established a new organization called Friends of the Wolf.

The Canadian province of British Columbia had decided to institute a wolf extermination project in the northern Peace River area. That decision was made by British Columbia's environment minister, Anthony Brummett, who hired a biologist named John Elliott to carry out the pogrom.

Action was needed to protect the wolves, and although my focus had been primarily on marine wildlife, I felt I had to intervene. I tried to secure a meeting with Minister Brummett, but he refused to meet with me. I had to find another way to get his attention.

I had learned that the key to making a bang with the media was to give the media what the media wants, and the mainstream media is interested in just four specific elements: sex, scandal, violence, and celebrity.

Right from the beginning I saw the violence—the shooting of wolves from the air and the inherent risk assumed by anyone who might interfere. And quite quickly I saw a second element: the bragging of big-game hunter and millionaire Bob Keen of Fort Nelson, who boasted that he had given Anthony Brummett a campaign donation of $10,000. I quickly spun this assertion into a bribe, giving the story the element of scandal.

All I needed now was sex and celebrity. I was able to recruit actress Bo Derek as the official spokesperson for Friends of the Wolf, and she was perfect.

At our media conference in Vancouver, the room was packed with reporters, cameras, and microphones. One reporter asked why Bo Derek was our spokesperson.

"What does Bo Derek know about wolves? Having her as a spokesperson is silly."

"Really?" I replied. "You guys make the rules. We're just playing the game. The fact is that if I had one of the two foremost wolf biologists in the world here—say, Dr. Gordon Haber or Dr. David Mech—this would be an empty room. But the fact that Bo Derek is our spokesperson is the reason the room is packed and the reason this story will be a headline on the front page of tomorrow's newspaper."

Now that I had the media's attention, my next move was to charter a small plane and fly to Fort Nelson, where—predictably— the town boss, Bob Keen, made it quite clear we would not be able to find lodging or purchase fuel. No lodging in Fort Nelson was a serious issue in subzero weather.

I was prepared for a situation like this and had our supporters contact the head offices of the fuel companies to accuse them of discrimination. My team and I then took our tents and sleeping bags and set up camp on the lawn of Royal Canadian Mounted Police headquarters to guarantee our safety. When the Mounties objected, we told them they had a responsibility to uphold the law and to stop local businesses, including the hotel owned by Bob Keen, from discriminating against us. They did so and I made a point of booking rooms at Keen's establishment.

Once we were able to set up a base in Fort Nelson, it was time to get a rise from the locals supporting the wolf kill, which was about 95 percent of the population. I rented a local auditorium and called a town meeting to debate the issue. I had no intention of convincing anyone in the town to side with the wolves—that was a lost cause—but the media had followed us in droves. Staying at the same hotel as my team and I were reporters from the CBC, the *Vancouver Sun* and *Province* newspapers, and independent television station CHEK-DT. BCTV even sent their anchor Pamela Martin to cover the story, and all the cameras were in place for the debate.

About 375 people crowded into the auditorium. There was a noticeable absence of children, and most of the attendees were men. Some were drunk and many were loudly yelling obscenities.

I turned to my friend David Garrick and said, "Well, this should be fun."

I walked up to the podium, took the mic, and with a smile prepared to address the crowd.

Right away the heckling began.

A guy in camo shouted, "You're nothing but a convicted criminal, ya bastard!"

Fortunately, a sympathetic local woman had briefed me on some of the ringleaders—especially this guy.

I looked at him and countered: "Yeah, I was arrested for saving seals. You, my friend, were arrested for beating your wife."

Another man jumped up, shouting, "Step outside, you piece of shit, and I'll kill you."

I ignored him and addressed a Mountie in the back of the room. "Please take down that man's name. If you find my body in the morning, kindly charge him with murder. He made the threat."

I then turned to the man who made the threat and said, "Don't you know that if you're going to kill someone, it is not smart to announce it in advance—unless, of course, you did not mean it and you're just trying to impress your fellow cavemen here."

I was trying to rile the men up, and I was quite prepared for any assault when the doors in the back flew open. A small group of locals shambled in, grotesquely parading two mutilated wolves. Both the bodies stank, and it was obvious that they had been dead for some time. The locals were laughing and dancing before the cameras, cursing and acting like they had just scored a major victory.

The reporters were horrified, and I was delighted. The locals had exceeded my expectations. I was planning on their attacking me before the cameras, but this was even better.

One of the men tried to work the jaws of one of the wolves to make it look like it was talking to the cameras as he shouted, "We don't need no fucking wolf lovers up here telling real men what they should do!"

The back doors were kicked open again, and another trapper dragged in two more dead wolves. The cameras immediately shifted to him.

"I just shot these two wolves today, asshole. They were lurking near my home, waiting to prey on my children. What do you think of that, you piece of shit?"

I smiled at him. "I think you just lost the war, you idiot."

Another trapper yelled, "We're going to kill every goddamn wolf in this province and you freaks ain't going to stop us."

Perfect. When the cameras turned on me, I simply said, "Welcome to Fort Neanderthal."

The next morning, the national news referred to Fort Nelson as Fort Neanderthal.

The challenge was to keep the media coverage ramped up to continue to pressure the federal government. I decided that my crew and I would trek a hundred miles into the bush off the Alaska Highway to search out the camp of John Elliott and his gang of wolf killers. We had flown over their camp and knew where it was, but the plane could not land anywhere and we could not secure a helicopter.

With snowshoes and backpacks, we headed off into the wilderness with a media crew filming our departure as we trekked across the ice of the Kechika River. I knew we would not be able to do much on foot, but it was dramatic—protestors striking out in subzero conditions to save the wolves.

We trekked all day and camped at night. The weather was so cold that we had to use an axe to chop potatoes and carrots. I dropped an orange on a rock, and it shattered like glass. The temperatures were down to –40 degrees Celsius.

As we journeyed down the frozen river, we were monitored by daily flyovers from the media. To keep the story going, I saw an

Leading a crew to disrupt wolf hunting in the Peace River area of northern British Columbia. Getting fresh water from the Kechika River.

opening in the middle of the river where the rapids had prevented the water from freezing. We all walked over to the edge and looked at the rushing black water. I then had everyone walk backward in their same tracks and back into the woods.

When the daily media plane flew over, all the reporters saw were tracks leading into the open water. They reported that my entire crew may have drowned in the Kechika River. The story was corrected the next day when they saw us on the ice as they flew over.

We managed to keep the story prominent in the media for almost two weeks. As a result, the provincial government was getting a lot of pressure, especially because of our evidence regarding the donations received by the environment minister from big-game hunting organizations.

Back in Victoria, my wife, Starlet Lum, had paid a visit to minister of environment Anthony Brummett. She was there to deliver a petition opposing the wolf slaughter that listed some forty thousand names. She went into the minister's office while the media waited outside the door. With her was our three-year-old daughter, Lilliolani.

Brummett snapped that he did not want any kids in his office, so Starlet asked Lani to go back outside, where our friends would take care of her. Brummett then angrily took the petition and dramatically made a point of dropping it into the trash can by his desk.

Outside the office, when Lilliolani came out by herself, the reporters asked her what was going on.

Lilliolani looked into the cameras and said, "That naughty Mr. Brummett does not like wolfies, and he hates kids."

It was too funny a statement to not make the news that evening.

A few days later, the premier of British Columbia, Bill Bennett, asked Brummett for his resignation.

A few weeks after Brummett resigned, I had arranged for a meeting with the new environment minister, Austin Pelton.

As I was walking up the stairs to the legislature, Anthony Brummett happened to be walking down the stairs toward me. Recognizing me, he stopped and said, "I hope you're happy that I was forced to resign."

I smiled and replied, "Mr. Brummett, I would really like to take the time to talk with you, but I'm in a bit of a rush. I have an appointment with the environment minister."

And the new minister was eager to listen. On March 28, 1985, the environment minister, Austin Pelton, announced that he would put a stop to the wolf hunt.

Chocolate Pie Cannons versus Bullets

THE FAROE ISLANDS

David McColl of Sea Shepherd Scotland first brought the horror of the *grindadráp* to public attention when he visited the Faroe Islands in 1983 to document the slaughter of pilot whales.

The term *grindadráp* translates from old Nordic as the "murder of whales" and is commonly called the grind. It involves driving entire pods of pilot whales or dolphins from the sea and onto beaches where the defenseless animals are viciously slaughtered with spears and knives. The hunters kill every single member of the pod: males, females, pregnant females, and calves. The grind is not done out of necessity or even for commercial reasons. It's done for sport, for fun and amusement.

My ship, the *Sea Shepherd II*, which was seized by the Canadian government during our 1983 campaign to defend the seals, was finally returned to me in the spring of 1985. Judge Yvon Mercier tried every trick he could to prevent the return of my ship, but he was overruled by the Quebec Court of Appeal, and that decision was upheld by the Supreme Court of Canada.

There was a great deal of damage done to the vessel, but with a crew of volunteers I set to work to make her ready for sea again.

At the same time, I initiated a lawsuit against the Canadian government for damages. It was a challenge to get the ship ready in time to make a crossing of the North Atlantic. I was short on cash with much work to be done.

One day the Halifax harbormaster dropped by with an offer. There was a small Colombian freighter in the harbor that had been brought in months before by the Mounties on suspicion of trafficking drugs. Nothing was found, but the crew deserted and the owner in Colombia wanted his ship towed to Haiti for repairs. The harbormaster asked if I was interested. I said sure, and he gave me only the man's first name—Carlos—and his number.

I called Carlos and told him I would tow his vessel. He offered $25,000 dollars for my work. I agreed but told him I needed a written contract and a waiver of responsibility if the ship sank while under tow.

A few days later, I received a very suspicious check for $25,000 from Joe's Garage in Caracas.

Within two weeks, I spent the funds on repairs and fuel and still had not received a contract or a waiver. I tried calling Carlos again, but the number was disconnected. I informed the harbormaster that I could not tow the ship and informed my crew of my intention to depart.

Some of the crewmembers were nervous.

"This guy is a Colombian drug lord," said Peter Wallerstein. "We're all going to get Colombian neckties."

"What the hell is a Colombian necktie?" someelse asked.

"What that means," I answered, "is they slit your throat and pull your tongue out the hole."

A couple of the crew turned quite white.

"But not to worry," I said. "I tried to reach him, and if he contacts me, we'll give him his money."

"But we spent his money," Peter protested.

"True. But we'll get it somehow—I could not tow his ship without a waiver."

By July 1985, the *Sea Shepherd II* was ready for departure, and I set my sights on the Danish Faroe Islands to oppose the slaughter of the pilot whales. However, I also intended to make a stop in Iceland to give the governing authorities a warning to abide by the regulations outlawing commercial whaling. If they did not, we would return to confront their whaling ships.

Our arrival in Reykjavík, Iceland, created quite a stir. There was a Greenpeace ship, the *Sirius*, in port and we were berthed directly behind her.

Greenpeace had been getting lots of attention until one of its media releases alerted the Icelandic authorities that I was an anti-whaling terrorist. This backfired on Greenpeace, because it focused all the Icelandic media attention on Sea Shepherd.

When asked by an Icelandic newspaper what Sea Shepherd would do if Iceland did not comply with the whaling regulations, I replied that Sea Shepherd would "sink the Icelandic fleet." This resulted in our being placed under guard and ordered to leave Iceland, which did not bother me—I had intended to stay in Iceland just long enough to issue a warning. My brief time there allowed my team and I to map out the harbor, the location of the whaling ships, and the location of the onshore whaling station in Hvalfjörður.

We left Iceland the first week of August, bound for the Faroe Islands, a small group of remote islands just northwest of the Scottish Shetland Islands.

Upon arriving in the Faroe Islands, I met with Prime Minister Atli Dam. When I asked him why Faroese people were killing pilot whales, he replied that the grind was a "gift from God" and that the Faroese did not care what the rest of the world thought about it.

My crew and I spent a few weeks hanging around the Faroes to make our presence known. At one point, a small boat approached and the occupants began to throw eggs at us, forcing me to disperse them with our water cannon.

During the month we were in the Faroes, no whales were slain. We departed, bound for London and planning to return in 1986.

I never did hear from Carlos from Colombia again. It was like he disappeared—and that was entirely possible, given the nature of his occupation.

Many months later, however, I could not resist calling up Peter Wallerstein.

When he answered the phone, I said in a thick Latino accent, "Hi, Pedro, this is Carlos. Do you have my money?"

Needless to say, Peter did not find it very funny.

In order to successfully protect the pilot whales in 1986, I needed to mount a solid campaign; for that I needed some powerful weapons, and there is nothing more powerful than cameras. Especially if those cameras belong to the BBC. Jeff Goodman was a director for the BBC, and he came aboard to make a documentary about the killing of the whales.

In June 1986, the *Sea Shepherd II* departed from England bound for Malmö, Sweden, where the International Whaling Commission was meeting. In Malmö, we attended what would be the last commission meeting that we were ever allowed to join.

At that meeting, I made it very clear that Sea Shepherd intended to take the moratorium on commercial whaling seriously and that we intended to do whatever it would take to enforce the moratorium. Japan, Norway, Iceland, and Denmark were all determined to defy the moratorium. Japan claimed it would do only so-called research whaling while the three Nordic nations vowed to disregard the moratorium.

With the meeting concluded, I took the *Sea Shepherd II* across the North Sea and back to the Faroe Islands. Upon arriving, we dropped anchor and cleared customs and immigration without issue. As soon as the customs officials left, three Faroese policemen boarded my ship. The BBC cameras were rolling as the policemen immediately ordered me to leave Faroese waters.

I replied, "We just got here, and we have cleared in legally. We are not ready to depart."

"Captain Watson, I have been told to inform you legally to leave Faroese waters. You, your ship, and your crew must leave Faroese territorial waters immediately. Neither you nor your crew are allowed to enter any harbor in the Faroes."

I looked at the officer. "I'm confused. We have just received customs clearance and we have been legally and officially admitted to the country, and now you tell me we must leave. What legal reason do you have to force me to leave?"

The senior officer looked a little uncomfortable as he stammered, "Well, ah—what do you call it?—the parliament . . . The parliament simply doesn't want you in Faroese waters."

"So, you are telling me that we are expelled without having done anything wrong?"

The officer fumbled for words. "You are requested . . . I am requesting you to leave Faroese waters."

"Oh," I said. "Then this is not an order but a request?"

"If you don't leave, you will get a proper sentence," the officer replied.

Surprised, I asked, "How can we get a sentence without being charged?"

"Well," he answered, pulling some papers from his briefcase, "you will get it from the government, and the government says that there will be no negotiations at all."

It was obvious that the officer was embarrassed. His argument was political and not legal, and my attempts to point out the facts were flustering him.

"You have your warning," he said. He stood up, closed his briefcase, and left my cabin to return to shore.

There was also a BBC crew on the shore, so I decided to test the policeman's warning. I sent three crewmembers ashore to meet with the government. As our small boat arrived in the inner harbor, the Faroese police immediately arrested all five of us and seized our boat.

I sent Rod Coronado and Nick Taylor in a second boat to retrieve the first boat, but they were also arrested, and our second boat was seized as well.

I was then ordered to leave the Faroes. I replied that I would not leave without my crew and my two small boats. In response, the Faroese sent out their one coast guard patrol ship, the *Olivur Haglur*. The gray converted fishing trawler had a gun mounted on her foredeck.

One of my crew burst into the wheelhouse looking very frightened. "They have a big gun and they are coming straight for us."

I laughed. "After staring down the barrels of guns on a Soviet frigate, this little gun is hardly an intimidation."

The *Olivur Haglur* came alongside us at a distance of approximately 165 feet. The captain radioed to us, telling us to give ourselves up.

I answered, "Give ourselves up for what? What charges do you have against us?"

The Faroese captain did not seem to understand my question. He responded, "You do not intend to give up?"

I picked up the receiver and replied with the words of Captain John Paul Jones: "I have not yet begun to fight."

That gunboat chased us around the Faroe Islands for five days, and the pursuit soon became tiresome. One morning, I decided to turn the tables on the *Olivur Haglur*. With the Faroese on my stern, I did a "Crazy Ivan" and pulled the wheel hard to port. The *Olivur Haglur* panicked and pulled hard to starboard as we completed the circle and were bearing down on her stern.

The radio crackled and a panicked voice intruded. "*Sea Shepherd, Sea Shepherd*, do you intend to ram us? Do you intend to hurt us?"

"No," I said, "we have no intention of ramming or hurting you. We just want to illustrate how annoying it is to be chased around all the time. Besides, why should you have all the fun? It's our turn to chase you for a change."

Seeing that we were not to be intimidated, the police contacted me to offer a deal. They would return my crew and my two boats if I agreed to sign an expulsion order barring me and my ship from any Scandinavian country for three years. I agreed with no intention of abiding by such an order, as I was signing under duress. We had not broken any laws.

The boats and crew were released, and I returned to Scotland but only to refuel and buy a couple of rolls of barbed wire to make it difficult for anyone to board the *Sea Shepherd II*. Within days, we were back in Faroese waters. We began to patrol off the beaches and sat each evening just outside the main harbor of Tórshavn, the capital of the Faroe Islands.

After a week of patrols, when we were off the southern tip of the island of Sandoy, we saw the *Olivur Haglur* approaching.

I radioed the ship, saying, "*Olivur Haglur, Olivur Haglur*, where have you been? Great to see you again! Are you ready to resume the chase?"

"*Sea Shepherd*, this is the *Olivur Haglur*. You are under arrest. Please stop your engines."

I ignored the order. We could see the crew of the *Olivur Haglur* lowering inflatable boats into the water. A few minutes later, four large inflatables, each carrying five uniformed Danish police officers, came racing toward us. I stepped out onto the starboard bridgewing as one of the boats came alongside the *Sea Shepherd II*.

"Do you wish to arrest us?" I yelled down to them.

For an answer, one of the policemen stood up and aimed a shotgun directly at me. I could see that the other officers were heavily armed, two of them carrying what looked like automatic weapons.

I laughed. "What are you going to do—shoot me?"

His response was immediate. His trigger finger moved, and I saw a spurt of flame as a whining buzz zipped by my right ear. There was an explosion behind me. Something struck me in the side of my neck, and I couldn't see—my eyes stung.

I heard a second shot, and the green running light above my head exploded in a shower of glass. I dove back into the wheelhouse.

"Everybody put on your gas masks!" I yelled as I reached for mine. I realized that the stinging in my eyes was from tear gas.

I found out later that the officer had fired a tear gas shell. It had shattered against the bulkhead only three inches from my head, causing a piece of the fiberglass to strike me in the neck.

I grabbed a parachute flare then stepped back onto the bridgewing with my gas mask on. The officer stood up to fire again. I aimed the flare, pulled the cord, and sent the rocket flying into the side of the inflatable, puncturing the side and deflating a pontoon. The officer dropped his shotgun overboard and dove into the bottom of the boat as it drifted back, half-sunk, in our wake. Meanwhile, on the main deck, Rod Coronado used a fire hose to stop another officer from boarding our ship.

There were two inflatables on either side of us, their occupants tossing tear gas canisters or shooting at us. It was time to bring out our secret weapon.

On the deck I had six barrels of surplus pie filling—in chocolate and banana cream flavors—from the US Department of Agriculture. It was strange stuff—I'd had it for more than a year and it had not gone bad. Our water cannon had an attachment that, when dropped into the barrel, would send out a forty-five-gallon shot of the sticky, sweet goo.

Rod quickly set it up. As a police inflatable sped up alongside with an officer preparing to shoot another tear gas canister onto the deck, Rod opened fire and sent a blob of chocolate pie filling straight into the boat, knocking the officer with the gun down to the deck and covering all the officers with chocolate.

He sent another shot of banana cream pie at the second inflatable. The shot missed the boat but splashed yellow goo onto the officer nonetheless.

That pie filling did the trick. Both boats fell back.

Jeff Goodman and his BBC crew captured the entire confrontation. The documentary that aired was called *Black Harvest*, and for the first time the world was becoming aware of the horrors in the Faroe Islands.

The first campaign to defend pilot whales and dolphins in the Faroe Islands. Repelling a tear gas attack by Faroese police.

The police officers accused me of shooting at them and splashing gasoline into their boats, but the BBC cameras captured the events and contradicted their story. Even the Danish public was amused by the pie-filling sliming.

1985

Pints with the Unspeakables

RENFREWSHIRE, SCOTLAND

It was Oscar Wilde who quite accurately described foxhunting as "the unspeakable in pursuit of the uneatable."

Foxhunting is not a sport—it's an excuse for a sport where the object is to terrorize and murder an innocent fox with a posse of horses and a pack of dogs.

I was aware that a group called the Hunt Saboteurs Association regularly attempted to disrupt these sadistic upper-class indulgences, so I asked the Glasgow chapter, the Glasgow Hunt Sabs, if I could accompany them on a sab. At the time, I was in Scotland and there was a hunt the next weekend near the village of Houston in Renfrewshire.

The hunters were distinct with their English-saddled horses, scarlet hunting coats, beige jodhpurs, polished black boots, barking dogs, and bugle. This fancy group was backed by a group of about a hundred more shabbily dressed countryfolk with sticks and Land Rovers. They were there to cheer on the hunters. To me, they looked like nothing more than a gaggle of servile peasants groveling for favors from their lords.

The third group was the one I was now part of—the Hunt Saboteurs—and honestly, we were just as shabbily dressed as the hunt's supporters, the only difference being that we sported longer hair and coats adorned with animal rights patches. Some wore balaclavas around their necks, to be donned in the event of a scuffle.

There were about thirty dogs accompanying the hunters. They looked rather skinny and dirty in contrast to the burnished coats of the horses and the meticulous attire of the hunters.

Finally, there were a couple of constables lurking about. They looked out of place and nervous. The hunt's supporters and the hunt sabs heckled each other while the hunters took pains to look indifferent to the those they considered members of the lower class.

The hunt's supporters formed a human wall between the hunt sabs and the horses. There was some pushing and shoving, but then a bugle sounded and, amid shouts of protest, the dogs took off noisily followed by the horses. About thirty supporters followed in their vehicles, and some forty hunt sabs, including me, were left to trail horses and cars on foot. I had to admit that following on foot seemed somewhat futile.

The hunt supporters' cars had to keep to the roads as the horses and dogs charged over the muddy fields with the hunt sabs far behind.

"This seems to be somewhat one-sided," I said to the hunt sabs. "Perhaps we should get horses to head the hunters off before they find a fox."

This pronouncement was met with astonished stares. "Riding horses is animal cruelty," someone yelled. Another voice chastised me, saying, "We're not upper-class toffs like them."

Defensively, I responded, "Sorry, I was thinking strategically." Then I asked, "By the way, can't they nail us for trespassing for walking over the fields? I assume they're private property."

A woman next to me answered in a thick Scottish accent. "We don't have trespassing laws here in Scotland—we have the right of free passage."

"So let's get motorcycles," I suggested.

"Absolutely not. Motorcycles are loud and obnoxious. That would scare the foxes," someone countered.

"Better scared than dead," I mumbled as we sluggishly moved across a muddy field and climbed over a small stone wall.

"What if I owned property?" I began again. "Could I stop the hunt from crossing my property?"

"Unfortunately, no. The hunters can legally cross private property without permission from the owner," the same young woman answered.

The sound of barking dogs was farther away by now. We were losing ground.

We finally caught up with the hunters when the hunt was over. They had failed to oust a fox from hiding, no thanks to us.

The dogs were not happy. The hunters, however, seemed jovial, saying it was a jolly good ride. The hunt's supporters seemed downcast. Their lust for blood was far greater than that of the those in the scarlet coats.

As the sun set on my first campaign with the Hunt Saboteurs, someone suggested we all hit the local pub. To our amusement, the establishment was called the Fox and Hounds.

As we approached, we could hear laughter and music coming from inside the pub. But when we entered, the music and laughter stopped. We were greeted by the angry faces of a few dozen hunters and their motley supporters.

The landlord rushed over and told us we were not welcome. But before we could turn to go, the master of the hunt approached, all smiles and good cheer.

"Now what's this, my good man?" he asked the landlord.

"I was just telling these hooligans they are not welcome here."

The master of the hunt looked at the landlord and said with an air of superiority, "We can be foes during the day, but come evening we can share a drink like civilized fellows, don't you think?"

"Whatever you say," replied the landlord with a frown.

The master of the hunt held out his hand to me, saying, "A pint each for these good gentlemen, if you please, landlord."

I had to admit, this man caught us all off guard. We were hardly expecting a free drink, let alone to be allowed to stay in the pub. The landlord was still scowling, but for the most part it was just friendly banter for the next hour.

The master of the hunt defended the foxhunting as tradition, and we said that any tradition that depended on cruelty and slaughter needed to be abolished.

"Why not a hunt without a victim?" I inquired. "You mentioned it was the chase you enjoyed. Why kill the fox?"

"That's a good question," he replied. "We could, I suppose, but I'm afraid most of these gentlemen would have none of it." He motioned to the hunt's supporters.

"What do they get out of it?" I asked.

The master of the hunt glanced at them with a condescending smile. "I think they just like to see blood, to be honest."

"And you're okay with that?" I pressed.

He hesitated, thinking. Then he said, "Never gave it much thought, I suppose."

A few free pints of beer later, we went our separate ways, with the hunt sabs promising not to relent and the foxhunters vowing not to quit and the hunt's supporters looking like they wanted to punch us all in the face.

That evening was an enlightening experience. Happily, a fox did not die that day, but I could not help noticing how each class held such differing and deeply entrenched viewpoints. I also felt that if we could have secured horses, we could have seriously disrupted these hunts—but that was apparently not an option for the hunt sabs.

I did suggest something for the next sab, though. "Get some butyric acid. It stinks like you can't even imagine. Soak a rag in it, hold your nose, and drag that rag across these fields. That will put the dogs off the fox's scent, and it will make the ride quite unpleasant for the toffs on the horses. It won't harm anyone, but it smells like rotten butter."

A few years later, I was happy to hear that my suggestion was used in other hunts in Britain. I hope it spared the lives of many foxes.

Raid on Reykjavík

ICELAND

had given my first warning to the Icelanders on the dock at Reykjavík, the nation's capital, in the summer of 1985. My message was clear: "Obey the International Whaling Commission moratorium on commercial whaling, or I will sink your whaling ships."

I gave my second warning to Iceland at the 1986 IWC meeting in Malmö, Sweden. Sea Shepherd waited for the United States to uphold sanctions as stipulated by US law. By September 1986, we had exhausted all conventional means of forcing Iceland into compliance with the IWC regulations. In fact, the only thing that the moratorium achieved was to relieve public pressure against whaling. The public now falsely believed that the moratorium was in effect and that there was no need for further concern or action. It was imperative that we strike a blow against whaling soon. We needed to dramatize the fact that whaling was continuing.

Rod Coronado was a teenager in 1979, the year I rammed the pirate whaler *Sierra*. That was when he first heard of Sea Shepherd. He had written me a letter back then, which I answered. In 1983, he sent me $200 for fuel for our campaign to protect seals. In 1984, after graduating from high school, Rod traveled north from his home near Gilroy, California, and searched me out in Vancouver.

In 1985, I sent Rod to Halifax to help prepare the *Sea Shepherd II* for the campaign to Iceland and the Faroe Islands. He had proven himself to be the most loyal, dedicated, and hardworking member of my crew. In the Faroe Islands in the summers of 1985 and 1986, he had tackled the whalers and the authorities with discipline and courage, and on our return to England he came to me with an idea. He wanted to undertake a campaign to Iceland to act against the Icelandic whalers. He knew that I had too high of a profile in Iceland, but he needed only one other crewmember—David Howitt.

David Howitt had joined us in March 1986 as an engineer. He was very quiet and at first glance he seemed more of an observer than an activist. This suited his training as a natural history photographer. He was also a proficient bicycle mechanic, a skill that had landed him in my engine room.

As Rod and I discussed his idea, we knew more research into the location and security of the Icelandic whaling station and ships would be necessary. On October 15, 1986, Rod and David landed at the airport in Keflavík, Iceland, and took the bus into town, where they registered at the Salvation Army's hostel. They spent hours drinking coffee at a small café across from the dock, keeping an eye on the four whaling ships and taking notes of the movements of the crew and security guards. Piece by piece they picked up tools from different hardware stores: a bolt cutter, a large Crescent wrench, and a heavy monkey wrench. They hitchhiked up the coast to the whaling station at Hvalfjörðhur, where the ships brought the carcasses of whales they had killed. Rod and David had heard that the factory gave tours, so they decided to play tourist. Howitt brought his camera, but when they arrived, they found the place deserted. It was closed for the season. They took pictures, sketched maps, and made plans to return.

On November 6, Rod and David mailed their photos, drawings, and notes to Sea Shepherd UK director Sarah Hambley. She was the only person aside from me who was aware that the two were involved in a mission to Iceland.

On Saturday, November 8, the planned attack on Icelandic whaling operations was set in motion. Rod and David's agenda was to rent a car, eat dinner at Reykjavík's only vegetarian restaurant, drive to the whaling station and sabotage it, return to the docks, sink the whaling ships, drive to the airport, and catch a plane to Luxembourg.

On November 10, I received a phone call from Sarah. She calmly said, "We've got two on the bottom and the boys are home."

I had the media releases ready to go. The Icelanders were furious. The operation was a complete success, and the international news coverage showed two whaling ships on the bottom of the harbor with just their wheelhouses and upper decks above the water. The news also reported the extensive damage to the whaling factory. Most importantly, no one was hurt.

Rod and David had driven to Hvalfjörður and arrived at eight o'clock at night, just as a snowstorm began. They parked their car in a nearby quarry, changed their clothing, slipped on day packs containing tools and flashlights, and walked toward the unguarded whaling station. The snow was falling heavily, giving them excellent cover. They circled the compound under the glare of the mercury-vapor lights that illuminated the entire facility. After confirming there were no people about, they entered through an unlocked door, located the main circuit box, flipped the switch, and killed the power.

They then began to systematically attack the machinery of the facility in a controlled assault. The objective was to inflict as much damage as possible. The first target was the computer room. The video monitors exploded under the heavy crescent wrenches. They smashed the terminals, the printers, the fax machine, and anything that looked expensive. They worked over the six huge Caterpillar diesel engines and electrical generators that powered the large refrigeration units where the whale meat was stored. They severed lines, breaking and dismantling expensive parts. They carried parts of the engine as well as long flensing knives to the pier and tossed them into the deep water of the fjord. They smashed the refrigeration units and then moved on to the whale oil centrifuges and hydraulic-driven equipment, cutting the hoses as they methodically dissected the robotic apparatus the Icelanders used to mutilate the whales.

Finally, Rod and David broke open the freezer doors and discovered tons of whale meat inside. They jammed the doors open to expose the meat to the warm air in the plant.

The destruction went on for some four hours. The storm outside kept people off the road and would have explained the blackout at the whaling station. The storm also muffled the racket from the destruction of the machinery. Rod and David left the plant, walked calmly back to their car, and proceeded to drive back through the pelting snow to Reykjavík's harbor.

They knew from their observations that there was one watchman for the three whaling ships. Unfortunately, the fourth ship was in dry dock. The three whaling ships were rafted alongside one another and moored to the pier. The watchman was on the outermost vessel and most likely asleep.

Rod and David made a quick dash across the pier toward the ships. The wind was howling, the water of the harbor was choppy, and the visibility was poor. Rod was delighted with the weather. He told me later that the storm was a blessing—it kept people inside and the wind masked the noise of the sabotage.

Before Rod and David's mission commenced, I instructed the two men not to take any action that would endanger any person. That meant Rod and David were free to attack two of the whaling ships: the *Hvalur 6* and the *Hvalur 7*.

The lights were on in all three ships. The doors were unlocked. David quickly entered the first ship and Rod took the second vessel. They had an interior drawing of each ship, and they were able to locate and check every bunk. There was no one aboard either ship. Rod stepped aboard the third ship and peered through the galley window. The watchman was lying on a galley bench, snoring.

With the check for personnel completed, both men entered the engine room of the *Hvalur 6*. Their experience working in the engine room of the *Sea Shepherd II* paid off. They lifted the heavy lower deck plates and quickly located the large seawater intake valve, which allows the cold ocean water to circulate through the engines' cooling system and provides water for the firefighting systems and toilets. David closed the sea valve, and then both men went to work removing the heavy bolts to dismantle the main seawater pipe from the valve. Pipes and valves on ships are easy to identify: seawater pipes and valves are always painted green as opposed to blue for fresh water, brown for fuel, orange for oil, black for wastewater, red for fire systems, and silver for steam.

With the *Hvalur 6* primed and ready to go, Rod and David boarded the *Hvalur 7* and did the same thing—with the pipes removed, they opened the valve and watched the seawater pour into the engine room under high pressure. A geyser of water hit the upper deck and gushed down, completely soaking them both. The roar of the water was unnerving, but they were undeterred. Jumping back on the *Hvalur 6*, they ran down to the engine room and opened the sea valve. Both ships were filling up fast.

Running back to the main deck of the *Hvalur 6*, they vaulted the rails and jumped back aboard the *Hvalur 7* and severed the mooring lines that attached the two sabotaged vessels to the third ship carrying the watchman. They threw the knives and tools overboard and jumped back across the decks of the ships to the pier. The guard was still sleeping as his ship slowly drifted away from the other two.

The two men ran across the pier to the parking lot and the safety of their car. It was 5:40 a.m. when they drove away, heading to the airport. They looked back one more time to see both ships beginning to list.

Just a minute out of the harbor, they spotted a police cruiser with flashing lights behind them. Rod, who was driving, muttered, "How can they be that quick? They can't be *that* good."

Rod pulled the car to the side of the road and stopped. Two police officers stepped out of the patrol car. One cop stayed next to the cruiser and the other walked up to the driver's side of Rod and David's rental car. He asked Rod to step out. It was then that Rod became acutely aware of his wet, grease-stained clothing. Nonetheless, he smiled and got out of the car. The officer asked him to sit in the back seat of the police cruiser, leaving David to remain in the passenger seat of the rental car. Rod handed the policeman his California driver's license with a smile.

In November 1986, we sank half of Iceland's whaling fleet and shut down their illegal operations for seventeen years.

The two police officers spoke to each other in Icelandic for a few minutes as Rod maintained his composure. One of the officers turned to Rod and asked, "Have you been drinking any alcohol?"

"Of course not," he replied. "I don't drink."

"Okay, have a nice trip."

"Thanks, officer."

Rod got back into the driver's seat and took off.

Unbeknown to both men, the police had received word of the sinking ships while Rod was sitting in the back seat of the patrol car. This was not surprising. The two ships were already on the bottom of the harbor. At the time, however, the police were not suspecting deliberate sabotage.

Rod and David's flight was at 7:30 that morning. They waited anxiously for the boarding announcement and even more anxiously when the flight was delayed because of the weather.

Back at the harbor, more police cars had arrived at the scene, and word was quickly spreading that Kristján Loftsson's ships had sunk. Loftsson was the owner of Iceland's only whaling company.

The investigation was underway, but by the time authorities realized what had happened, Rod and David were in the air and bound for Luxembourg. From there, they took a bus to Belgium, boarded the ferry to Dover, and caught the train to London.

Rod and David had called Sarah from Luxembourg. From the United Kingdom, Sarah called me in Vancouver, and I issued a media release claiming responsibility and stating that our objective was to cripple illegal Icelandic whaling operations.

The attack was expensive. Icelandic officials conservatively estimated the cost of damage to the ships at $2 million, the damage to the plant at $2 million, and the destruction of the whale meat at $4 million. It was an $8 million hit, and I knew it was actually more than that because I was certain those two sunken ships would never again kill whales.

And it had gotten Iceland's attention.

Prime Minister Steingrimur Hermannsson called for an emergency cabinet meeting and a debate in the Althing, the Icelandic parliament. Afterward, Hermannsson made a statement. "The saboteurs are regarded by the Icelandic government as terrorists," said the prime minister. "All efforts will be made to get the people who are responsible prosecuted for this inhuman act."

Icelandic attorney general Hallvardur Einarsson said that he would use all possible channels to have the saboteurs extradited and prosecuted in Iceland.

In response, I immediately contacted the Icelandic police and members of the international media to inform them that I would welcome extradition proceedings and the opportunity to defend our actions in an Icelandic court.

Back home in British Columbia, the provincial attorney general, Brian Smith, forgetting his place as a provincial rather than a federal leader, announced that he would have me investigated for conspiracy, terrorism, and anything else he could get me on. He claimed he would then send me to Iceland himself. He was not too pleased when

I responded by telling him to investigate his own powers first. This was not a matter of concern to the provincial government. It was a federal matter.

A day later, I was a guest on the radio show of Dave Barrett, a former British Columbia premier. Barrett was questioning me when the radio station's manager announced that the building had to be evacuated. A caller had said that a bomb had been planted in the radio station to protest my violence in sinking the whaling ships.

I was laughing at the absurdity of it as we exited the station.

On the sidewalk outside the station, reporters from all over the city descended for an impromptu press conference with me and the former premier. I told them I thought it was somewhat puzzling that someone would threaten to kill innocent people to protest our "violence" in sinking whaling ships. Then a reporter thrust a microphone toward me and asked, "What is your response to Greenpeace issuing a media release condemning your actions as terrorism?"

I defended myself with a quick sound bite. "Well," I said, "what do you expect from the door-to-door salespeople of the environmental movement?" I was referring to the army of door-to-door Greenpeace canvassers that beg for money for their bearing witness to ecological atrocities.

My offer to surrender to Icelandic authorities went unanswered. I asked Rod Coronado to fly to New York City to meet me, so that we could do the media rounds. Rod handled himself brilliantly before the media. He never wavered from the position that Iceland was a hooligan whaling nation in violation of international laws. We received positive write-ups in *Time* and *Newsweek* and favorable coverage on television.

After the media blitz, I typed a letter to the president of Iceland to address possible charges against any of us. The Icelandic government had promised to prosecute, and I agreed to cooperate. We wanted our day in court.

The letter went unanswered. I wrote a second letter and a third, both of which also went unanswered. A reporter for an Icelandic newspaper called me and said the authorities in Iceland were determined to have us extradited. I told him there was no need to do that. They simply had to invite us. We would come on the date and to the place of their choosing.

Nothing. I heard nothing at all. For more than a year, absolutely nothing.

So in early January 1988, I let the Icelandic media know that I intended to arrive in Iceland on January 21.

Early in the evening of January 21, I arrived in Keflavík on an Icelandair flight from Luxembourg. I stepped off the plane wearing my black dress uniform and was greeted by two dozen police. An officious man in a gray suit approached me.

"Captain Watson, I am the chief immigration officer. How long do you intend to stay in Iceland?"

I laughed. "Well, I don't know, really. Five minutes, five hours, five days, five months, or perhaps five years—I'm afraid only Iceland can answer that question."

"I see." He seemed confused but added, "Please come with us to the police station for questioning."

I smiled and answered, "That's what I'm here for."

The drive to the police station in Reykjavík was pleasant. The officers were friendly and pointed out the sights. At the station, they brought me coffee as I waited for two prosecutors, the Canadian consul, a state-appointed lawyer, and some additional officers to arrive.

When everyone had arrived, one of the prosecutors addressed me. He got straight to the point. "Is the Sea Shepherd Conservation Society responsible for sinking the two whaling ships and damaging the whale-meat processing plant?"

"Of course," I said. Then I added, "And we intend to sink the other two ships at the first opportunity."

"What was your role in this action?"

"I was responsible for all activities undertaken in the name of Sea Shepherd. I gave the orders."

"Did you give the orders to sink the ships?"

"I did."

"But"—the prosecutor paused before continuing—"you yourself did not actually sink the ships."

"No, of course not. I'm too well known in Iceland, and at the time I was under an expulsion order, which has since expired, from the Faroes that would have prevented me from entering Iceland or any Scandinavian country."

Appearing clever now, the prosecutor exclaimed, "Aha! So, the people who did this thing, the people that we want to arrest, will not come to Iceland."

"They will both come if you ask them to. You have not officially requested any arrests or charges. I have repeatedly requested charges and my requests have been ignored. Give me a phone and I'll ask them to come here on a plane tomorrow."

The other prosecutor's face flushed red with anger. "It's not your place to decide who we charge and when we bring charges. That is our prerogative. We don't have to respond to your requests simply because you make them. Our investigations dictate our actions."

I chuckled. "What investigations and what actions? The situation is simple. Iceland illegally kills whales. We retaliated by sinking two of your illegal ships. What do you need to investigate? A deed was done. We perpetrators admit to doing it, and we throw ourselves before you to do as you will and you respond by doing absolutely nothing. Frankly, gentlemen, I'm a trifle confused."

One of the police officers interrupted. "Captain Watson, are you hungry?"

"No, I'm not." He looked disappointed, so I added, "Unless, of course, you're all hungry."

The officer laughed and said, "We are."

"Well then, let's eat," I responded.

All in all, it was great fun, this questioning. We chatted through dinner about whales and whaling, and after dinner the prosecutors continued with their questioning.

"So," began the first prosecutor, "you admit that you did not directly participate in the sinking of the ships."

"That's correct. I did not do it myself. However, I did conspire to do so. I did support the actions, and I will continue to do so."

"But," he resumed, smiling, "you did not actually board the ships and help sink them."

"No, I did not."

"Thank you, Captain Watson. That will be all. We'll talk to you in the morning."

A prison guard took me to one of the most comfortable jail cells I had ever seen. *If this is prison*, I thought, *it isn't half-bad.*

The next morning, after a pleasant sleep and breakfast, I was escorted to a police car. The officers said I was to be taken to the airport and deported.

There were some reporters outside, being kept at a distance by the police. One of them yelled out, "The police say you denied any involvement with the sinking of the ships. Is that true?"

I managed to shout back that it was not true before the police pushed me into the car and we made our way back to the airport.

Two Icelandic police officers escorted me on the plane for the trip back to New York. They were quite friendly. One of them said to me, "You know, we have not seen this kind of thing in Iceland since the days of the Vikings. I do disagree with your sinking the ships, but it is a good spirit—a spirit we once had and have long since lost."

I sent an open letter to the people of Iceland that was published in *Dagblad* explaining why we did what we did, and I was pleased that the paper published it.

I found out later that while I was being driven to the airport, the Icelandic attorney general, Hallvardur Einarsson, gave a speech before the Icelandic parliament that made a mockery of his earlier position that all efforts would be undertaken to make sure we, the "terrorists," would be brought to justice for our "inhuman" act. Before the parliament, Einarsson expressed consternation that I would ask to be arrested and said that he refused to play by my rules. He recommended that I be deported and banned from entering any Scandinavian country for five years.

There were never any charges, never any arrests, which meant that no crime had been committed. The governing authorities in Iceland knew that if they put Sea Shepherd on trial, they would be putting themselves on trial for criminal whaling activities.

1987–1992

Curtains of Death

THE BERING SEA, THE NORTH PACIFIC OCEAN, AND THE CARIBBEAN

Between 1987 and 1992, Sea Shepherd launched several campaigns to oppose and shut down high-seas drift netting. I took three ships into these confrontations: the *Divine Wind*, the *Sea Shepherd II*, and the *Edward Abbey*. They were campaigns of intense confrontations. We rammed drift netters and confiscated and destroyed their nets, and with every campaign we focused more and more attention on this incredibly destructive industry.

The drift nets we found ranged from ten to more than one hundred nautical miles in length. They were set in panels from the surface and hung to a depth of about fifty feet. Buoys held them up at the top and lead weights weighted down the bottom. The drift nets were massive, devastating weapons of ecological destruction, and every day enough drift net was being set to encircle the globe three times.

In 1987, Sea Shepherd challenged Taiwanese and Japanese drift netters in the North Pacific and the Bering Sea, covering ground all the way past Adak in the Aleutians to within sight of the Soviet Union's coastline.

The early 1990s were filled with confrontations over drift nets. The most dramatic of our drift-net campaigns began on Sunday,

August 12, 1990, when we barged into the midst of a fleet of six Japanese-registered drift-net ships about a thousand miles north of Hawaii. The vessels were just completing the setting of their nets—between them, there was nearly two hundred miles of monofilament drift net in the sea.

Each of the Japanese ships were about two hundred feet long, equal to my ship, the *Sea Shepherd II*. Their hulls were a dirty white color and encrusted with scaly rust. From the stern of each ship shot streams of brine to allow the continuous net to be laid with greater ease.

I began to follow the *Shunyo Maru 8* as she spread her weblike netting behind her like a water spider. This net, stretching for miles behind the ship's stern, was a weapon of mass ecological destruction, a literal curtain of death. As we watched, we knew that thousands of fish, sharks, marine mammals, turtles, and seabirds were struggling in the tightening folds of this insidious web of death.

We watched as the ship set the net and, upon completion, turned and began to head back forty miles to the location where the crew had begun the set. When the ship returned to that point, the drift netters began to retrieve the net and its victims.

The Japanese skipper called me on the radio and warned me to stay away from his net. In response, I brought the *Sea Shepherd II* alongside the *Shunyo Maru 8*, close enough to film the fishermen on the deck.

The radio sputtered, "What you want? What you want?"

I replied, "I want you to stop drift-net fishing."

He did not seem to understand, asking, "Why are you crossing my ship?"

"Because," I answered, "you're killing too many dolphins, whales, birds, and turtles, and you're taking too many fish."

This was followed by an outburst of angry, shrill Japanese.

We continued to follow the drift netter, filming the activity on her deck. Just after midnight, the Japanese crew attached the net and began to haul it in. I was surprised at how fast they were pulling it in.

We filmed the operation, documenting every squid, bird, and marine mammal they hauled in. We documented evidence of the taking of protected birds, a Dall's porpoise, and an unidentified species of dolphin. With that evidence, I was ready to act. I just needed to wait for the dawn, when there would be enough light for the cameras.

By six o'clock that morning, we had the light. A media crew from Citytv in Toronto, under the direction of my friend Bob Hunter, was in position on the monkey deck above the wheelhouse. Our photographer, Marc Gaede, was also ready.

I took the wheel. I ordered the engine room to give me maximum power, and we then charged across the swells toward the port side of the *Shunyo Maru 8*. I was approaching from behind at a close angle to her starboard side. My objective was to destroy the large power block the ship was using to haul in the net. I needed to crush that block without sinking the ship.

With the distance closing between the *Sea Shepherd II* and the *Shunyo Maru 8*, I sounded three loud, long blasts of the horn to warn the fishermen of our intentions. Our bow rose on the swells. I could see some of the fishermen looking up, wide-eyed. They then retreated from the port side, abandoning the net. Our bow wave came on before us, colliding with the wake of the drift netter. An eruption of spray shot up between our hulls, and like a hammer we struck. The power block exploded in a shower of sparks. The gunwales of the Japanese ship crumbled as the steel plates buckled. The ships ground their steel hulls together, creating a cacophony of tortured metal. The net was severed and the power block crushed.

Not a single person was knocked off their feet on either ship. One of the fishermen threw a knife through the air, and it passed over the shoulder of the cameraman on the monkey deck. Bob Hunter reached down, picked up the knife, and with a laugh said, "Hey, got a souvenir."

Over the intercom, I notified my crew to be prepared for our next target, the *Ryoun Maru 6*, which was located about two miles away.

As we approached the *Ryoun Maru 6*, we could see her crew hauling in a huge shark. After I sounded a warning on the horn, the fishermen dropped the shark and the net and ran to their starboard side as we rapidly approached the vessel's port side, my bow aimed directly at her power block.

Searching out and destroying destructive drift net in the North Pacific, the Caribbean, and the Bering Sea.

Once again, the *Sea Shepherd II* struck where I had intended her to strike, crushing the power block and the rails and buckling the plates on the main deck.

The third and fourth drift netters were fleeing, and we were unable to catch them. But they had dropped their nets. When the fleeing fishing vessels were out of sight, we began the tiresome task of hauling in and destroying the nets.

The entire confrontation was documented and sent to the media, including the Japanese media. Upon berthing in Honolulu, I was prepared for Japan to lay charges in response to our high-seas attack or to publicly denounce us. Instead, surprisingly, the Japanese government refused to even recognize that an incident had taken place. We contacted the Japanese consulate and declared that we had attacked Japanese ships and destroyed Japanese property. I delivered the video documentation to the consulate and provided the same to the Japanese media contacts in Hawaii. I stated that we were ready to accept charges, be they in the International Court of Justice in The Hague or in Tokyo. The consulate told me that he had no idea what I was talking about.

The video was aired on Japanese television, but still the official Japanese response was to disclaim all knowledge of the incident. It seemed obvious that Japan wanted to keep the controversy of drift-net fishing as quiet as possible. The Japanese authorities realized that they would gain nothing by taking us to court and that, in fact, any publicity would only serve to illuminate their questionable activities before the eyes of the international public.

A day later, the US Coast Guard raided the *Sea Shepherd II* to look for "safety violations." Most of the men complimented us on a job well done, and a couple apologized for the harassment, saying that it came from "up top."

We had fired the first shots in the drift-net wars. I was confident that what we set in motion led to the 1992 international ban on drift-net fishing.

In November 1991, I bought the retired US Coast Guard patrol vessel *Cape Knox* in Charleston, South Carolina, and renamed it the *Edward Abbey* in honor of the late author of *The Monkey Wrench*

Gang. I took the vessel north to Norfolk, Virginia, to be repaired and to meet up with the Sea *Shepherd II.*

It was quite amusing when the *Sea Shepherd II* arrived in Norfolk. I had appointed John Huntermer as captain while I was working the *Edward Abbey.* John brought the ship into Norfolk's harbor and, because of miscommunications with the pilot, the big black ship flying the Canadian Red Ensign was berthed in the United States naval yard.

The Sea Shepherd crew was quite impressed with the arrival. Trucks moved in to remove garbage and waste oil and to bring supplies we had not ordered. The crewmembers were given passes to depart and enter the gate to the yard, and it seemed like an ideal berth.

Three days later, some officers arrived to inquire about the nature of our visit. Their suspicions had been aroused by the unmilitary bearing and dress of our crew. For three days, it was assumed we were a visiting vessel from the British navy. It was embarrassing to the US Navy that we had been berthed in the yard without anyone noticing. It was also illegal, but the officers realized that charging us would be even more embarrassing—doing so would mean having to explain why our presence had not been noticed sooner. The navy quietly arranged for a berth at a commercial dock in downtown Norfolk, and we were not charged for the move or the stay.

A few days later, both the *Sea Shepherd II* and the *Edward Abbey* departed for Key West, Florida. I took the *Edward Abbey* down through the inland waterway to Savannah, Georgia, and then out to sea and down the coast to Key West.

From Key West, both ships departed for the Panama Canal and then sailed on to Cocos Island, where we anticipated there were several poachers. When we found the poachers, we ordered them to leave the waters around Cocos Island. When they refused, we attacked them with pie cannons, stink bombs, water cannons, and paintballs.

One particularly stubborn poacher refused to budge. I had a replica of a US Civil War cannon aboard, and as the poacher watched, I loaded it with black powder but no cannonball. We swung about until the poacher was staring at the mouth of the cannon. I lit the fuse and by the time the smoke dissipated, he was moving out to sea rather quickly.

We returned to the western coast of North America. From California, I flew off to attend the United Nations Conference on the Environment and Development in Rio de Janeiro, Brazil, where wonderful promises were made without any hope of realization. So, once again, Sea Shepherd harassed fishermen and confiscated nets.

Upon our return to North America, the *Sea Shepherd II* was ordered into Ucluelet on Vancouver Island by the Royal Canadian Mounted Police. The police officers conducted a fruitless search of the ship for weapons and drugs.

When the harassment was over, I was readying to leave when I was handed a pilotage bill for $7,500. That's when I realized that now would be the best time to retire the *Sea Shepherd II*, something that I had been contemplating for a while. I didn't know it then, but this decision would link the fate of the *Sea Shepherd II* to that of the *Farley Mowat* years later.

1988

Rascally Rabbits

SOUTHERN CALIFORNIA

The Animal Liberation Front is not an organization. It's more of a movement without any organization or strategy. People who act on behalf of the Animal Liberation Front share only one trait: a desire to intervene against humanity's practice of inflicting cruelty and death to animals.

In the mid-1980s, some friends of mine who identified themselves as Animal Liberation Front activists asked me if I would like to participate in a raid on a rabbit breeding facility in Southern California. They said they needed a getaway van and a driver; and because I had the van, I was designated as the driver.

Assuming that very little could go wrong, I agreed. A few nights later, five of us were driving down a dark and dusty country road. I noted the distance from the road, pulled over, and checked my watch. It was two o'clock in the morning. We all got out of the van and covered the headlights and brake lights with masking tape. We then continued down a long driveway toward a field and a barn. On the other side of the barn was a house. There were no lights on. My four accomplices put on black ski masks to match the rest of their black clothing. They exited the van and made their way across the field to the barn. I turned the van around and kept watch.

About ten minutes later, the four rescuers returned with three bags full of rabbits. They placed them in the back of the van and went back for more. After their second trip, we heard a dog barking. Suddenly a light came on in the house. Everyone jumped into the back as I started the van and drove slowly and carefully back to the road. The road was hard to see in the blackness. Someone said a car's headlights had come on near the barn. I took a fix on a star and moved faster, remembering that it was a straight road. It was an uneasy feeling, navigating in total darkness. When we reached the point where I remembered the road being located, I took out a flashlight and quickly checked to be certain. The others jumped out and removed the tape from the headlights, and then we sped off. A few miles down the road we removed the tape from the brake lights and then drove out from the Morongo Valley area on Route 62 until we reached Interstate 10 headed toward Riverside.

Feeling good and cruising westward, we suddenly noticed that a couple of the rabbits had escaped the bags and were curiously hopping about in the back.

"What the hell, you guys?" I yelled. "These are some damn big rabbits."

Each of them was as big as a medium-size dog.

Jonathan laughed. "Heavy bastards also."

Rod added, "They are bred large for experimental purposes."

I laughingly asked, "Where do we unload a van full of monster rabbits? These guys are not some cuddly bunnies. It's going to be hard to place them."

Janice saw a sign for the Whitewater rest area. "Damn, I have to piss bad," she said. "Me too," said Jonathan.

I pulled into the rest area parking lot and quickly found we were not alone. It was spring break, and the place was full of partying students. Loud music was blaring and the smell of pot was in the air.

I parked and we went to the restrooms. As we walked back to the van, we saw two cops standing and looking at it.

As we approached, one of the cops tersely asked, "Is this your van?"

I felt a knot in the pit of my stomach, and my mouth went a little dry as I mumbled, "Yeah, officer, it is."

Somehow the report of our raid had reached the cops, and I felt for sure we were in deep shit.

"So what the hell is going on inside?"

That's when we noticed that the van was rocking slightly and we could hear the sounds of humping and thumping. The damn rabbits, now free of their individual cages and comingled in the back of the van, were loudly fornicating.

Janice's face went pale.

"Well, officer, there are a bunch of rabbits in there. They seem to be making out. I can show you if you like, but they might escape if we open the door," I explained.

"Why do you have a van full of rabbits?" the officer asked.

I had to think quickly. "It's for a film project we're doing called *Rascally Rabbits*," I said.

The thumping was growing louder. The cops looked amused. "What you're saying is that you have a bunch of fucking rabbits and they're fucking in the back of the van."

"Yep," I answered. "Do you want to check it out?"

"Yeah, maybe we should," one of the officers said. Just at that moment a fight broke out between two students a few cars over. The officers turned quickly to address the commotion as we quietly got into the van and slipped away.

"Damn, that was close," Jonathan said. "What were you thinking telling him there were rabbits in the van? We could have been arrested."

"What else could I say? The best way to stifle an inquiry is to make sure your story has a foundation in truth. I could not tell them there was nothing going on inside—they may have thought someone was being abducted. By telling them there were rabbits in the van, I could guarantee that if they opened the door, they would see rabbits, which would demonstrate that we did not have anything to hide."

Janice was still nervous. "Yeah, but what if they knew about the rabbits and we just told them we had a van full of rabbits?"

I laughed. "Well, there was that possibility, and it was a risk. But hey, we're on the road. And more importantly, how do we stop all these rabbits from humping? Damn, but they are a horny bunch."

When we got back to Topanga, the sun was coming up and we got a good look at our rescued rabbits. They were indeed big and not so cute. We also noticed that they all had tattoos inside their upper lip.

"Now what?" asked Janice. "What are we going to do with them?"

"There is only one thing we can do with them," I replied. "We can let them go."

Jonathan was doubtful. "We can't just let them go—coyotes or dogs will get them."

"Yes," I said, "they might get caught by coyotes. But there are already rabbits in these hills and they survive—and these guys are bigger and look tougher and they have each other, sort of like a giant rabbit gang. I think they'll get by fine."

So we drove the rabbits up to the top of a ridge as far from the houses as the road would allow. There was nothing but a remote telecommunications tower.

When we opened the van door, most of the rabbits jumped out, tumbling into the dust. They looked around and then dashed off in different directions into the shrubbery. Rod decided to take some of the rabbits to release in Northern California.

Janice seemed upset. "Why did we go to all this trouble to rescue these rabbits when now they may just be meals for the coyotes?"

I smiled and said, "Well, they may be caught by coyotes, hawks, or eagles—but until that happens, *if* it happens, they will be free in the wild. And that is a hell of a lot better than where they were. I think they'll be happy here. I'm happy we did this. Thanks for inviting me along."

Eco-Hawks

ALBERTA, CANADA

In January 1990, the Canadian Cattlemen's Association (now the Canadian Cattle Association; CCA) made the recommendation to the Canadian ministry of agriculture that the entire population of more than four thousand wood buffalo be exterminated in Alberta's Wood Buffalo National Park.

It was a shocking proposal but hardly surprising coming from the CCA. Of course the cattle ranchers would like to see the buffalo eliminated. A cattle rancher is a person who strings barbed wire across the prairies; drills wells and digs stock ponds everywhere; drives off the elk, bison, antelope, and bighorn sheep; poisons coyotes and prairie dogs; shoots eagles, bears, cougars, and wolves on sight; replaces the native grasses with tumbleweed, cow shit, cheat grass, snakeweed, anthills, povertyweed, mud, dust, and flies; and then leans back and smiles broadly, a beer in hand, as they leer into the television cameras and tell us how much they love the land.

Cattle ranchers brag about taming the west by fencing it off in an orgy of greed and materialism that defies the very laws of nature. The 1990 proposal was laughable to conservationists but not to the government of Canada. The Ministry of Agriculture accepted the proposal of extermination as the approach it would implement to address the problem.

But what exactly was the problem? Some of the bison were infected with bovine brucellosis, a contagious disease of livestock, typically caused by *Brucella abortus*, which may also infect people. The disease causes pregnant cows to abort or give birth to unhealthy calves. The bison had to go, they argued, in order to maintain the disease-free, grade A quality of Canadian beef.

As expected, the government ignored the concerns of Indigenous people in and around the area of Wood Buffalo National Park. Canada gave the nod to the boys with the bucks—the ranchers. A special federal panel set up by the Ministry of Agriculture refused to hear a report from the Parks Canada Agency. A special-interest group with the specific special interest of eradicating buffalo had successfully roped the bureaucrats into using tax dollars to benefit their own industry.

The bison herd had been exposed to brucellosis since the 1920s, when park officials shipped 6,673 plains buffalo from overgrazed areas in the south. The Canadian Wildlife Service knew that many of the animals were diseased, but the demands of the ranchers to remove the buffalo from the land they wanted exclusively for grazing cattle prevailed. Ironically, these buffalo had contracted brucellosis from cattle. A healthy wolf population would have sorted out the problem naturally, but because of earlier political lobbying from the same ranchers, the wolves had been hunted to the brink of extinction.

In the early 1970s, the buffalo numbered between ten thousand and twelve thousand, and the animals began to die from disease. Nothing was done by the government to stem the disease. Twenty years later, the disease appeared to have run its course. And now the ranchers and the government wanted to kill the survivors of a disease caused by the cattle industry and allowed to get out of control by the same industry that was now demanding a final solution—a solution that would mean complete eradication of a subspecies of bison without discrimination between diseased and healthy animals.

The mainstream Alberta media was also championing a policy of extermination. An editorial in the August 31 edition of the *Calgary Herald* ended with the pronouncement: "The herd must be destroyed."

Quick to smell the stench of easy money, Alberta politicians and sport hunters were falling over one another to share in the profits of an investment in extinction. A legislator from Fort McMurray, Norm Weiss, had recommended that hunting licenses be sold to hunters who are "eager to bag a buffalo." Weiss went so far as to say, "I really believe that the hunt could be a good revenue generator."

The Alberta Fish and Game Association stated that opening the park to hunters could save the federal government an estimated $20 million, according to Nels Damgaard, the senior vice president of the group.

However, Parks Canada was opposed to the idea of sport hunting in a national park. And even a federal panel stated its desire that there be "a systematic and sensitive elimination of the diseased herd."

"Letting Bungle-o Bill out there with his big heavy gun is neither humanitarian nor systematic," declared Pam Barrett, the New Democrat house leader in Alberta. In 1990, the bison in and around Wood Buffalo National Park made up the largest free-roaming herd in the world. The second largest free-roaming herd of about two thousand bison was in Yellowstone National Park, and those buffalo also had brucellosis. Fortunately, the option of killing them was unacceptable to Americans. A Montreal newspaper summarized the words of Marsha Karle, a spokesperson for Yellowstone National Park: "Experts at Yellowstone question if killing the bison would eradicate the disease."

Indians and Metis who lived around Wood Buffalo National Park, many of whom hunted the bison for food when the animals wandered out of the park, were the most vocal opponents of extermination. Native spokesperson George Kurszewski, who lived in Fort Smith and hunted buffalo, railed against the federal review panel's decision to slaughter the animals. He called the decision "a mad rush to kill all of the bison." According to the *Calgary Herald*, Kurszewski, along with a University of Calgary professor, said the recommendations are "based on insufficient, inaccurate, and exaggerated data."

Kurszewski said that the statistics supporting the proposal of slaughter were less than factual. "They are saying that 30 to 50 percent of the herd are diseased. But this is based on figures that were arrived at 35 years ago," he told the *Calgary Herald*. He also cited the example of an earlier hunt by Native people, after which it was discovered that only 6 out of the 200 buffalo killed by hunters were actually sick.

Valerius Geist, an international wildlife biologist and professor of environmental design at the University of Calgary, agreed with Kurszewski. According to the *Calgary Herald*, Geist maintained that "the diseased-bison problem is somewhat 'contrived.'"

"They . . . are a minimal threat and can be easily managed," stated Geist. He went on to say that the assumption made by the federal review panel that the disease would not fade away naturally was "questionable." The *Calgary Herald* reported, "Geist charged the government has 'jumped on the Wood Buffalo bandwagon' because of a hidden agenda that favors game ranching."

The newspaper summarized Geist: "A venison and dead wildlife parts market—drawn from elk and domestic bison—could be generated with control of Canada's wildlife resources."

Chief Pat Marcel of the Chipewyan native band agreed. His tribe's reserve bordered Wood Buffalo National Park. A journalist for an Alberta newspaper, the *Edmonton Journal*, reported that Chief Marcel said, "We can't accept what's been presented to us, by no means. It's more evidence of the arrogance of the federal government pushing their agenda on us. It's not acceptable anymore."

Other Indigenous leaders had recommended in January 1990 that the bison be rounded up and the diseased animals removed. "Total extermination is not the way to go," they said.

Marcel also expressed his concern at what he believed was "the government's hidden agenda to get rid of the bison to open up the park for agriculture and forestry," the *Edmonton Journal* stated.

"This is not just a plan that would be resolved in 15 years by restocking the park area with disease-free animals. You're looking at grazing land in the future, 50 or 60 years from now, in the lower end of the park. As the agriculture belt moves north, they're going to be needing land. It's as simple as that," Marcel declared.

Marcel's point of view was contrasted by University of Saskatchewan wildlife biologist Francois Messier, who was advocating for the herd to be slaughtered for the long-term health of all ungulates in the area, including cattle.

The *Star-Phoenix*, a newspaper in Saskatchewan, summarized Messier's opinion. "There's a cattle pasture about 100 kilometers west of Wood Buffalo park," the paper reported. "If any cattle are infected, the industry could lose an estimated $200 to $500 million over the next decade, [Messier] said."

In the same article, the *Star-Phoenix* also mentioned R. D. Lawrence, a Canadian naturalist and spokesperson for the Canadian Federation of Humane Societies, who didn't share Messier's assessment of the situation. "It would be an international disgrace to eliminate the single largest bison herd in the world to accommodate cattlemen," according to Lawrence in the *Star-Phoenix* article.

The *Star-Phoenix* also reported that Ken East, the superintendent of the national park, argued that culling all the bison would not be simple. "The suggestion has been made without sound knowledge of the size of the area and the logistics," East was quoted as saying. "The bison herd isn't just in the park—this is 50,000 square miles of rugged, mountainous countryside."

According to the newspaper, acting park superintendent Bart Hartop added, "We're talking 20 years and millions of dollars."

Francois Messier fired back that he believed the cost and difficulty would be justified: "It's disconcerting to kill 4,000 bison, but in the long-term perspective, there's no other alternative."

"Canada is one of the few countries with disease-free status, so losing this premium status means a drop in import meat prices," reported the *Star-Phoenix*, summarizing Messier.

Messier had hit the nail on the head. This controversy was all about a choice between beef prices and the survival of a species.

Wood Buffalo National Park was and still is a wildlife sanctuary, a UNESCO World Heritage Site, and a nesting habitat for migrating birds. It would be absurd to have a national park without the species that gave the park its name.

Listening to all of these arguments, I said to myself that enough was enough. If the cattlemen wanted to go to war with the buffalo, we would need to go to war with them first in a preemptive strike.

I was scheduled to give a lecture at Ryerson University (now Toronto Metropolitan University) in Toronto and decided to invite the media to my lecture, saying that I had a special announcement pertaining to the buffalo of Wood Buffalo National Park.

I had an idea, but I was aware that not only was the idea highly illegal but that it was illegal to even publicly advocate for it. So I created a fictional group: the Eco-Hawks.

At the media conference prior to my lecture on ecoactivism, I made the announcement. Addressing both the students and the journalists, I began: "I have been asked to join a radical group of scientists who wish to take action against the proposal to exterminate all the buffalo of Wood Buffalo National Park in Alberta. I refused to join this group, but because their intentions are illegal, I believe it's my civic duty to inform the public of this group's intentions.

"I would like to state clearly that I do not endorse what this group is planning, because what they are intending to do is illegal and I do not endorse or support or involve myself in illegal activities.

"This group calls themselves the Eco-Hawks. They met with me yesterday here in Toronto. They invited me to join their campaign, but after hearing their plan, I had no option but to refuse.

"The leader of the group says she is a graduate biochemist from the University of British Columbia. She says her name is Monika Lewis, which I presume is not her real name. She said to me, 'I'm sick of seeing my profession degraded by academics for hire. You can always find an institution willing to justify any ridiculous, politically motivated scheme if the price is right.'

"Her colleague, a naturalist who calls himself Derek Milner, added, 'If wilderness is outlawed, then only outlaws can save the wilderness.'

"Milner and Lewis told me they are part of a small band of scientifically educated 'outlaws' and that the group has decided to take action in defense of the buffalo. They told me they have a plan, and when they told me what the plan was, I realized that it would be extremely controversial and frightening to the cattle industry: they told me that they have both the knowledge and ability to culture a disease called brucellosis and that they have the knowledge and ability to intentionally infect cattle with the disease.

"If the plan to exterminate the buffalo in Wood Buffalo National Park goes ahead, the Eco-Hawks informed me that they will deliberately inoculate cattle from Manitoba to British Columbia with brucellosis.

"Milner told me that once the killing begins, Canada's disease-free status will be the cost of implementing this perverse proposal.

"I told Lewis and Milner that this was extortion, and they admitted that it was. Lewis told me that it was tit for tat, and if the government wishes to operate immorally to cater to special-interest groups, then it is high time to challenge the status quo.

"'Extortion is a crime against the state,' Milner told me. 'But destroying a species is a crime against nature and humanity.'

"When I asked him if they were worried about being caught, Milner told me that there are lots of cows between Manitoba and the Pacific Ocean."

When I finished making the statement, the journalists hit me with a barrage of questions, asking if I had informed the authorities, if I could describe the two, and if I had pictures.

I told them that I considered this announcement as informing the authorities and that I did not have pictures or any other details to share.

One journalist was not buying my story and asked if I was actually leading this group, to which I said, "Of course not—I'm not a criminal."

Another asked, "How do we know this story is even true? You could be making it all up."

Hmm, a good nose for bullshit on this one, I thought. But I answered simply, "Well, you don't know—you just have what I'm telling you."

The story was picked up, and to my surprise the police did not question me. They most likely held the opinion that I had made the whole thing up, and of course I had. But the entire point of the exercise was to plant the idea that it was possible to deliberately infect cattle with a disease that would cost the cattle industry tens of millions in losses by undermining their grade A beef status.

The very idea was enough to shake up the cattle ranchers. The plan to exterminate the buffalo of Wood Buffalo National Park quietly went away.

As of this writing, some three thousand buffalo live within the borders of the park, a number that is likely greater than it would be had the slaughter gone forward but a far cry from the millions of bison that once roamed free across North America.

Pigeon Purgatory

HEGINS, PENNSYLVANIA

From 1934 to 1998, a perverse annual massacre took place every Labor Day in Hegins, Pennsylvania.

An August 25, 1992, article in the *Washington Post* described it as such:

> Like Spain's running of the bulls at Pamplona, the Hegins pigeon massacre is a day of down-home festivities. More than $35,000 was raised last year for local civic programs from the sale of beer and barbecued eats. It's a day of lawn chairs, picnics and tailgating. Then blood lust takes over and gunners line up to blast away at hapless pigeons. Shooting fish in a barrel is about the only form of killing less demanding of talent from the shotgun set.

This description made it into the *Washington Post* because my colleagues and I had intervened the year before. That's when an organized protest held by numerous animal rights groups descended upon Hegins to help commemorate Labor Day. In 1990, fifteen animal rights activists had been arrested for interfering with the pigeon shoot. Because of that protest, a much larger crowd of protesters had arrived for the 1991 Hegins pigeon slaughter day.

I went to Hegins, along with Cleveland Amory and Heidi Prescott of the Fund for Animals, Ingrid Newkirk and Alex Pacheco of PETA, and Wayne Pacelle of the Humane Society of the United States.

I arrived early as the crowd was having the traditional breakfast of ham and eggs. Dozens of gun-toting, camo-wearing men were strutting around, fancying themselves as Clint Eastwood or Bruce Willis. A few of them sneered at me and one stopped to ask me what I was doing there.

"I've come to see just what compels grown men to shoot birds in a basket. You call this a sport?"

"Yes, it's a sport, and it's *our* sport—you should mind your own fucking business."

"It ain't a sport," I replied. "You're just a sexually frustrated coward that's replaced your penis with a shotgun."

He turned a deep shade of red and made a move to strike me.

"Wait a minute before you hit me. There is something you need to do," I warned.

"What's that, asshole?" he asked.

"You might want to smile for the state troopers over there."

"Asshole," he muttered as he walked away.

I had to be very careful during this "festival," because I was not a US citizen in 1991 and an arrest would cause me problems when I wanted to return to the United States or apply for US citizenship.

The primary tactic of the animal rights activists was to run out on the shooting field to block the killers with their shotguns. Alex Pacheco ran out to the field, grabbed a cage full of pigeons, and began to flee as police officers pursued. He managed to smash the cage to release the birds, all of which were able to escape before he was caught and arrested.

I recognized Neal Barnard, MD, as he stepped up to the line with his shotgun. None of the organizers knew that Dr. Barnard was an animal rights activist, and those of us who did recognize him pretended not to know him because he was there with a gun for a reason. He had paid his fee; thus, he was a legal participant. He called for the pigeons to be released, shouldered his shotgun, and fired, and the birds flew away.

"Damn. Could you set up another cage for me, please?" he requested.

Once again Dr. Barnard took aim and fired. And once again the birds flew away unscathed.

A couple of grounds boys were laughing. "That guy can't shoot worth a damn," one of them said.

Dr. Barnard had loaded his gun with blanks and thus successfully spared the lives of numerous pigeons.

My job was to film Wayne Pacelle as he ran out on the field to release the pigeons from a trap. I held the camera as Wayne dashed out. A bunch of shooters began screaming for the police and shouting insults at him when they noticed that I was filming the action.

"Hey, he's one of them!" a large burly man yelled as he pointed at me.

Suddenly a couple of hunters began to reach for my camera.

"Break his fucking camera," one of them yelled.

With my eye on the camera, I could see Wayne rushing to grab a trap.

A hand hit the camera. "Gimme that, ya asshole."

Without taking my eye from the camera's viewfinder, I yelled, "Back off now—FBI!"

They stopped. Wayne grabbed the trap and smashed it as the police were closing in on him.

"You ain't no fucking FBI," said one of the shooters. "Show us yer badge."

Again, without looking at them, I loudly said, "If I must show you my badge while I'm gathering evidence, I'll bust you for obstruction. Now back off."

And they did.

One by one, the activists were handcuffed and transported to the local jail and charged as the killing went on. I saw Heidi Prescott from the Fund for Animals and Ingrid Newkirk from PETA arrested and carried off the field to the police vans.

With a number of activists removed from the killing grounds, I decided to leave. But before leaving I went to the public restrooms. In my pocket was a small glass bottle carefully wrapped in a few layers of cloth. I went into a stall and carefully unwrapped the bottle. With the cloth, I wiped my fingerprints off the bottle and flushed the cloth down the toilet. Then, using some toilet paper to grasp the bottle and avoid leaving more fingerprints, I carefully poured the liquid on the floor beside the toilet. I quickly left the bathroom—I did not run but just walked briskly into the crowd and made my way to the grounds' exit.

A few minutes later, there was a disturbance near the restroom and people were yelling. I heard one man exclaim that there was a horrible smell coming from the men's bathroom. A couple of state troopers ran toward the building but stopped as the stench hit their nostrils.

I smiled and said to myself, "Good old butyric acid—smells like rotten butter on steroids."

I found out later that eighty-five protestors were arrested, hauled off to the local jail, and charged with trespassing and theft. I wasn't sure how freeing pigeons was theft. The birds were not stolen, just liberated.

The article in the *Washington Post* that appeared a year later stated:

> James Diehl, a former trapper boy who is now the lawyer from the Hegins Park Association that hosts the shoot, argues that the event is legal. "I pretty much echo the sentiments of my clients," Diehl said in a phone interview. "You have a constitutional right to voice your opinion. You have no constitutional right to come into a community, violate the law, desecrate property and commit a criminal act. That's what [local people] find offensive."
>
> It's also what offends furriers, whalers, lab researchers, circus owners, horse carriage operators, slaughterhouse managers and other users or abusers of animals who see shifts in public opinion threatening the old way of having fun or making a buck. The legal argument is weak: what's legal isn't necessarily moral.
>
> The good citizens of Hegins, like the good operators of zoos where animals are imprisoned or the good medical researchers who torment and kill mice, rats, chimps or whatever, point to the history and benefits of their practice. Cock fighting and bull fighting were once legal in the United States. No more. Public sentiment changed.

Who changed it? The same kind of defenders of animals who went to Hegins for the past five or six years and who will be back this Labor Day. Live-bird target shooting has been outlawed in most states where it was once accepted as a sport. Pennsylvania is one of four holdout states that let the blood keep flowing.

In 1998, Hegins, Pennsylvania, held its last Labor Day pigeon massacre. I was proud to be a part of the movement that shut it down.

1992

Columbus, Make My Day

PUERTO RICO

As a boy, I once fantasized about going back in time to 1492 so that I could be offshore in the Bahamas with my ship to welcome Christopher Columbus and his gang of vicious thugs to the "new world."

My welcome would not have been very friendly. I'd have given the sailors a warning to abandon ship. Then I would sink those accursed little caravels, after which I would rescue the crews and ferry them back to the coast of Spain with a warning to stay put and not bother the gentle Carib and Taino people anymore.

It was a nice little dream, but—alas—it was only a dream. The reality was that the landing of Columbus ignited the greatest genocide and mass extermination of humans and cultures in the history of humanity. So I was especially irked to discover that Spain was sending three replicas across the Atlantic to commemorate the five hundredth anniversary of the arrival of this mass-murdering monster.

I called up my old friend Bob Hunter, who was hosting his own environmental awareness show on Citytv in Toronto. I asked him what he thought of the idea of intercepting the replicas of the *Niña*, the *Pinta*, and the *Santa Maria*. He loved the idea.

My friend, journalist and writer Terry Glavin, had written a book in 1990 entitled *A Death Feast in Dimlahamid*, which dealt with the struggles of the Gitxsan and Wet'suwet'en peoples of British Columbia. Through him I met with some of their leaders, like Chief Wii Seeks and Gordon Sebastian. I ran the idea of disrupting the Columbus celebration by them. They said they would like to be involved, and I was thrilled by their response.

My ship, the *Sea Shepherd II*, was in Key West, Florida, and ideally situated to set forth to intercept the replicas. For the campaign, I temporarily changed the name of the ship to *Aligat*, the Gitxsan and Wet'suwet'en word for "warrior." Fourteen members of the Gitxsan and Wet'suwet'en Nation arrived in Key West to join my crew. We set forth in early December, bound first for the Bahamas and then for the waters just east of Puerto Rico.

When we reached the Bahamas, we landed on San Salvador, deciding not to clear customs and immigration on the grounds that Indigenous peoples should not be obligated to ask for permission to land in territory unlawfully seized by the likes of Columbus.

My crew flagged down a tour bus and requested that the driver take them to the Columbus monument on the island. Instead of paying the driver, they officially declared him to be their new governor for the Bahamas. The driver excitedly accepted the honor and took them straight to the monument, smiling as the warriors took a crowbar and pried the bronze plaque from the statue. Today that plaque is on display in the council house in Gitxsan and Wet'suwet'en territory.

With the visit to the Columbus monument complete, the crew returned to the ship, and we set off for Puerto Rico. We entered the harbor of San Juan and tied up to one of the industrial piers. I called immigration and received a control number and permission to go ashore. All fourteen of the Native crewmembers went ashore. A half an hour later, US customs arrived and was not very happy to discover that they had gone ashore without clearance.

I was dealing with an officer named Garcia, telling him that I had an immigration control number.

Angrily, Garcia yelled, "I didn't hear anything about anything! Therefore, nothing happened. Got it? You better get everybody who left this boat back on this boat right away. That's an order. Your crew is confined to the ship until further notice, and I'm inclined to fine any crewmember not aboard now three thousand dollars."

Garcia and his armed buddy retreated to their jeep. A few minutes later, a dozen officers in army camouflage arrived and took up positions at strategic points on the pier.

When the Indigenous crew returned and were ordered back aboard, they were told they would be fined. That is when Gordon Sebastian, the Gitxsan Frog clan lawyer, observed that each one of the individuals facing the $3,000 fines was a Native person. "Of course, it's just a coincidence that we were all headed off to look for a hotel," he said carefully. "We all know that. But to the outside world, it must look awfully suspicious that not a single white person on this crew has been charged, only the Natives. All we have to do is get the message out."

After listening to some angry threats of fines and deportation, I explained to the officials that deporting all fourteen Indigenous crewmembers that came to protest the Columbus celebration would not look very good on the news. My explanation was backed up with the arrival of the local media, which had been contacted after Gordon's suggestion.

A grumbling Officer Garcia left.

The next morning, officers from the US Coast Guard arrived to ask what our intentions were. I told them we intended to blockade the replicas of Columbus's ships to protest the quincentennial celebration of his arrival.

The officer in charge, in all seriousness, asked me, "Don't you think it's somewhat unfair to block those small boats with your larger ship?"

I looked at him and laughed. "Really? Are you seriously saying that we're the bullies here?"

"Your ship would be seen as a very intimidating threat to the Spanish crew on those little boats," he replied with a look of concern on his face.

"Look," I answered, "I have no intention of damaging those boats. This is a legitimate protest by Indigenous peoples against five hundred years of injustice that began with that mass-murdering maniac arriving here in the Caribbean to begin the greatest genocide in world history."

His face reddened. "That's one way of looking at it—another way of looking at it is that if not for Columbus, the United States would not have become the freest and greatest nation on the planet."

"You can't stop us from leaving, and you can't stop us from protesting the arrival of these obscene boats. We have every right to navigate those waters, and we intend to do so."

We left the harbor and headed to the eastward side of Puerto Rico to await the arrival of the caravels. The Coast Guard had raced ahead to provide protection to the Spanish ships, in addition to the Spanish naval frigate accompanying the Columbus expedition.

We knew the replicas were close, because on our radio we had picked up Spanish voices and the words "*Santa Maria*, read you loud and clear."

I sent crew up the foremast with binoculars. We knew the boats had to pass north of the Virgin Islands to reach Puerto Rico and we could hear them. They had to be close.

The Coast Guard was monitoring our movements and relaying our position to the Spanish navy. Early in the afternoon, a US Navy nuclear submarine surfaced behind us, overtook us, and passed across our bow.

"Now, that's a definite show of power," I said with a laugh. "Here we have a nuclear submarine defending the reenactment of the voyage of the man who ushered in five centuries of genocide. Very appropriate!"

It also occurred to me that this was how the US Navy had been monitoring us all of yesterday and today, and I realized that the submarine would not have revealed herself unless the caravels had passed us.

I grabbed a chart and there it was. The Coast Guard must have guided the caravels through the Anegada Passage to get around us.

"They are ahead of us," I said to the crew. "Maybe we can catch them before they reach Puerto Rico."

At full throttle we set off toward where the replica ships most likely were heading: the northeastern coast of Puerto Rico. It was not long before we spied the three sails moving toward the marina of Puerto del Rey.

As we were closing in, we saw the Spanish warship turn and head directly toward us at full speed, belching thick black smoke and aiming her deck guns straight at us.

The frigate and the *Aligat* were on a collision course in slightly rough seas. Each ship was sending white sheets of spray over the other's bow as they rapidly approached each other.

I turned to Bob Hunter. "I think they want to play chicken with us. This should be fun."

Bob did not look convinced. "I don't know, Paul—this is looking very dangerous."

"Don't worry, Bob, the frigate is going to move. They always do. I've played this game with the Soviets and the Canadian Coast Guard—they'll move."

"How can you know that for sure?" Bob replied nervously.

"Because I won't move and, in a few moments, the captain is going to realize just that."

As the two ships came closer, the US Navy submarine surfaced not far off to witness this high-seas drama.

As I watched the frigate through my binoculars, Bob asked, "Is this a collision course?"

With a laugh I said, "Well, yes, but only if they don't move. They will."

And they did. The frigate moved to starboard and went thundering by our port side, so close we could have hit her with a spitball.

The frigate passed and began to turn around to pursue us, but I turned hard to port and crossed their bow. With a smile I informed Bob that we had just crossed the T and noted the fact that we were flying the British flag, the very same flag that Admiral Horatio Nelson flew when he did the same at the Battle of Trafalgar. "They will get the message," I assured him.

I then launched a Zodiac with a Native crew and a camerawoman to follow the caravels into the marina.

It appeared that we had failed. The three caravels were safe in the marina. We had not stopped them, and there was no way we could enter that marina with the *Aligat*, as she was too large.

"Time to send in the marines," I said.

We returned to San Juan and docked the ship. I called a couple of taxis, and a Native crew of three led by Arthur Loring, Gitxsan wing chief of the Eagle clan, headed off across the island to Puerto del Rey. Bob Hunter and a handful of crewmembers, armed with cameras, followed.

The morning raid evolved into a comedy. When my crewmembers arrived at the marina, they were greeted by four armed guards; but Bob passed himself off as a yacht owner with his crew. They even called for a golf cart to drive him down the docks to the Spanish ships.

With Bob sitting in the front seat of the golf cart, the Native crew put on their war paint and headdresses. When they arrived on the docks, they found the three ships tied up alongside each other with the *Santa Maria* on the outside. The crews were sleeping in their hammocks as our war party crossed over the *Niña* and the *Pinta* to the *Santa Maria*, where a large Spanish soldier was guarding the gangway. When the guard saw Arthur and his crew sporting war paint, feathers, and drums, he sprinted to the dock to run for help.

Meanwhile, our crewmembers took their positions and began drumming and chanting. The obviously hungover Spanish crew woke to what must have appeared to be a bizarre sight. Arthur Loring had their full attention as he proclaimed, "My name is Gu Tsagan from Gitwangak." He jabbed his chest with his thumb and said, "I am from the Eagle clan, and I claim the *Santa Maria* for our people in North, South, and Central America."

One of the sailors who could speak English began to translate to the others. Arthur picked up on this and spoke slowly with pauses. "I'm seizing this ship. I am staying on it. We will see that corrections are done right by our people."

Not a single Spanish sailor moved or ordered any of our crewmembers to get off the ship. They just stood and stared until a police officer arrived. This cop was quite perplexed about what to do with the situation. A group of hostile people had just confessed to seizing the boat in a blatant act of piracy, but the fact that they looked like Indians, talked like Indians, and were in fact genuine Indians caught him off guard just as it had the sailors.

With the crews from the other two replica ships now on the deck of the *Santa Maria*, Arthur boldly announced, "I am not giving this ship back until the Spanish consulate comes down here and apologizes to our people."

Meanwhile, at the marina's entrance, two army trucks arrived with armed soldiers. The soldiers jumped out of the trucks and surrounded the *Santa Maria*. Snipers took up positions overlooking the marina.

On the other side of the ships, there were bubbles in the water. The police had deployed divers, who were approaching.

Members of the local media had begun arriving at the gate of the marina and were being denied entry. But by the time the captain of the *Santa Maria*, Santiago Bolivar Pineiro, who was supposedly a direct descendant of Christopher Columbus, came on deck, the media outlets had made it past the marina's gate and were now on the dock, their cameras recording every moment.

Captain Pineiro was trapped. He was aware of the history of his own nation, and the last thing he needed was to violently expel a group of Native American protesters.

Finally, the Spanish consulate arrived. The consul and Captain Pineiro sat down at a small table across from Chief Wii Seeks and Gordon Sebastian. The four of them spoke for twenty minutes, and then the consul took out a piece of paper, signed it, and handed it to Wii Seeks.

And with that the tension was eased—the drumming stopped and Wii Seeks proudly proclaimed that the Spanish consul had officially apologized in the name of Spain for five hundred years of injustice.

Arthur Loring stood up to say, "Justice has been obtained. I obey the will of my chiefs and thereby release this ship."

As the media departed and the Spaniards got back to work, our crew of Natives and reporters walked back to catch a taxi, only to find the media had commandeered them all. The police force's detective superintendent approached the crew with a smile and offered to drive everyone back to San Juan in patrol cars. He was apologetic. "Please forgive us for overreacting. We did not know if you were peaceful or not. The message that went out to all the police and military forces was not good. It said, 'Terrorists have seized the *Santa Maria.*' So we came prepared to shoot."

He then laughed and said, "But fortunately this all ended peacefully— no one was hurt, and many of us are sympathetic to your cause."

When everyone arrived back in San Juan, the detective super- intendent treated everyone to a meal at a Chinese restaurant.

Most of the Native crew flew back to Canada, and I prepared to take my ship back to Key West, satisfied that we had accomplished something significant in receiving an official apology for five hundred years of genocide and destruction that began with that ignoble rapist and murderer, Captain Christopher Columbus.

1992–1994

Battle in the Lofoten

NORWAY

S ea Shepherd had helped shut down Iceland's illegal whaling operations, but Norway was killing more whales illegally than Iceland.
So, in 1992, I made the decision to intervene against the outlaw
activities of the Norwegian whaling fleet.

Toward this end, I recruited a very competent accomplice. I
knew that Dwight Worker had the courage and resourcefulness for
the job. He was the only person since Pancho Villa to have escaped
from Mexico's notorious Lecumberri prison. He made his escape
after serving two years of a five-year sentence at Lecumberri, where
he had been subjected to numerous abuses by both guards and
inmates. He was tough and ideal for a midwinter commando raid
north of the Arctic Circle.

Our objective would be one of the whaling boats in the Lofoten
Islands in the far north of Norway. We decided to make a state-
ment on Christmas Day 1992. My job would be to locate the target.
Dwight's job would be to sink it.

I landed at Arlanda Airport in Stockholm, drove across the
Swedish border to Norway, and then traveled up the coast of Norway

to the Lofoten. Dwight took the train north to Kiruna, Sweden, where he also rented a car.

I took a female volunteer with me so we could pose as a married couple on vacation. If we were asked about our plans, we would say that we were interested in spending the holidays in the Arctic.

The Lofoten Islands are extraordinarily beautiful, but in the dead of winter there were only a few hours of twilight each day. Darkness defines the high north's winter, and each day was dark, bitingly cold, and deathly quiet.

We discovered two whalers in the town of Steine, one of which was the *Nybraena*. Both ships were owned by a notorious family of whalers.

With the target vessel located, I contacted Dwight in the town of Andenes and gave him directions.

On Christmas Day, a little after midnight, Dwight boarded the *Nybraena* armed with a hefty monkey wrench and bolt cutters. He closed the seawater intake valve, cut through the green seawater pipe, reopened the valve, and invited the sea into the engine room, which quickly began to flood.

A few moments after Dwight left the dock, two Norwegian fishermen, just leaving a party, spotted him. They approached him, and Dwight, being neither Norwegian nor fluent in the language, knew he would be hard-pressed to explain why an American would be on the dock beside a whaling ship in such a remote place.

One of the Norwegians called out, and Dwight, thinking very quickly, bent over, stuck his fingers down his throat, and vomited onto the snow.

The two fishermen laughed. The man was obviously drunk, they assumed, which was not unusual in a town in which people were having Christmas parties.

When the men passed out of sight, Dwight looked back and saw that the *Nybraena* was visibly lower in the water. He returned to his car and drove back to Kiruna to catch the train to Stockholm and then a flight to the United States.

I drove through Sweden, caught a ferry to Denmark, and connected with a train to Amsterdam, where I notified the media that we had just delivered a Christmas gift to the whales. I called Norwegian police inspector Elisabeth Kaas of the Lofoten and Vesteralen police to officially inform her that we had sunk the *Nybraena*. I gave her my information and told her to contact me if any charges were forthcoming.

A few months later, Inspector Kaas flew to Seattle, where the FBI had arranged for her to interview me in their offices. I answered her questions and she returned to Norway, and I heard nothing more until 1997.

In January 1994, Sea Shepherd disabled a second Norwegian whaler, the *Senet*, in the south of Norway. Once again we claimed credit for the sinking.

A Norwegian reporter called me to ask why my organization was sinking whaling ships. I replied that Norwegian whaling was a violation of the International Whaling Commission's regulations, and we were simply enforcing the regulations.

"But there are many small whaling boats in Norway," he said. "Sinking one or two is not going to stop whaling."

"That is true," I replied. "However, the object of these campaigns is to hurt the entire fleet. Because of the sinking and disabling of these two vessels and our announced intention to sink more, ship owners are now obligated to pay much higher insurance premiums, specifically war insurance premiums. Sinking one or two impacts the entire fleet financially."

In the summer of 1994, I launched a new ship that I named *Whales Forever*, and I announced that Sea Shepherd intended to disrupt Norwegian whaling at sea with the continued objective of forcing the whalers to pay war insurance premiums and publicizing Norway's continued illegal activities. My crew and I departed Amsterdam and headed north along the coast of Norway, making sure to stay outside of twelve miles. I took a dozen European journalists with me. I carried a bright yellow mini submarine on the back deck—I didn't intend to use it, but I wanted the Norwegians to think I would.

Norway sent the warship *Andenes* to monitor our progress. She did not attempt to contact us; she just stayed close, looking ominous with her big guns. By midday, I expected us to be off the coast and near the whaling station at Skrova.

At 5:50 a.m., I was startled to hear the radio squawk. A thickly accented voice was hailing us: "*Whales Forever*, this is the Norwegian warship *Andenes*. You have just entered Norwegian territorial waters. Please stop your ship. You are under arrest."

I took a quick glance at my GPS and radar and noted my ship's position on the chart.

"*Andenes*, this is the *Whales Forever*. We have not entered Norwegian waters. We are in international waters."

The Norwegian commander responded, "You have entered Norwegian territorial waters. Stop your ship. You are under arrest."

I ignored him. Instead, I hit the alarm button to signal my crew to man their battle stations. Within minutes, all thirty-four crewmembers and media people were on deck. The crewmembers were manning fire hoses and the members of the media prepared their cameras and tape recorders. I sent a crewmember with a camera to the deck above the wheelhouse.

The Norwegian warship's captain continued to call us and I continued to ignore him. He had no authority over us in international waters; thus, I had no intention of submitting to him.

Suddenly, without warning, the *Andenes* turned to port and began to cross in front of us. I saw the nearly 220 yards of heavy yellow nylon rope she was towing. We had anticipated this. The Norwegian ship was attempting to foul our prop. In the Netherlands, I had the dry dock weld three triangular teeth to the bow along with a dozen stainless steel cutting blades around the prop shafts. Still, I knew it was best to avoid the possibility of entanglement, so I cut the main engines and threw the bow jet thruster hard to starboard, keeping our stern away from the rope.

The warship circled us and cut across again. Once more I was able to take evasive action to protect my vessel's prop. After my third successful evasive measure, the Norwegian commander was noticeably frustrated and angry. He came around a fourth time, cutting much closer than before. He turned hard to port and attempted to cross the bow of my ship once again when I noticed he was heeling far over to port.

I heard our cameraman yell from the top deck. "He's going to ram us!"

Inking outlaw whaling vessels in Norway and confronting the Norwegian navy off the coast of Northern Norway.

From my position at the controls of the bow thruster, I could see that the *Andenes* would hit us amidships at twenty-four knots. At that speed, she would cut us in half if she hit us. I threw my bow thruster into full starboard and ordered the main engines into reverse.

This maneuver saved my ship, but there was no avoiding a collision. The *Andenes* ripped across our bow, and the inch-thick steel hull collapsed and tore away like paper.

The *Whales Forever* heeled far over to port as the *Andenes* roared past us like a runaway train. The jagged steel of our torn bow ripped along the side of the warship, buckling railings, snapping cables, and cutting into the hull.

The impact swung the *Whales Forever*'s stern directly into the path of the towing rope. Our port engine prop snatched the rope and came to an abrupt stop. I shut down the starboard engine. The rope had been cut by the bow teeth and the crew began to haul it in.

A large helicopter appeared above us, and it looked like soldiers were going to rappel down to our decks. I grabbed a parachute flare and triggered it, sending a rocket skyward as a warning to the pilot to back off. He did.

We were dead in the water. We had to get underway before the Norwegians sent a boarding party over. I started up the engine to move ahead when a large piece of the rope was seized and pulled tighter into the prop. I ran from the wheelhouse with a fire axe and began violently hacking at the thick line to sever it.

With the port engine going, we managed to limp away as the warship approached. With the *Andenes* almost on top of us, the line in the port prop broke free. We started the port engine and lurched ahead at thirteen knots. I changed course, heading directly out to sea with the Norwegian warship in pursuit.

The Norwegian commander angrily came back on the radio. "*Whales Forever*, this is the *Andenes*. You are under arrest. You *will* stop."

"*Andenes*, we did not enter Norwegian waters and we have not broken any of your laws," I replied. "You have no authority to arrest this ship in international waters."

The Norwegian captain responded, "You will be arrested—there is no dispute about this. You will be arrested. Stop your ship."

"Negative, Captain, I will not stop this ship and we will not be arrested. I will not submit to your illegal demands."

I paused and then continued. "Captain, are you prepared to sink this ship and kill my people?"

The enraged commander responded, "By whatever means, I intend to fire upon you. This is your first warning shot."

The awesome 57-millimeter turret gun pointed our direction. We saw a puff of smoke and heard a deep boom. A fountain of water erupted some sixty-five feet on the other side of our ship.

The radio crackled again. "*Whales Forever*, please order your crew to the stern. I will be firing a shell into your bow. Let me know when your crewmembers are on the stern."

Without waiting for my orders, the crew deployed along the starboard side of the ship facing the guns. They stood in a line from the bow to the stern.

"Captain Watson, I see you are not obeying my orders and you are willing to order your crew into danger instead."

"*Andenes*, I did not order my crew to do anything. They've read quite a bit about Gandhi. I can't do a damn thing with them in this regard. Some of them have stood down bulldozers and whaling ships. They will not submit to your guns."

In anger, the commander snapped back. "I will hold you responsible for any deaths or injuries."

I answered, "Who do you think you are—Pontius Pilate? You can't wash your hands of this. You've got the guns, sir. It's your finger on the trigger. We are unarmed. Oh, and did I mention there are a dozen European reporters with cameras aboard my ship? If you shoot, you alone will be responsible for killing people. The world will hold you responsible."

Undeterred, the captain said, "Tell your people I will be firing a second shot."

I relayed the message. The crew replied that they understood the risks and agreed to stand their ground.

The big gun barked again, and a shell whistled through the air and over the *Whales Forever*, landing about a hundred feet away from her port side.

The commander then ordered me to evacuate the ship's engine room. "I intend to put a shot into your engine compartment. You're ordered to evacuate the engine room."

As calmly as possible, I answered, "Negative, sir, I will not do that. If you fire into the engine room, you will kill people. I have five engineers down there, four men and a woman."

There was no one in the engine room when I said that.

"Captain Watson, I have ordered you to evacuate your engine room."

"I heard you, *Andenes*. You have no authority over this ship. We have no intention of submitting to your guns. We have broken no law;

we have not invaded your territory. You're acting irrationally and we will not comply."

"*Whales Forever*, this is the *Andenes*. You will submit. You will be arrested, we will take you to Bodø, and your ship will be confiscated. I order you to stop your ship."

"*Andenes*, we will never submit to you. The answer—for the final time—is no."

Putting down the transceiver, I turned to my first officer, Bjørn Ursford, a veteran of the Royal Norwegian Navy, and said, "They don't seem to understand that we will not stop."

Bjørn answered, "Nobody has ever said no to them before. They have not been given orders on how to deal with a negative reply."

"Do you think they will actually sink us?" I asked.

"It is possible. It is obviously the only way to stop us."

I triggered the ship's emergency position-indicating radio beacon, sending a Mayday signal.

The *Andenes* stopped briefly and lowered a rigid-hull inflatable boat crewed by commandos. It raced up alongside us and crossed our bow as one of the men tossed a heavy blue canister over the side only six feet before our bow.

"What the hell is that?" I asked Bjørn. But before he could answer, a horrendous explosion lifted the bow of the ship out of the water, rocking us violently from side to side.

"Depth charges!" shouted Bjørn. "Here they come again!"

Our cameraman tracked the inflatable boat as it approached. Three men were aboard and as they prepared to make a second pass, the sailor holding the depth charge bumped against the driver of the boat and stumbled, dropping the device at his feet.

The reaction would have been comical except for the realization of an impending tragedy. All three commandos stared open-mouthed at the fumbled canister. The two not at the wheel dove for it and managed to roll it over the side into the water. It had already been triggered and the second blast was much closer to the bottom of our hull.

They made two more passes and dropped two more depth charges. The *Whales Forever* was a former seismic-testing vessel, which meant she boasted a reinforced bottom; but I knew the depth charges must be inflicting some damage.

My choices were simple. I could surrender and lose both ship and submarine in addition to being arrested, or I could carry on and risk the warship attacking us, thus losing both ship and submarine and also endangering the lives of the crew. If we survived, we would be arrested.

I decided to call the *Andenes*'s bluff. There was no way Norway would risk killing people, especially European media people. It would be a nightmare for them, especially since we had not actually committed a crime.

I set a course for the Shetland Islands. The *Andenes* chased us for the next twenty-four hours until we came within sight of the Shetland Islands. She then fell back and we cruised into Lerwick Harbor, knowing that we'd humiliated the Royal Norwegian Navy and brought worldwide attention to the illegal activities of the Norway's whalers.

The Nazi Bear Hunter

TOFINO, BRITISH COLUMBIA

The beefy loggers jeering at us from the government wharf in Tofino fearfully dove for cover. Our US Civil War cannon shot reverberated across the harbor and echoed back to us, reflected off the forested slopes of Vancouver Island's Clayoquot Sound. My ship, the *Edward Abbey*, a former US Coast Guard patrol boat painted black and flying Sea Shepherd's version of the Jolly Roger flag, moved alongside the pier as the embarrassed loggers got to their feet before the small battalion of media cameras. It was all smoke and noise, a salute to the spirit of the besieged ancient forests.

My team and I were in Clayoquot Sound to bring attention to plans to clear-cut one of the island's most amazing old-growth forests. I had been an activist in the Clayoquot area for some time. I had formed a group called Le Coeur des Bois (the Heart of the Woods), and the year before we had spiked more than twenty thousand trees.

Tree spiking was an idea that I came up with after hearing about a Vancouver Island sawmill that had been shut down for days in the late 1970s after one of its saws struck a cannonball embedded in a tree. Word had it that the ball had been fired two centuries earlier from one of Captain James Cook's ships and had lain within the guts of the ancient cedar until it was discovered by the destructive probing of the saw, which had shattered on impact. I viewed tree spiking as the inoculation of trees against a disease called clear-cutting.

In 1982, a small band of friends and I spiked two thousand trees on the southern slope of Grouse Mountain overlooking the city of Vancouver. We had called ourselves the North Vancouver Garden and Arbor Club and spoke through our fictional leader, Wally Cedarleaf. In response to our weekend activities on the mountain, the sawmills canceled their agreements to purchase the trees, and the forested slopes survive to this day as direct evidence that the tactic of tree spiking does save trees.

There were lots of activists in Tofino, and most were not happy to see us. In their view we were too aggressive, and they were also upset that I had an invitation to address Chief Francis Frank and the Nuu-chah-nulth Tribal Council, and they had not.

Paul George, founder of the Western Canada Wilderness Committee, was pissed. His organization had just asked to address the council and had been refused. George wanted to know why, and the tribe was not telling him.

"Well, Paul, did you ask permission to enter their territory?" I asked him.

"What do you mean? I asked to speak to the council."

"Yes, you said that," I replied. "But before we left Seattle to come here with the *Edward Abbey*, I sent them a letter asking for their permission to enter Nuu-chah-nulth territory. It was only when they replied that we departed."

Paul George looked at me and said, "You know you're not welcome here—people want you to leave."

"Who said I'm not welcome here? The Tia-o-qui-aht and Ahousaht First Nations say I'm welcome. I'm sure the loggers are of the opinion I'm not welcome. Are you saying that you and the other groups believe I'm not welcome here?"

"Yes, we do believe you're not welcome here. You're a troublemaker; we don't need you stirring up trouble here. You don't belong here."

"Look, Paul, if the Nuu-chah-nulth say I should leave, I'll leave. But as to not belonging here, why is that? I'm a Canadian and I'm not telling you that you don't belong here just because you're an American. We all have a concern and an interest in protecting old-growth forests."

"Why don't you just go back to saving whales?" he replied. "When did you become interested in saving trees, anyway?"

I laughed. "I think it began when I climbed my first tree. That was some time ago, I believe."

As I was getting ready to speak to the council, I was on the pier near my ship doing an interview with a television reporter. Suddenly I saw a gruff, bearded man in his sixties quickly approaching me. He looked angry.

In a thick German accent, he yelled, "Go back to where you came from, you bastard! We don't want your kind here. You don't belong here—now fuck off."

The reporter was taken aback but her cameraman kept the camera rolling. The man said he was a bear hunter and did not appreciate outsiders coming and telling locals what to do.

I looked the man over, smiled, and calmly said, "How many Jews did you kill in the war?"

The reporter was shocked. "You can't accuse someone of something like that just because he has a German accent. That's quite narrow-minded and offensive."

"But it's not offensive if it's the truth. This man is a war criminal."

The bear hunter got angrier and clenched his fists, his face turning red. "I was not in Germany during the war. I never killed anyone. Fuck off and go back to where you came from."

"I am a Canadian, so I am where I came from. You may be a Canadian also—I don't know—but I do know you were in the German army. In fact, you were in the Waffen-SS. So I'll ask again, how many Jews did you kill in the war?"

The reporter turned to me and said, "He says he was not in Germany during the war. You can't just accuse a man of being a war criminal without proof."

"He's lying," I replied. "But then again, he may have been in Poland. But he was in the SS for sure, and the proof of it is standing right before us."

"What do you mean?" the reporter asked.

"Look at his right hand. He's missing his trigger finger. I've heard the Soviets cut off the trigger fingers of SS soldiers they captured. He certainly was not an officer. Captured SS officers got shot in the back of the head. He's the right age, he has a German accent. He was in the SS. So, Herr Bear Hunter, how many Jews did you kill in the war?"

The man turned and walked away without another word.

1993-1995

Cod War

NEWFOUNDLAND GRAND BANKS

As a boy raised in the Canadian Maritime province of New Brunswick, I was very much aware of the adventurous history of the Newfoundland Grand Banks. I had read *Captains Courageous* by Rudyard Kipling, and every Maritime boy knew about the adventures of the schooner *Bluenose*.

In 1993, I had the opportunity to be a Grand Banks Captain Courageous with the difference being that instead of catching cod-fish, I went there to save the cod.

I had been warning Canadians since 1985 that the cod fishery would collapse. The exploitation had been relentless, but the Canadian government department of Fisheries and Oceans did not want to hear any concerns. In 1992, the cod trawlers returned with empty holds, and reality slapped the government and the fishermen in the face. The fishery had collapsed.

Yet foreign trawlers continued to fish on the Nose and the Tail of the Grand Banks, the two areas just outside of the Canadian two-hundred-mile economic exclusion zone. This meant that any international fishing outside of the economic exclusion zone was out of Canada's control.

Even though the cod fishery was closed and thousands of fisher-men were out of work, nothing in the way of a serious protest had occurred. Newfoundland's fishermen's union staged a ridiculous protest by taking a Canadian dragger out to the Grand Banks and making a show of throwing a traditional dory into the storm-tossed sea. The Canadian media made a big deal about the anger of the fishermen and called it the Cod Wars.

I had just purchased an old Canadian Coast Guard buoy tender called the *Thomas Carleton* in Halifax, which I renamed the *Cleveland Amory* in honor of the man who helped me secure my first ship in 1978, the *Sea Shepherd*.

I had been preparing the ship for a campaign to Iceland and Norway to protect the whales. The Grand Banks was directly on my course toward Iceland, so I decided to escalate the very quiet Cod Wars on the Grand Banks by announcing a showdown with the for-eign trawlers.

The *Cleveland Amory* flew the Canadian flag and I, as a Canadian captain, would fully meet the qualifications of proper Canadian repre-sentation. I would not be representing the fishermen, however. I would be representing the cod.

We departed Halifax in late July and headed toward the Grand Banks. I had publicly announced that it was my intention to insti-gate an international incident to bring attention to the decline in cod populations and to point out that foreign draggers were continuing to diminish the cod populations even further.

In the early morning hours of July 28, we entered the area known as the Tail of the Bank. We found other ships immediately, although not the foreign draggers we were looking for. Instead, there was the Canadian Coast Guard ship *Sir Wilfred Grenfell*, the Fisheries and Oceans patrol vessel *Cape Roger*, and the European Economic Community patrol vessel *Ernst Haeckel*. I called the ships as we moved past them, but they refused to respond. Nonetheless, I continued to hail them, saying, "Thanks for joining us to stop these draggers from wiping out the cod. I assume we share the same concerns."

Still no reply.

My first officer, Richard Eurich, asked, "What's with the show of force? They can't be out here protecting the foreign draggers from us, can they?"

"That's exactly why they are out here," I answered. "You don't know my government. They will think nothing of spending millions of dollars to prevent one of their own citizens from doing something they haven't got the guts to do themselves."

By midmorning, with the government ships on our tail, our radar gave us a new target and we headed for it. As we approached, the target was positively identified as a dragger, the Cuban-registered vessel *Rio Las Casas*, and she was preparing to lower her net.

I contacted the ship over the VHF radio. "*Rio Las Casas*, this is the conservation ship *Cleveland Amory*. Under the authority of the United Nations World Charter for Nature, we are requesting that you cease fishing and return to Havana. Do you understand?"

The Cubans did not argue. All they could see was a large black ship leading a squadron of Canadian government vessels with government air support overhead. They agreed to leave without argument.

The feds then ruined the day.

The radio squawked. "*Rio Las Casas*, this is the Canadian Fisheries and Oceans patrol vessel *Cape Roger*. You have every right to continue fishing in this area. That black ship is under the command of an environmental terrorist. You do not have to do what he says."

The Cubans were obviously confused. They requested clarification. The *Cape Roger* once again gave them assurance that they could continue fishing. They began to deploy their net again.

I was hoping that fishermen in Newfoundland were monitoring the communications. On one hand, their government was telling them it was opposed to the foreign draggers fishing the Grand Banks, and now they could hear the government inviting the Cuban ship to set her nets.

On the *Cleveland Amory*, I again requested that the Cubans cease and desist, and then I crossed their stern, which forced the Cubans to retrieve their gear. The Cuban trawler stopped, and I maneuvered alongside to allow the documentary crew to shoot footage of the ship. To avoid physical contact with the *Rio Las Casas*, I ordered my ship to go astern, pulling us slowly back behind the dragger.

Chasing Spanish and Cuban cod trawlers off the Tail of the Grand Banks of Newfoundland with the *Cleveland Amory*.

As we moved backward, my crew tossed bottles of foul-smelling butyric acid onto the Cuban vessel's decks. The fishermen recoiled in disgust from the stench.

The *Cleveland Amory* slid backward with only inches between her hull and the hull of the *Rio Las Casas*. When we were off the Cubans' stern, we watched as they got underway and headed south out of the area.

The Canadian Coast Guard ship *Sir Wilfred Grenfell* radioed the fleeing Cuban trawler, and a voice identified itself as representing the Royal Canadian Mounted Police. This was the first indication that the Mounties were aboard the *Sir Wilfred Grenfell*.

At first, the Cuban captain wanted nothing to do with the Canadian authorities. He just wanted out of the area. However, after two hours of negotiations between the Mounties and the Cuban embassy in Ottawa, the Cuban captain gave permission for the Mounties to board his ship.

Undeterred by the Mounties, we carried on and found a second trawler, a Spanish-registered ship with her net in the water. Again, I ordered the vessel to leave and cited the United Nations World Charter for Nature.

Once again, the fisheries patrol vessel *Cape Roger* intervened to inform the Spanish ship to ignore my warning. My crew and I were quite amused when the Spanish captain radioed back a simple, "Fuck you."

But this time the Mounties radioed me to inform me that I was under arrest and that they intended to board my ship. As a Canadian commanding a Canadian-registered ship, I had no choice but to agree to have them come aboard.

Three inflatable boats, each carrying a heavily armed party of Mounties, approached the *Cleveland Amory*. My crew tossed down the boarding ladder and they boarded my ship. Despite looking like they came prepared for a gun battle, they realized that they were unopposed—I presented myself to them to be arrested, although they would not tell me on what charge.

I turned over my command to my first officer, and the Mounties then transported me to the *Sir Wilfred Grenfell*, where I was confined to a cabin for the thirty-hour trip to Saint John's, Newfoundland.

The *Cleveland Amory* was taken under tow to Saint John's and, although my crewmembers were not arrested, they were ordered confined to the ship while she was in port.

When the Coast Guard ship approached the port of Saint John's, I was transferred to a helicopter. Much to my surprise, hundreds of fishermen were demonstrating on the dock—this time, they were not against me but for me. For two decades, I had been the hated villain in Newfoundland for protecting harp seals, and now I was a hero for defending the cod. I realized that the helicopter transport was to ensure that the fishermen would not see me.

"We can't have you being welcomed as a hero now, can we?" the constable said to me.

The helicopter lifted off into the fog and flew above it. I saw the stone fortress and surrounding antique cannons on the top of the mist-shrouded Signal Hill. We descended into the milky haze and landed at the airport. I was handcuffed, hustled into the back seat of an unmarked car, and taken to Royal Canadian Mounted Police headquarters to be photographed and fingerprinted. After being officially identified and booked by the feds, I was hustled out the door, transferred to a car, and driven to the jail in downtown Saint John's.

"What have we here?" the Newfoundland constable asked as the Mounties escorted me through the archaic entranceway of what was called the Saint John's Lockup.

One of the Mounties answered, "Watson will be staying over the weekend."

The jailor said, "Ye think he would be chasin' some real criminals. He was only tryin' to protect our fish."

"He broke the law," the Mountie replied sternly.

I interrupted. "That's a matter of opinion, and it would be nice if someone would inform me as to what law I broke."

The jailer was clearly on my side. "You feds are more enthusiastic about some lawbreakers more than others. What are you going to do about the bandits stealing our fish?"

"That's not up to us," replied the Mountie. "But you can't have citizens taking the law into their own hands."

I laughed. "I can see why. The public might begin to think they can do a better job than you."

I was ushered into my weekend retreat. It was a small, rather primitive rectangular concrete room with a steel bunk—sans mattress—and an odd sink-and-toilet combination unit. The walls were a dirty yellowish-green color, decorated with soot-smudged cryptic script, the artistic representations of the uneducated proclaiming gutter-minded trivialities. The sewer art had been applied with burnt matches. The floor was red. *Good for masking bloodstains*, I thought. The ceiling contained a plastic half sphere housing a monitoring camera. Inset into the ceiling were fluorescent lights that were never turned off.

On Monday, I was escorted to the courthouse to be booked on four charges of mischief, the charge that the government used to harass people when it can't find evidence of a real crime. Sometimes it was coupled with other typical harassment charges, like conspiracy or obstruction.

I had not injured anyone nor damaged any property, but I was being charged with two counts of mischief endangering life, with a maximum penalty of life in prison, and one count of mischief endangering property, with a maximum charge of ten years in prison. It was absurd, but I estimated that the government of Canada had just spent some $3 million to arrest one person for protecting fish from foreign fishing operations that the government itself had called pirate fishing.

After years of defending seals from Newfoundland fishermen, I was astounded to see some two hundred fishermen protesting outside the courthouse demanding my release. "Save Paul Watson! Ban the dragger! Save Paul Watson!" I could hear them shouting.

As we left the courthouse, one of the men approached me and said, "Thank God, you're helping save our fishery."

I didn't argue. My concern was for the fish, not the fishermen. However, they were good allies, and I was not about to discourage them.

In the courthouse a few moments earlier, I had been ordered to post $10,000 in bail and to reappear in court in six months for a preliminary hearing.

On September 12, 1995, I went on trial in Saint John's before a judge and jury. The government spared no expense to win a conviction. It paid to fly a crew from Cuba to testify against me. It brought in a law professor from the University of Toronto to argue that the United Nations Charter for Nature was not valid in Canada. The chief prosecutor of Newfoundland, Colin Flynn, was personally taking on the case. In addition, the trial was being held in a province in which I had been unpopular for decades.

I was prepared. I had asked a lawyer friend of mine, Marvin Storrow in Vancouver, who in his opinion was the best damn lawyer in Newfoundland. Without hesitation he recommended Brian Casey.

Brian Casey was a legal artist. He opened with this statement: "Ladies and gentlemen of the jury, my client is not saying he did not do this; in fact, he is very proud of his actions and denies none of it. If need be, he will do it again."

I thought the courtroom was a bit archaic. I had to sit in a cage-like box in the middle of the room with the jury to my left and lawyers for both sides to my right. The defense's strategy was to plead justification under a legal principle known as color of right. Casey told the jury that Sea Shepherd acted under the belief that the United Nations World Charter for Nature authorized nongovernmental organizations and individuals to uphold international conservation regulations and laws. The prosecution attempted to portray me as a reckless pirate who endangered the lives of Cuban and Spanish fishermen as well as the lives of my own crew.

Ironically, several months before my trial began, the Canadian minister of Fisheries and Oceans, Brian Tobin, staged a media stunt of arresting a Spanish trawler in the same international waters in which we had intervened against the Cubans. Tobin was lauded as a hero for doing exactly what I had been arrested for, except he'd used his political power to make the arrest.

Casey compared my nonviolent approach to the use of guns and tear gas by the Canadian authorities to achieve the same ends. To no one's surprise, Judge Derek Green ruled that my lawyer could not compare my actions to the government's actions. But he surprised everyone with his reasoning. "It has not been determined," he said, "if the actions by the government were proper, justifiable, or legal."

Prosecutor Colin Flynn did not do his case any service when he compared my actions to the Nazis: "What Watson did in ordering the Cubans off the Banks was no different than what the Nazi thugs did in painting swastikas on synagogues. It sends the wrong message."

The trial lasted until October 10. At one point, the local newspaper, the *St. John's Telegram*, wrote, "Everyone in the courtroom seemed to be under stress except for the defendant who appeared to be having a good time."

After seventeen hours of deliberation, the jury found me not guilty on all charges except for a misdemeanor charge stemming from allowing my crew to hurl stink bombs at the *Rio Las Casas*.

I was fined thirty-five dollars.

Standing Up to an Angry Mob

THE MAGDALEN ISLANDS, QUEBEC

I have been fighting the brutal slaughter of baby harp seals on Canada's east coast since 1975, and the justification for the continued killing was always the jobs it provided, despite the entire industry's dependence on government subsidies to survive. In fact, it would have been cheaper to pay the sealers not to kill seals. That option would have eliminated the huge annual costs for the deployments of icebreakers and the enforcement of regulations, although enforcement was usually directed at those of us trying to stop the killing.

One alternative to killing seals was tourism. People wanted to see the newborn seal pups on the ice. The government reluctantly granted some permits to allow tourists to fly out by helicopter to spend an hour or two with the whitecoat pups. Tourism was fine, but it offered relatively few jobs for the sealers themselves.

But something that I noticed in 1983 gave me an idea. I had observed that three-week-old baby seals naturally molted their white fur, and the hairs—although still attached to the emerging new hairs below—could be easily brushed off the body.

The whitecoats' hairs are not really white. Each hair is transparent and hollow, similar to polar bear fur. This allows for the air inside each hair to be heated by the sun during the day and provide warmth through the night until the pups can increase their body fat from their mothers' rich milk.

The thought came to me that the whitecoats' hairs could be collected and used as an insulating fiber in sleeping bags or winter jackets. In other words, it would be a nonviolent and humane alternative to the bloody sealing industry.

I was able to get a government permit to do the research on this idea. In March 1994, I took a small team to the Magdalen Islands, a small group of sandy islands in the Canadian Gulf of Saint Lawrence. Once on the island, I hired two sealers to come to the ice. I traded their clubs for dog grooming brushes, and we collected eighty bags of whitecoat seal fur. Most importantly, we discovered that the seal pups not only did not mind being brushed but also seemed to enjoy the brushing just as dogs and cats often enjoy it. Each pup yielded some two ounces of molted hair.

I had earlier contacted a representative of a German company that specialized in organic fibers, and they asked me to send them samples of the material. The result of my small research expedition was that I was confident we could develop a nonlethal, cruelty-free, stress-free form of sealing—a gentle alternative that could also supply jobs to the commercial sealers.

The idea was met with a lukewarm response from the Canadian media and the sealers. Tina Fagan, the executive director of the Canadian Sealers Association, said that if the idea had come from anyone but me, she might have considered it a viable option.

Mark Small, the president of the Canadian Sealers Association, said that he was concerned that the brushing would be inhumane and a cause for stress to the seals. He argued that clubbing the seals was more humane than brushing them, to which I responded by asking him which he would prefer: to have someone gently brush his hair with a hairbrush or to have someone bash in his skull with a baseball bat.

I requested another permit to return to the ice in 1995. Tobias Kirchhoff of the German company Kirchhoff Bedding Fabrics of

Exploring a nonviolent, nonlethal form of sealing by brushing naturally molted fur from baby seals to be used in making clothing.

Germany would come with us, and we would hire more sealers to collect more samples. I also invited my friend Martin Sheen to participate. I thought that having a celebrity with us would bring needed attention to the alternative idea. And because Sheen was with us, this brought reporters to the Magdalen Islands from Canada and Europe.

I knew this seal-fur alternative could benefit both the seals and the sealers. The baby seals would not have to die, and the sealers could continue to make money. I put the word out in the sealing community that we would pay cash for the collection of the seal hairs. To the government I said that this idea would be creating jobs for an economically depressed region of Canada.

The sealers were not enthusiastic about the idea. They refused to meet with us and instead called a meeting of the Magdalen Islands

Sealers Association. They quickly reached a consensus that they wanted no part of what they considered a wimpy form of income.

"Seals are meant to be clubbed, not coddled," said Gilles Theriault, a leader of the sealers association. "Who does this guy Watson think he is? Does he think we will exchange the club for the hairbrush? We are men, sealing men—we are not women."

Organized by a few agitators, the meeting had turned ugly before it even started, with reporters being ousted and warned not to interfere. By late afternoon, fired up on beer, the sealers left the meeting to march to the hotel where most of the reporters and my crew and I were staying. They occupied the lobby and told the manager that no one was to enter or leave.

We called the Quebec provincial police (QPP). They refused my request to order backup from the mainland. However, six officers arrived but made no attempt to disperse the crowd, the members of which were in the lobby drinking, smoking, and screaming that they wanted no part of my alternative idea. Officer Pierre Dufort of the QPP informed me that the sealers were also personally angry with me for disrupting their sealing operations on the ice between 1976 and 1983—now was their opportunity for revenge.

Martin Sheen bravely ventured into the lobby to speak with the sealers and to invite them to the church across the street to discuss the idea. They threatened to lynch him if he did not leave. The police advised him to return to his room because they could not guarantee his safety.

"I was in fear for our lives," Sheen told reporters. "This is the ugliest, most violent mob that I have ever witnessed."

With the mob downstairs trashing the lobby of the hotel, my crew, the media reporters, and I were in our separate rooms. Photographer Marc Gaede was standing in my room, and Officer Dufort and another QPP officer were sitting in the room's two chairs as I sat on the bed. We could hear men walking and talking loudly in the hallway outside our door, some yelling, "Where's Watson? Bring the bastard out! We want to talk to him!"

I looked at Dufort and said, "What do you intend to do if they come through that door after me?"

The officer shrugged. "There is not much we can do. We're quite outnumbered."

I was astonished. "You call yourself a police officer?"

He said nothing.

A few minutes later, the sealers started banging on my room's door. Dufort actually smiled. "Well, looks like they found you."

The sealers began to smash in the door with a fire axe. As the door broke open, I dashed into Marc's room, which was connected to mine; locked the door; and pushed the bed up against it.

I could hear the commotion in my room: The door cracked, the door's frame collapsed, and a screaming mob of drunk, barbaric locals surged in. "Where the fuck is Watson?" they demanded. They forced Marc Gaede into a chair and threatened to gouge out his eyes. They threw his camera to the floor and stomped on it.

Marc said nothing but Dufort pointed to the door leading the room that I was in. One of the sealers swung the axe three times, smashing his way into the room.

I braced myself, my shoulders against the bed, my feet firmly against the wall. It was like attempting to back a human avalanche. The force on the door was so powerful that my feet were driven into the drywall. The door splintered under the repeated blows of the axe and then broke apart as a flow of arrogantly ignorant humanity poured into the room, stinking like a burst cesspool after a booze party. Their faces were wild and contorted as they screamed in rage.

I stood up and, with my back to the wall, faced them. At least thirty men stormed into the room with another thirty in the room behind them and two hundred more filling the lobby and hallways of the hotel. The vile madness in their eyes communicated their desire to kill me, and I felt with absolute certainty that I was a dead man. There was no escape.

In my hand I clutched my only means of defense, a stun gun, a device that could knock down a man without inflicting serious injury. Stunning thirty of these thugs was impossible, of course, but I'd be damned if I would die without a struggle.

The sealers stared at me for a few seconds, seemingly unsure about what to do. The ringleader, Gilles Theriault, leaped forward and punched me in the side of the head. Slightly dazed, I dropped him to the floor with the stun gun and struck another man, a sealer named Langford who was coming at me from my right.

Langford fell with a thud to the floor and this confused the other men momentarily; but then a third sealer grabbed me by the hair and began to punch and kick me. I zapped him as two others spit in my face.

They pushed me closer to the window. One of them yelled, "Toss the bastard out the window," as they began to push. We were on the second floor and I moved desperately away from the window. A sealer went to punch me. I ducked and his fist went through the glass. His blood spurted onto my clothes.

The only thing that saved me was one sealer with the sense to know his comrades were going too far. He turned his back toward me to block the others, and this maneuver stopped the mob long enough for two uniformed police officers to push their way into the room. The officers screamed at me to leave the island. I said I would not.

One of the cops yelled at me. "You will leave, or you will be a dead man in one minute!"

"I will not submit to this mob. I will not go into that crowd. No way."

The two cops grabbed me and pulled me through a gauntlet of punching, kicking, and spitting sealers. My legs were kicked from beneath me. I fell, got up, and stumbled down the hallway and down some stairs. Someone stabbed me in the side with their keys.

The two cops dragged me outside and across a parking lot. They threw me into the back seat of a police car. As the two officers got into the front seat, a sealer jumped into the back with me and began punching me. I elbowed him in the gut and another officer dragged him out the door.

Suddenly a brick smashed into the car's side window near my head, spraying the right side of my face with shards of glass. The cop in the driver's seat jumped out of the car to chase the assailant. As the mob began to surround the police car, one of the sealers jumped into the driver's seat; fortunately, it was the sealer who had defended me earlier, whom I now suspected of being a cop himself. He slowly drove the car through the mob and out of the parking lot. As the car departed, I saw the mob attack a photographer from London's *Daily Mirror* paper. They smashed his cameras and punched him in the face.

The police car drove to the airport with dozens of cars filled with sealers following behind. After we arrived at the small airport, the officers quickly took me through the door and behind the glass security partition as the crowd surged into the small building. I noticed that there were women in the crowd, most likely the wives of some of the sealers. There were only three officers with me and more than three hundred angry people hammering on the glass.

The mob demanded that I wipe the blood from my face. I was not sure why they were asking that, but I refused. One of the officers told me I needed to cooperate, or they could not do anything to guarantee my safety.

"What kind of cop are you? You want me to take orders from this ignorant lynch mob? I don't think so. You should be ashamed of yourself."

With an angry look, he said, "You're damn lucky you're not being charged."

"Really, what the hell for?"

"Stun guns are illegal in Canada."

I looked at him. "You guys really are a fucking joke. If not for that stun gun, I'd be dead now."

Other officers approached me and pulled me outside. A small plane was landing.

"Get into that fucking plane and get your ass out of here."

The mob, however, was pushing its way through the partition, so I had little choice. I boarded the plane.

The plane flew across the gulf and landed in Moncton, New Brunswick. The pilot told me I was free to go.

"Where? I don't have any money or identification, or even a coat."

"Not my problem," he answered.

When I entered the airport, I saw a tactical unit of the QPP getting ready to board a flight to the Magdalen Islands. However, I decided to approach an airport police officer for assistance, and he arranged for me to be taken to the hospital.

Back in the Magdalen Islands, the media and my crew were under siege. The local cops were demanding that the reporters turn over their tapes. Bob Hunter and his cameraman had already buried their tapes in a snowbank, and the European media were refusing to comply despite threats from the cops. The situation was defused somewhat with the arrival of the QPP tactical unit that had been flown in from Quebec City, the same unit I saw boarding the plane in Moncton.

I later found out that Martin Sheen had called his agent, who then called the US consulate in Quebec. The consulate demanded that the tactical unit be sent.

The sealers thought they would get their revenge on Martin Sheen. They smashed in the window of the local video store, confiscated all the Martin Sheen films they could find, piled them in the middle of the street, and set them on fire.

Officer Donald Bouchard of the QPP informed the reporters that they were free to leave but they would have to turn over their tapes. The Europeans gave up blank copies. When the cops asked why the tapes were blank, the reporters said that Europe had a different system and that European tapes could not be played on North American equipment.

The QPP reported to the Canadian media that nothing much happened. Bouchard said, "There was a peaceful demonstration but no violences and Paul Watson voluntarily left the Magdalen Islands when politely requested to do so."

A few days later, the authorities were embarrassed when the tapes they tried to confiscate aired the truth about what happened that night.

1997

Hotel Lelystad

GERMANY, THE NETHERLANDS, AND MONACO

The lock's gates opened, and the *Sea Shepherd III* moved slowly forward. Her high steel prow pointed eagerly at the choppy cold waters of the Firth of Forth. After six months of preparations and refitting work, the seven-hundred-ton North Atlantic trawler moved briskly eastward, leaving the city of Edinburgh, Scotland, behind. Ahead of us lay the waters of the North Sea and our destination: the German port of Bremerhaven.

In the spring of 1997, I purchased the *Sea Shepherd III* in Scotland. We would complete her refitting in Germany.

The weather was good, and we docked two days later. We had been here before, and many friends and supporters came down to the dock to welcome us. A policeman stopped by, asked for newsletters, and said he was pleased to see us again.

My team and I were certainly aware that the Norwegian government was keeping tabs on our movements in Europe. This was the fifth year that they were preparing to kill whales in defiance of the International Whaling Commission (IWC) moratorium on commercial whaling. A new Sea Shepherd ship only a few hundred miles from

Norway's shores was most likely making the whaling industry nervous. We had sunk whalers in Norwegian ports in 1992 and 1994, and we had also engaged in a confrontation with a Norwegian navy ship in 1994.

A few hours after clearing customs and immigration, I left the ship to use the pay phone across the street from the dock. When I was about three hundred feet from the ship, a German police officer, clad in a green uniform, walked quickly toward me and held out his hand. "Captain Watson, I am sorry, but I must inform you that I have the unpleasant task of having to arrest you," he announced.

I looked back at my ship to see a half dozen police cars approaching the berth. They stopped and each discharged a couple of officers.

I asked the officer what I had done.

"It is not a German matter; we have been requested by Norway to arrest you in response to an Interpol warrant seeking your extradition."

"Okay, I guess you have to arrest me," I replied.

The jailers were friendly. They held me overnight and most of the next day. My lawyer, Manfred Ernst, discussed the case with the state prosecutor of Bremen and the case was dismissed. I was released and greeted by dozens of German supporters and a marching Bavarian tuba band.

I was free for just one day. My understanding from the German prosecutor was that the decision to release me would be binding in other European countries.

The German prosecutor was wrong. I had to return to the United States, and as I was going through immigration in Amsterdam's airport, I was told there was a warrant out for my arrest. I tried to explain that the German authorities had ruled that the warrant was not valid. The Dutch disagreed.

I was held overnight. The next morning, the judge said that he disagreed with the German assessment and ordered me to be held for an extradition hearing. The date for the hearing was eighty days away. I was transported to the Lelystad prison to await the date for an extradition trial.

Being a prisoner in the Netherlands was quite the experience. I spent 120 days in Lelystad, and I can honestly say I had no complaint about the place. It was the most civilized prison that I've ever seen or heard of. The guards, both men and women, were all very polite and none of them carried weapons.

One of the things I found fascinating about Dutch prisons is that it was not illegal to escape. When I asked the warden about this, he said, "We believe the instinct to escape captivity is natural, and we can't punish people for doing what is natural." Despite the Netherlands' recognition of a natural desire to escape confinement, however, Lelystad was supposed to be a maximum security prison. I was placed in a cell for twenty-three hours each day, with one hour in the common area with the other prisoners. Twice a week we had access to a gym or the football field. The cell was comfortable and offered a view of the courtyard that was filled with tulips and sculptures. There was a television, a small refrigerator, a sink, and a toilet. In addition to the food served by the prison, prisoners were allowed to order in their own food. I always ordered rice and spices so that during the one hour a day we prisoners were in the common area, we could pool what we had for a common meal. Strangely enough, almost half the prison population in my section were Africans. Most of them were on immigration violations or drug charges. There were only three Dutch men. And some of the Africans were great cooks, so the meals were always a treat.

On my second day, two of the guards came to my cell and asked if I wanted to do a work detail.

"What does that involve?" I inquired.

"Boxing flowers," one of them said. The other guard said I would be paid one guilder per hour for the work.

"And what if I don't want to do it?" I asked.

The guards laughed. "Well, then you don't have to do it."

"Okay," I said. "I think I'll just stay in my cell and read."

My arrest was making news, and numerous requests from the media for an interview resulted in the prison warden allowing me one hour a week for a media conference. He even supplied coffee and doughnuts.

The media attention came with varied reactions: one Dutch magazine described me as Holland's only political prisoner, and Rutger

Hauer personally came to visit me. In addition, I received thousands of letters from around the world, and I kept busy answering them with handwritten replies. However, when Greenpeace condemned me and said that it supported the Norwegian extradition request, the organization also denied that I was a Greenpeace cofounder.

This turn of events motivated my friend and fellow Greenpeace cofounder Robert Hunter to fly to the Netherlands from Toronto to hold a media conference at Lelystad to confirm that I was indeed a Greenpeace cofounder and that I had his absolute support.

All in all, it was a pleasant stay at Lelystad.

When my trial date arrived, I stood before a panel of three judges, to whom I admitted to organizing the sinking of the pirate whalers *Nybraena* in the Lofoten Islands in 1992. However, I denied ramming the Norwegian warship *Andenes* in 1994. She had rammed us.

There was also a charge that I had issued a false Mayday call during the confrontation with the *Andenes*. My defense was that we had been rammed, we had been depth charged, and we were being fired on by the Norwegians—that was a legitimate reason to issue a Mayday. In addition, the Mayday was proof positive of our location, and that location was outside of Norwegian territorial waters.

The Dutch judges made a diplomatic decision: because the Norwegians had already tried me in absentia and sentenced me to 120 days—and because I was only a week short of having served 120 days in Lelystad—they ordered my release in a week's time. More than two hundred protesters were outside the courthouse demanding my release, but I sent word to them that the outcome was acceptable. The Norwegians were not happy about it and we had made our point. The entire affair received some great media attention, and it recruited hundreds of Dutch citizens as Sea Shepherd supporters.

I shook hands with all of the prison guards and returned to my ship in Bremerhaven to prepare for my voyage to the Mediterranean to attend the IWC meetings in Monaco. Since 1994, I had been banned from attending the IWC, but that did not keep me from showing up. In fact, Sea Shepherd received more attention being on the outside than on the inside. When I brought the *Sea Shepherd III* into the harbor of Monte Carlo, we quickly became the premiere attraction.

Arrested in the Netherlands on a Norwegian warrant requesting extradition, released from Lelystad Prison after 120 days without extradition.

Prince Rainier III gave us a prime location to dock without charge and provided a police security detail for us.

My primary focus that year was to prevent the Makah Tribe of Washington State from resurrecting whaling operations. The US government had financed the travel costs for the Makah whalers just as it had for the IWC conferences in Ireland in 1995 and Scotland in 1996. The Makah whalers also had the support of the Japanese and Norwegian whaling commissions, which saw an opportunity to force the United States to back off on its opposition to commercial whaling. The US government was not financing those elders of the Makah nation who were opposed to whaling. Thus, Sea Shepherd was financing the costs and working with Makah elders Alberta Thompson, Dottie Chamblin, and Jeff Ides so their voices could be heard.

Prince Rainier III delivered an official invitation for me to attend the reception for the IWC. With an invitation from the prince, I could not be refused entry.

I put on my dress uniform and entered the reception area of the Hotel Hermitage, where the party was taking place. I deliberately arrived late for special effect. The Icelandic delegation glared at me, as did the Greenpeace delegation.

IWC secretary Ray Gamble approached me. "I told you yesterday you are not welcome."

I smiled in response. "Yes, I understand—I'm not welcome at the meeting, but this is a reception hosted by the Principality of Monaco and here is my official invitation."

I showed the invitation to him, pointing out my signature as well as the prince's.

He walked away.

I was enjoying the hateful stares as I went over to speak with Alberta Thompson and Dottie Chamblin. However, Brigitte Sifaoui, the scientific adviser for the French delegation, approached me, saying, "I see you have made an impression on our Norwegian and Japanese friends."

That's when I noticed that the Norwegian and Japanese delegations were following the Icelandic delegation walking out of the reception in protest that I was there.

I was absolutely flattered.

With a laugh I said to her, "When you can make a Norwegian whaler walk out on free booze, you must be doing something right."

The next night, marine-mammal advocate Will Anderson came to my ship, speaking on behalf of all the nongovernmental organizations. He asked if I would please not attend the NGO reception for the delegates—the NGOs wanted the whalers to attend, and they would not if I was there. I agreed not to attend.

The NGOs had their reception without me, and the whalers did not attend.

However, as I was walking with a couple of my crewmembers, we saw five members of the Japanese whaling delegation sitting at an outdoor café. We went over and said hello. They had been drinking and were more than a little happy; surprisingly, they invited us to sit down for a drink. It was the first time we'd ever spoken face-to-face with Japanese whalers, and they seemed curious to know more about us.

I quietly asked one of my crew to go to the ship and bring back some Sea Shepherd shirts, which I presented to the Japanese delegation. They actually put them on. The picture of whaling delegate Tadahiko Nakamura wearing one of our shirts was priceless.

A couple of other NGO delegates walked by and were shocked to see us drinking with the Japanese delegation. I believe that the next day the Japanese delegates were quite embarrassed to see that we published pictures of them wearing our shirts.

A Whale for the Killing

NEAH BAY, WASHINGTON

The beginning of 1998 found me aboard the *Sea Shepherd III* in the port of Wilmington, North Carolina, preparing to once again venture into the Canadian Gulf of Saint Lawrence to oppose the slaughter of seals.

I decided to take a new approach this year. The objective was to focus international attention on the slaughter. Toward this end, I had invited Canadian writer Farley Mowat; Paul Mitchell CEO John Paul DeJoria and his daughter Alexis; and Bronwen Booth, the sister of Cherie Blair, the wife of British prime minister Tony Blair. Brigitte Bardot had also planned to join us, but her plane experienced mechanical problems and had to return to France. Nevertheless, photographer Bernard Sidler from *Paris Match* joined us along with other media representatives.

With these celebrities aboard the *Sea Shepherd III*, the Canadian government left us alone. Whenever we approached sealers on the ice, they immediately left. There was very little drama but lots of publicity and the opportunity to once again bring this perverse annual massacre to the attention of the international public.

We left the Gulf of Saint Lawrence, making sure to drop more net rippers onto the Grand Banks to foil the destructive draggers, and headed south to the Panama Canal. From there, we sailed up the Pacific coast of Central and North America to a small bay at the tip of Washington State's Olympic Peninsula.

My objective was to intervene against plans by the Makah Tribe to resurrect whaling. The Makah Tribe had not killed a whale for some seventy years, but after a visit from Japanese fishing executives, the possibility of making money from selling whale meat had motivated some on the tribal council to exercise their treaty whaling rights.

The Japanese and Norwegian whaling industry had provided funds to establish the World Council of Whalers on Vancouver Island with the objective of getting both the Makah and the Nuu-chah-nulth peoples to return to whaling. If the world would accept the legitimacy of aboriginal whaling, the Japanese, Norwegians, Icelanders, and Faroese could use the same aboriginal claim to legitimize their illegal whaling activities.

Sea Shepherd had been invited to intervene by some of the Makah tribal elders like Alberta Thompson, Dottie Chamblin, and Jeff Ides. In their opinion, the resurrection of whaling had little to do with tradition and everything to do with profit.

I had originally become involved in this issue in 1995, when the tribal elders invited us to come to Neah Bay. I arrived on our patrol boat, *Edward Abbey*, with two TV crews. Upon entering the harbor, we were confronted by a traditional whaling canoe with a crew of Makah decked out in feathers and warpaint, something that struck me as very odd because these items were regalia used by Indigenous plains people and not West Coast societies.

I stopped in the middle of the bay as the canoe approached. A young man stood in the bow and yelled up to me. "White man, you come with evil in your heart when my brother the whale wishes to give himself to us so that the people may live!"

I replied, "I just have one question: Do you intend to sell whale meat to the Japanese?"

The young man looked at me quite angrily and said, "When my brother gives himself to me, it is a secret in my heart between my brother and me."

"That's all well and good, but my question is, Will you be selling whale meat to Japan?" I replied.

We were both aware that the TV cameras were rolling. He glared at me. "I have nothing more to say to you, white man. You speak with forked tongue."

The whaling supporters then turned the canoe around and left. I thought, *That will not look good.* But we had come at the invitation of tribal elders, and two of them, Alberta Thompson and Dottie Chamblin, came aboard and were interviewed by the reporters.

One of the reporters said, "Your shaman was saying that Sea Shepherd is evil. Do you agree?"

Alberta laughed and replied, "Shaman? What shaman? Everyone is Christian here."

The reporter played the tape back for them. Alberta laughed. "Oh, that's Spencer McCarthy—I think he saw *Dances with Wolves* too many times."

Stopping the resurrection of whaling by the Makah Tribe in Washington State.

The reporter relayed to Alberta and Dottie that the wannabe whalers said they wanted to resurrect their traditions.

Dottie replied, "Weaving baskets and picking berries is part of our tradition. Speaking our language is part of our tradition. Killing a whale with an anti-tank gun is not part of our tradition."

I saw Alberta, Dottie, and Jeff over the next few years when we all attended the meetings of the International Whaling Commission in Dublin, Aberdeen, and Monaco. Each time, they spoke against any plans to bring back whaling.

In 1998, the US government gave the Makah Tribe permission to kill whales, and that brought Sea Shepherd back to Neah Bay with two ships. We were joined by numerous other groups to obstruct any attempted whaling operations.

It became a media circus that lasted from October through December, with dozens of journalists camped out on the reservation and the US Coast Guard mobilized to defend the whalers. The media was falsely casting it as some sort of cowboys-versus-Indians story, completely ignoring the Japanese connection and the voices of the opposing elders.

Every time the whalers set forth, we would obstruct their operations. I brought a miniature submarine painted as an orca to broadcast orca sounds underwater, which was a workable plan until the Coast Guard passed a regulation banning the broadcasting of orca sounds in the sea.

The Coast Guard established a security zone around the whaling canoe, prohibiting anyone from coming within a thousand yards of any whaling activity. But despite that, we were able to prevent every attempt by the Makah to kill a whale.

We returned to Neah Bay in the spring of 1999, and this time the whalers were more aggressive—one whaler threatened us with a .50-caliber rifle, and in the harbor a mob attacked us with stones while the Coast Guard watched and did nothing to stop the violence.

Some other groups, like the SEDNA Foundation, suffered quite a few arrests and some injuries. Thus, I made the decision to do everything within the law to obstruct the whale hunt—by staying within the law, Sea Shepherd's efforts could have maximum effect in protecting the whales. One workable tactic was to cruise my vessel at high speed in circles around the whaling canoe, keeping outside the exclusionary zone. While I was doing this, the Coast Guard radioed to warn me against violating the regulations and to tell me to stop generating waves.

I picked up the radio. "US Coast Guard, this is *Sea Shepherd*. Is this a no wake zone?"

An officer replied, "Of course not, it's the open sea."

"So you are in agreement that I am not breaking any regulations?"

He responded, "You are creating a dangerous situation. Please desist."

"But am I doing anything illegal?" I asked.

"No, sir, you are not. But I am advising you to not create waves."

My reply: "Thank you, sir, for your advice—but my job *is* to make waves."

We stopped all attempts to harpoon and shoot a whale that day.

It was inevitable, however, that with the full support of the US Coast Guard, the Makah whalers would eventually shoot a whale. They did so while I was refueling in Friday Harbor, Washington.

She was a juvenile gray whale that Alberta Thompson named Yabis, the last whale that the Makah people killed until 2007 when five Makah whalers illegally slaughtered another whale. Since then, not another whale has been killed. In the courts in Seattle, Sea Shepherd continues to challenge any attempt to kill whales.

Surviving Hollywood

LOS ANGELES AND THE NETHERLANDS

After the successful pursuit and sinking of the notorious pirate whaler *Sierra* in 1979, I sold the feature film rights to my life story to producer Tony Bill and Warner Brothers in 1980. Those funds allowed me to purchase the *Sea Shepherd II* in 1981.

Since then, I have either renewed the rights or sold them when they expired. Over the years I have sold the rights to numerous companies and filmmakers, including Marble Arch Productions, Wes Craven, Sony, Kingsborough Greenlight Pictures, and Galatée Films. With an average payment of $25,000 a year for the rights, I have made more money by the movie not being made than I will ever realize when or if the feature film is produced.

Dealing with Hollywood was an interesting experience—lots of promises but not much action. I did get to spend time with various actors that were under consideration to play me, including Jon Voight, Christian Bale, Rutger Hauer, Sean Penn, John Cusack, D. B. Sweeney, Scott Glenn, and Aidan Quinn.

My experience with Sony was illuminating. After the company owned the rights for two years, I came to realize that Sony had purchased the rights with the purpose of not making the movie. I realized this when the rights came up for renewal in the third year. I was sitting in the office of the Sony agent, waiting for him and biding my time by reviewing the titles on his bookshelf behind his desk. I saw some Greenpeace books, and I knew Sony was negotiating with Greenpeace for a movie.

When the agent came in and sat down, he presented me with the contract to sign. I told him I did not intend to renew. He asked me why.

"Well, I've been looking at your bookshelf, and it appears to have the titles for films you've made and for films you're making or intend to make. But I don't see any of my books on that shelf."

"I have your books at home," he said, clearly lying.

"Perhaps you do, but I have another offer from another company that I'm inclined to accept. Unless you double the option fee."

He glared at me. "You should accept that offer." He got up and indicated where the door was. I left.

A few days later, he called me and very tersely inquired if I intended to renew the contract.

"No, I told you I had another offer. I took it."

There was a pause on the line. "You really did have another offer?"

"Yes," I answered. "I told you that."

"I thought you were bluffing," he replied.

"I don't play your Hollywood games. Besides, you never had any intention of making the movie."

The new offer was from Wes Craven, the producer of horror movies. He said he wanted to try another genre to get away from the horror business.

He ended up screwing me over also when he decided to sell my rights to a television production company and pointed out the spot in the contract that gave him the right to do so. He sent me a check for $45,000 for the TV rights. I refused to cash the check, but that did not stop him from making demands on any other production company to pay him hundreds of thousands of dollars for the rights he literally stole from me.

The closest the movie came to being made was in 2000 when Kingsborough Greenlight received some €15 million from the Dutch government. The company most likely paid off Wes Craven with some of the money. The company had purchased ships and robotics, hired a production crew, and flown actors Aidan Quinn and Anne Heche to the Netherlands when it all collapsed—the producers were unable to secure the additional funding after spending most of the Dutch tax dollars.

Kingsborough Greenlight had also hired my ship, the *Ocean Warrior*, for the film. I voyaged from the Pacific to the Netherlands to be available for the production; but while I waited for the cameras to roll, I decided to sail to the Faroe Islands to once again oppose the horrific grindadráp.

This time I took Dutch actress Kim Van Kooten, two Dutch comedians—Hans Teeuwen and Theo Maassen—and members of the Dutch media. Bob Hunter from Citytv in Toronto and *Guardian* journalist John Vidal joined the campaign also.

I was under a Danish court order not to enter Faroese waters, but I blatantly ignored the order and dropped anchor just outside of Tórshavn's harbor. Immigration came aboard and gave us clearance. The police then came aboard and informed me that we were not allowed to land in the Faroes. They ordered us to depart.

I had been through this charade before, so I simply ignored the police and spent two weeks patrolling Faroese waters, followed continuously by a Danish warship, annoying the hell out of the authorities.

One day while we were cruising past Tórshavn, Hans Teeuwen, Theo Maassen, and John Vidal asked to be sent ashore in a small inflatable so they could confront the politicians. Of course they were all arrested, which got a great deal of publicity in the Netherlands and Great Britain. They were locked up and released a few days later. John Vidal was able to get about to interview the locals after he was set free. None of the men were fined. The Faroese wanted them gone with as little fanfare as possible, as soon as possible.

It was a good campaign, and we returned to Amsterdam to resume our part in the production of the movie on my life story, only to find that the project had fallen apart. We also discovered that a few people, especially those in the Dutch government, were not happy—the Dutch-funded movie producers had spent millions of euros without much to show for it. Of that sum I got absolutely nothing except to inherit some of the creditors, including a local shipyard that had done work on the prop ship the producers brought to the Netherlands from Great Britain.

My charter fee for the *Ocean Warrior* was also not paid. That ship was now lying alongside us—abandoned—so I sent my crew over to plunder it for anything that was useful. Afterward, I quietly slipped out of Amsterdam.

Although Sea Shepherd was not liable for the debts of the film company, we were the only material asset associated with the failed production, so the vultures were out to get us. Fortunately, I was one step ahead of the angry, money-hungry mob.

It was a mystery to me what the producers had spent the millions on, and the entire scandal made its way into the Dutch courts. The courts even put a lien on my film option rights, which caused a few obstacles for me going forward. After that, although I continued to shop the option of my life story, I decided to also shop around an idea for a television show. The experience in the Netherlands led me to be very wary of Hollywood promises and even warier of Hollywood tricksters.

I went to numerous production companies and networks. My approach was this: if the biggest show on Discovery Channel was a bunch of people taking boats into a remote, cold, and hostile area every week to catch crabs, I could give the network men and women of many different nations taking boats into a much colder, more hostile, and even more remote part of the planet to save whales. It had to be more compelling than catching crabs.

Thankfully, Animal Planet decided to take a chance. Their TV production of *Whale Wars* began in 2007 and lasted seven seasons, until the Japanese whaling fleet retreated for good from the Southern Ocean Whale Sanctuary.

Since *Whale Wars*, I have worked on or participated in documentary films, starting with *The Cove*. I have worked on *Sea of Shadows* for National Geographic, *Seaspiracy* for Netflix, and a documentary about me called *Watson* for Discovery.

The option to produce the feature film is now with Galatée Films; regrettably, producer Jacques Perrin, whom I had worked with for two decades, died in April 2022, before the movie could be made. However, his company is continuing to pursue the project.

2002

Treasure Island

COCOS ISLAND, COSTA RICA

"Carlos, tell those bastards that they are illegally killing sharks in Guatemalan waters."

Carlos Pérez Cembrero nodded, picked up the VHF transmitter, and said in Spanish: "*Varadero I, Varadero I,* please stop your fishing activities. You are unlawfully fishing in Guatemalan waters."

The fishermen ignored us and continued to pull in their long-lines, which had captured sharks. The fishermen removed the sharks from the ocean, sliced off their fins, and tossed the living, finless bodies back into the sea to sink to the bottom and die slowly.

Carlos looked at me in frustration. "They have no intention of stopping, Captain."

"It appears so. Carlos, see if you can contact the Guatemalan government and report this. Ask them what we can do."

We continued to follow the Costa Rican longliner, watching with a mixture of anger and frustration as they pulled in one shark after another.

For filmmaker Rob Stewart, it was an excellent opportunity to document these poachers. He was in the process of making a documentary

Stopping a Costa Rican shark-finning vessel in Guatemalan waters.

film on sharks called *Sharkwater*, and we were coproducers. He had joined me and my crew in Los Angeles a few weeks before because we were bound for the beautiful Cocos Island, which lies about three hundred miles off the coast of Costa Rica.

This was not the first time that Sea Shepherd had intervened against poachers near and around Cocos Island. We had tangled with them in the '80s and '90s, chasing them out of the marine reserve every time we passed by that beautiful island. We confiscated their longlines; freed all the living turtles, sharks, and fish we could find; and reported their activities to the Costa Rican government.

In 2001, I secured and donated materials and equipment for the rangers at Cocos Island, including generators, rifles, tools, clothing, boots, and a radar surveillance system. Sea Shepherd was also working on securing a patrol vessel for the rangers, which we intended to deliver by 2003.

Also in 2001, we had intercepted the Ecuadorian longliner *San Jose*, operating illegally just offshore of Cocos Island. While the Cocos Island rangers watched helplessly from the shore, the poachers set miles of baited hooks around the entire island. When we arrived, the Ecuadorians were in the process of pulling in the sharks.

We radioed the rangers and asked if they needed assistance. They were relieved to hear from us. At first, they thought our big black ship, the *Ocean Warrior*, was another fishing boat.

The poachers were just as mystified as the rangers. But our ship was bigger and looked mean, and when we ordered the poachers to stop their fishing operations, they did so without any argument. We rounded up their small boats, pulled in the lines, and freed the few sharks and fish still alive. Then we and a couple of armed Cocos Island rangers boarded the *San Jose*. Peter Brown was the onboard filmmaker that year, and he turned a copy of the documentation over to the rangers as evidence of where we'd caught them and what they were doing.

The *San Jose* was taken to the mainland, the catch was seized, and the ship was ordered confiscated by the Costa Rican courts. It was the first court-ordered confiscation of an illegal foreign fishing vessel in Costa Rican legal history.

We had already established a working partnership with the Galápagos park rangers and the Ecuadorian police in 1999 to help defend the Galápagos Marine Reserve. Sea Shepherd provided a patrol vessel, communications equipment, and a trained canine unit to detect smuggled wildlife products, and we had built a complete automatic identification surveillance system to cover the marine reserve.

Because of our success in 2001 with the seizure and confiscation of the *San Jose*, the government of Costa Rica had asked us to sign an agreement of cooperation to help protect Cocos Island. I met with Claudio Pacheco, the head of the Costa Rican Coast Guard at the time, and he helped with arrangements for this agreement with the Costa Rican Ministry of the Environment and Energy. Pacheco warned me that the risk of signing such an agreement would be that we would make some very powerful enemies.

Despite that implied risk, my team and I were returning to Costa Rica in 2002, feeling very positive about the prospect of working in cooperation with the Costa Rican government to protect sharks and marine wildlife. But just two days before the meeting, an unexpected incident would change all that.

In April 2002, we were on our way from Seattle to Costa Rica to sign the contract with the Costa Rican government to help control poachers in Costa Rican waters. While en route to Puntarenas, Costa Rica, we passed through the waters of Guatemala. There, we came across a Costa Rican fishing vessel, the *Varadero I*, finning sharks. Without authority to act, we could do nothing but watch and film the carnage, angry and frustrated that we could not stop the slaughter of the sharks.

We contacted the fisheries department in Guatemala, and the authorities asked us to stop the poachers, escort the *Varadero I* to Puerto San Jose, Guatemala, and turn the poachers over to the authorities.

With that permission secured, we ordered the *Varadero I* to stop fishing. The fishermen refused. We made numerous runs to cross their bow to persuade them to stop. We turned on our water monitor to intimidate them into stopping.

The captain of the *Varadero I* was operating his vessel in a very erratic manner. Although I did not want to collide with the boat, I did move close enough to intimidate the captain.

At one point, as the *Ocean Warrior* was passing on the starboard side of the *Varadero I*, the fishing boat abruptly turned to the starboard, colliding sideways with the port side of my ship.

I immediately asked my crew to assess the damage and check each person for injuries. Thankfully, there did not appear to be any damages or injuries. The *Varadero I* stopped and agreed to be towed to Puerto San Jose.

I sent two crewmembers over to the *Varadero I*. They asked if everyone was okay. The *Varadero I* crew replied that everyone was safe and agreed to be towed. The *Varadero I* crew took the towrope and tied her bow to the *Ocean Warrior*.

The *Ocean Warrior* towed the *Varadero I* eastward toward Guatemala. When we were still some thirty miles from shore, the port captain from Puerto San Jose radioed the *Ocean Warrior* to say a gunboat was coming to arrest the Sea Shepherd ship instead. He would not say why, but it was obvious that money had changed hands on shore—the *Varadero I* crew had bought their immunity from prosecution.

I ordered the towline on the *Varadero I* to be dropped and recovered. We carried onward toward Costa Rica to meet with the Costa Rican environmental minister to sign our agreement to defend the sharks.

Upon arriving in Puntarenas, Costa Rica, we were boarded by the police and the prosecutor. They informed me that there had been a complaint from the fishermen that my ship and I had endangered their lives.

I was charged with eight counts of attempted homicide.

I appeared in court the next day, bringing with me Rob Stewart and his video evidence and numerous members of my crew as witnesses. The court viewed the video and interviewed the witnesses, and I was informed that the charges were dismissed.

Two days later, the *Ocean Warrior* was boarded a second time. This time I was charged with eight counts of assault. Once again, I was ordered to appear in court, where once again I presented video evidence and my crewmembers were interviewed. And once again I was told that the charges were dismissed.

Finally, my crew and I were given official clearance to depart for Cocos Island. We spent a week removing toxic waste and garbage from the island and sealing it in barrels for transportation to the mainland. As we were returning, we encountered some Taiwanese longliners inside Costa Rican waters. I radioed Claudio Pacheco to ask for advice; he said that he could do nothing about the Taiwanese vessels.

"Sir, these vessels are fishing illegally in your waters. Surely we can order them to leave," I pressed.

"Unfortunately, although I agree with you that they should not be fishing there, we can do nothing if they are Taiwanese."

"Why not?"

"I cannot answer that, but you cannot interfere with them."

I was also informed by the rangers of Cocos Island that the shark-finning mafia in Puntarenas had placed a bounty of $25,000 on my head. It was not safe to return to mainland Costa Rica. Thus, we departed for Panama, our agreement with the Costa Rican government effectively scuttled. Later, the *Varadero I* shark-finners would be featured in the award-winning, internationally released film *Sharkwater* by Rob Stewart—much to the embarrassment of the Costa Rican government.

Nearly a decade later, in October 2011, a warrant was issued from Costa Rica for my arrest through Interpol. Why was this warrant issued ten years after an incident in which no one was hurt, nothing was stolen, and there was no damage to property? The warrant was dismissed by Interpol on the grounds that there was an appearance of political motivation.

I was not aware of the warrant until I landed in Frankfurt, Germany, in May 2012 en route to France. When I was told that there was an extradition request from Costa Rica, I was totally surprised. For what reason and why would Germany give credence to a warrant that had been dismissed by Interpol?

I found myself being transported from the airport to a prison. I was held for eight days until I was freed on a bond set at €250,000. Releasing me on bond was an unusual decision for a country that normally denies bail and absolutely denies bail for a foreigner facing extradition. I was ordered under house arrest, and I had to report to the Borheim police station every day. I was free, although I was restricted from leaving Germany, as I awaited extradition to Costa Rica.

I met with the Costa Rican foreign minister in Stuttgart and told him that I would be willing to go to Costa Rica with my evidence and my witnesses if a trial date was set. But, I told him, I did not feel it fair that I should be extradited and imprisoned for an indefinite time awaiting trial in a situation that would be both pretrial punitive and highly dangerous because of the bounty on my head set by the shark-finners in Puntarenas. For this reason, I had no alternative but to fight Costa Rica's extradition demand and seize the opportunity to use this case as a way to focus international media attention on the continued unlawful trade in shark fins from Costa Rican waters.

The evidence was clear that the shark-finners continued to enjoy immunity from prosecution for their crimes. The crew of the *Varadero I* were never charged despite the evidence Sea Shepherd provided the courts.

About a year prior to my arrest, on January 8, 2011, biologist Jorge Ballestero from the Costa Rican organization PRETOMA attempted to expose continued shark-finning in Puntarenas. He attempted to film a large number of shark fins being dried on racks and on the ground at a dock on the east side of the Puntarenas municipal market. According to PETROMA's report, Ballestero was physically confronted and threatened by a group of five men who tried to take his camera and forced him to flee into the market. When a police patrol got involved, the officers sided with the criminals. However, another environmentalist was able to record the evidence.

In a similar confrontation shortly after Ballestero's ordeal, without the presence of police, celebrity chef Gordon Ramsay was also threatened by a gang of shark-finning criminals who doused him with gasoline and held him at gunpoint. Ramsay was simply told by Costa Rican authorities to flee the country for his own safety.

2003-2006

The Siesta Conversation Club

SAN FRANCISCO

In May 2005, I participated in a debate with Carl Pope, the executive director of the Sierra Club, held by the Mountainfilm festival in Telluride, Colorado. I found Pope to be an example of what was wrong with the US environmental movement: tons of talk and little action. But I was content to live and let live. The Sierra Club did its thing, and I did mine; that is, until Pope accused me of being an embarrassment to the environmental movement because in his opinion my activities were radical and extremist.

At the end of the debate, there was a final question: "What can one person do?"

Pope said, "The best thing a person can do is to talk with their neighbor. That's the best way to educate others about the environment."

I looked at him. "Seriously, am I debating Mr. Rogers here? Talking to your neighbor, that's it?"

Addressing the audience, I said, "What can one person do? Find out what you're passionate about and then harness that passion to the virtues of courage and imagination. Get active and take action to defend life, diversity, and interdependence on this planet."

A month later, I was speaking about this incident with my friend Benjamin Zuckerman, PhD. Ben was a professor of astronomy at the University of California, Los Angeles, and a national director of the Sierra Club. Ben suggested that I join the Sierra Club, and he would then nominate me to run for the board of directors. He said, "The club has been hijacked from the spirit of John Muir and David Brower—it's become more of a support club for the Democratic Party, afraid to speak out about overpopulation, immigration, and pretty much anything controversial."

Taking Ben's advice, I joined the Sierra Club and made a run for the board. In the spring of 2003, I was elected to the fifteen-person board. I had to admit I was amused when Carl Pope himself called to officially inform me that I was elected.

"I look forward to working against you," I said.

Besides Ben Zuckerman, there were some other great people on the board, like Marcia Hanscom, Lisa Force, and Doug La Follette. Unfortunately, they were in the minority.

I got my first taste of how things were when one of the quarterly board meetings of my first year was held at a ranch in Montana where the meals consisted of buffalo, elk, and beef. When I tried to point out the contradictions of eating meat while protecting the environment, I was told that the Sierra Club supported hunting, fishing, and the livestock industry. I was also told that they had a portobello mushroom entrée for the vegetarians. In addition, I was surprised to be shut down whenever I brought up the issues of population growth, plastic pollution in the sea, and climate change.

During the three years I served on the board, we would have two annual board meetings in San Francisco, California—where the Sierra Club was headquartered—and two annual meetings in other locations. During my time, those locations included Billings, Montana; Boston, Massachusetts; Halifax, Nova Scotia; Charleston, South Carolina; San Juan, Puerto Rico; and Albuquerque, New Mexico.

I certainly remember the dinners. Lobster in Boston and Halifax, with portobello mushrooms for vegetarians. Blue crabs in Charleston, with portobello mushrooms for vegetarians. The portobello mushrooms were always consistent, and there was so much talk about the food from the nonvegetarian directors that I began referring to the club as the Siesta Conversation and Gourmet Club.

I was admonished, along with two other directors, for exposing to the *Los Angeles Times* that a donation of $100 million had been given to the club by businessman David Gelbaum. Carl Pope accepted the donation, which Gelbaum had made on the condition that the club become neutral on the issue of population and immigration. Pope did not want that information given to the public, and we had been warned not to provide it to the media. Of course, we did let the media know, resulting in a lecture from Pope and the punishment of admonishment by the board, which seemed nonsensical.

"What does that actually mean?" I asked. Nobody seemed to know other than the declaration by the board that we were admonished.

After being admonished, I had the word *admonished* printed in yellow on the black T-shirt that I wore to the next meeting.

One of the directors asked me point-blank what I hoped to achieve as a director.

"Well, I would like to know how the eighty-five million in donations received every year is spent, because I see a lot of administration and political lobbying but very little action, so I guess I would settle for ousting Pope. Maybe things would change somewhat if we had a new executive director who would not whore out the club's principles."

I was part of promoting a slate of candidates who wanted to restore the Sierra Club's concern about population growth. This effort resulted in a major response by Carl Pope, who disallowed our candidates to access the membership rolls while informing the membership that our candidates were motivated by racism—a curious thing given that an all-white board was accusing our candidates of being racist, yet our candidates included Ben Zuckerman, who is Jewish, plus an African American man and a Hispanic woman. Ultimately, however, Pope had control of the narrative through the membership list and his connections with the media.

One morning I received a phone call from a reporter for the *San Francisco Chronicle* wanting to know why I was opposed to Mexicans in California.

"Why would you say that?" I asked. "I don't care if California is one hundred percent Hispanic. Spanish was spoken here hundreds of years before English was spoken."

The reporter told me that many in the Sierra Club were concerned that we were running an anti-Hispanic, anti-immigration campaign.

"Absolutely not," I replied. "We simply want the club to drop their neutrality position on overpopulation and immigration. Our position is that the goal should be population stabilization. It has nothing to do with where immigrants come from."

Things came to a head at the Albuquerque meeting when Carl Pope brought in representatives from the inner city and the barrios to lecture the club's board on what our priorities should be. Pope wanted the club to address social justice issues like poverty. The all-white board, except for a couple of us, sheepishly listened to the chastisement from the social justice advocates.

This made me angry, and I spoke up. "I joined the Sierra Club to protect old-growth forests, wetlands, national parks, and endangered species. There are plenty of organizations addressing social justice issues. People-oriented charities get ninety-nine cents of every charitable dollar donated. I think they need to keep their greedy hands off our penny."

Predictably, this remark was not well received. One of the social justice advocates angrily denounced me as a racist, expecting me to be contrite and apologetic.

"Don't call me a racist. I'm a misanthrope. I dislike everyone regardless of race. This planet is being destroyed by humans, and I don't discriminate."

A couple of the other directors thanked me for defending the environment as a priority, but the majority were offended.

I did not run for reelection in 2006. I'd had about enough of the Sierra Club after three years. I decided to make an issue of it by resigning from the club in protest of an essay contest that asked young people to write about why they liked to hunt.

John Muir, the founder of the Sierra Club, was an anti-hunter who once described hunting as "barbarous slaughter." I made it very clear to my fellow board members that John Muir would be ashamed of the Sierra Club promoting hunting.

Two years after I resigned, six directors quit in protest after Carl Pope accepted a $1.3 million deal from Clorox. Between 2007 and 2010, Carl Pope—on behalf of the Sierra Club—accepted $25 million in donations from the natural gas industry. Finally, in 2011, Carl Pope resigned as executive director of the Sierra Club because of mounting protests over his leadership role in partnering with polluters and companies contributing to climate change.

I was gratified to see the new executive director, Michael Brune, openly participate in civil disobedience protests against the Keystone XL pipeline, the first civil disobedience protest action in the history of the Sierra Club. In a dramatic change from Carl Pope's "just talk to your neighbor" approach, Michael Brune was arrested on February 13, 2013, for opposing the pipeline. He publicly stated, "We are watching a global crisis unfold before our eyes, and to stand aside and let it happen—*even though we know how to stop it*—would be unconscionable."

Ten years after I was elected to the board to which I made my views clear about taking dirty money and advocating real action, the Sierra Club changed for the better. The changes were very gratifying.

2005

Ice Charades

THE GULF OF SAINT LAWRENCE AND THE COAST OF LABRADOR

In late January 2005, my crew and I departed on the *Farley Mowat* from Bermuda bound for Portland, Maine. Upon our arrival, I asked the US Coast Guard to do an inspection of the ship. They did so and reported no violations, no guns, and no drugs.

We then moved on to Halifax, Nova Scotia, where we were met by police cars and Canadian customs vehicles when we arrived. A dozen uniformed customs officers and police stormed the *Farley Mowat* looking for contraband, weapons, and drugs. For three hours they searched the cabins, tossed personal belongings onto the deck, and investigated every nook and cranny for whatever they were pretending to be looking for.

For ten days, Canada's customs authorities delayed our departure with inspections and harassment. Finally, on March 3, I and my crew of thirty individuals from ten different nations were able to depart. We headed for the Gulf of Saint Lawrence, where we would pick up television star Richard Dean Anderson by helicopter.

On March 6, we were in the gulf amid a large herd of harp seal pups. Once again, our presence in the gulf was meant to challenge the government's support of the cruel slaughter of baby seals. It was an easy challenge. It just involved pointing a camera at the sealers, an act that the Canadian government considered in violation of the Canadian Seal Protection Act, which made it illegal to photograph, film, or even observe the killing of a seal by a sealer. These arbitrary regulations were designed to protect the sealing industry and provided absolutely no protection for seals at all. I had previously been convicted of violating the regulations, and I was about to violate them again.

It was wonderful to be among the seals with not a sealing vessel in sight. Unfortunately, my delight was interrupted—the *Farley Mowat* suffered ice damage and a minor hull breach, forcing us to put into Channel-Port aux Basques, Newfoundland. Alex Cornelissen dove under the ship and located a very small hole on the bottom. All he could do was insert a tiny plug. Unable to complete the repairs in Newfoundland, we brought on some large pumps to keep the bilges from flooding.

A reporter called and asked Richard Dean Anderson, who played the character MacGyver on television, why he did not make the repairs with chewing gum. Richard laughed and said, "I don't have my writers with me."

After making sure that the pumps would keep the *Farley Mowat* from flooding, we returned to the Gulf of Saint Lawrence to confront the sealers. However, we discovered that the government had announced a delay in the opening of the seal hunt: it would begin on March 29 in the Gulf of Saint Lawrence and on April 12 off the coast of Labrador. With that knowledge, we returned to Liverpool, Nova Scotia, to wait for the opening day of the hunt.

The slaughter began on March 29, and we were able to document numerous violations by the sealing vessel *Newfoundland Leader*. As soon as my crew began documenting the killing of seals by the crew of the *Newfoundland Leader*, the Canadian Coast Guard icebreaker *Amundsen* came charging through the ice toward us. I quickly put my main engine into full reverse to avoid a collision with the icebreaker. The *Amundsen* ordered us to stand down and proceeded to shadow us throughout the day.

Confronting sealers in the Gulf of Saint Lawrence.

The sealing vessel *Gulf Clipper* approached quickly and would have hit us if I had not backed down to avoid a collision. The captain of the sealing vessel brought out a high-powered rifle with a scope and aimed it at my wheelhouse. I immediately reported this threatening gesture to the Coast Guard and was warned to stop harassing the sealers or I would be arrested.

"The bastard is pointing a rifle at us," I pushed.

The Coast Guard responded that the sealing captain would not be doing that if we were not here.

I called the Coast Guard again with a question. "What are you guys doing out here?"

"We're here to protect the sealers from the likes of you, Captain Watson."

"So who is responsible for protecting the seals?" I asked.

There was short silence and the officer on the bridge replied, "That is what you're here for, are you not?"

The officer's response caught me by surprise. "Thank you, sir, for acknowledging that. Someone must protect these seals, and it is obvious that it is not going to be the Canadian Coast Guard."

The next day, March 30, we approached the sealing vessel *Brady Mariner*. I sent out a group of crewmembers to document the sealers who were on the ice, clubbing seals. Almost immediately a Canadian Coast Guard helicopter flew over and informed us that we were in violation of the Seal Protection Act's regulations.

A few hours later, the *Amundsen* began to circle our ship again, breaking up the ice and forcing our crew to retreat to the *Farley Mowat*. The officers on the *Amundsen* made a couple of attempts to board the *Farley Mowat*, but we were able to avoid being boarded. The *Amundsen* had been maneuvering dangerously close, with only a few feet separating the two ships at times.

Things changed for the better that day when a full-scale gale moved into the gulf. Storms meant no sealing, and that was fine with us. The *Farley Mowat* was built for heavy weather. The sealing vessels, on the other hand, weren't made to withstand gales. Some of them were in trouble.

But instead of watching over the sealers, the *Amundsen*—with a party of Mounties aboard—was standing off from our position. She was joined by the Coast Guard icebreaker *Edward Cornwallis*.

I informed the Coast Guard that we would continue to document infractions by sealers and asked why the sealers were not being cited for illegal actions. "I saw a sealer kick a pup in the face," I reported.

The fisheries officer replied that he had more pressing concerns than the sealers' actions.

Later in the afternoon, the crewmembers of the *Farley Mowat* were able to prevent a sealing crew from killing seals on a large pan of ice. Sixteen of my crewmembers fanned out across the ice between the seals and the sealers. The sealers, after pointing their guns at the crew on the ice floe, returned to their boat and left the area.

Looking around at the carnage was painful. The tranquil blue-white ice fields that had served as a harp seal nursery for the last three weeks had been turned into a Dantean portrait from hell. Streams of blood flowed and pooled on the ice, which was littered with the vacant-eyed, cruelly skinned corpses of thousands of seal pups. In the open leads, bleeding bodies were bobbing, many sinking and going unrecorded in the quotas. The seals were being shot, kicked in the face, and bashed with clubs and spiked hunting tools called hak-a-piks.

I turned to two of my crew on the bridge and said, "If ever there was a portrait of humanity's remorseless cruelty, this mass slaughter is it."

The day ended with a standoff between the Coast Guard and the crew of the *Farley Mowat*. The *Farley Mowat* had been ordered out of the area, but we refused to leave. The Coast Guard's intimidation of the crew had not worked, and no further actions were taken to board the ship and arrest any of us.

The next day, I sent nineteen crewmembers across the ice toward a group of seals. The *Amundsen* dispatched a helicopter toward the crewmembers as they were walking across the ice. My crew was about a half nautical mile from the *Farley Mowat*. I informed the fisheries officer on the *Amundsen* that they were not in violation because no one was sealing. The fisheries officer replied that the sealers were hunting. We saw no evidence of this. The Coast Guard helicopter had just flown over the *Farley Mowat* toward the crew and landed near them, then it took off again.

At 2:05 p.m., seven of our international volunteer crewmembers— Lisa Moises, Lisa Shalom, Jon Batchelor, Jonny Vasic, Jerry Vlasak, Adrian Haley, and Ian Robichaud—were assaulted by sealers from the sealing vessel *Brady Mariner*. A group of sealers from the *Brady Mariner* approached my crew on the ice. They were angrily swearing, making threats, and demanding to know why the volunteers were there and why they thought the seals needed defending.

One of the sealers barked, "This is our ice. We kill seals, it's what we do—now fuck off."

Jon Batchelor replied, "We save seals, it's what we do. So perhaps you should fuck off."

With that, one of the sealers swung his sealing club toward Jon, who blocked it with his walking staff. Another sealer swung his club at Lisa Moises but slipped and fell on his ass. Jerry Vlasak was struck in the face with a club and was bleeding. My crew defended themselves from the blows with their walking staffs but did not fight back—I'd told them any attempt to physically defend themselves would result in assault charges against them and not the sealers.

The Coast Guard helicopter approached. Some officers got out and began to chase my crew, completely ignoring the fact that they were the ones being assaulted by the sealers. I called the crew back, and as they were returning, the Coast Guard began landing Mounties to arrest them.

Eight of the crew I'd sent out managed to make it back to the *Farley Mowat* despite the *Amundsen* trying to break up the ice to prevent them from reaching our ship. The other eleven crewmembers were arrested and charged with taking pictures of sealers on the ice.

I radioed the *Amundsen* and officially requested that assault charges be brought against the sealers. The authorities ignored my request. We had video evidence of the assault and the minor injuries that the crew had suffered.

The eleven arrested crewmembers were flown by Coast Guard helicopters to the jail in Charlottetown, Prince Edward Island. After posting bail, they were released. I rented a helicopter to ferry them back out to the ice to rejoin us. Sea Shepherd's attempts to bring charges against the sealers were denied.

The next day, the *Edward Cornwallis* passed close by the *Farley Mowat*, leading a line of sealing ships through the ice. As they passed, the sealers were yelling obscenities at us. We saw one sealer aboard the *L. J. Kennedy* standing on the top deck above the wheelhouse— he dropped his pants to his ankles and began to masturbate. Others were dropping their pants and mooning us.

I turned toward Alex Cornelissen. "That has to be the most bizarre thing I have ever seen out here. What the hell?"

"Well, it is April Fools' Day," said Alex, "and this is a parade of fools."

A reporter called me and asked what the sealers were doing. I reported that they were not killing seals, but they were mooning us and pleasuring themselves on the deck. "I know that's hard to believe, but we filmed it," I said. "We've seen enough Newfie rear ends to last a lifetime and it was not a pretty sight. These guys are rude, nude, and have a mean 'tude. What a credit to Canada they are!"

With the nasty weather and the thick ice, most of the sealers had decided to go home. Of the thirty sealing vessels, two had sunk while others were damaged by the pressure from the ice. The *Brady Mariner* was one of the ships that had suffered damage, and her crew, whom we were now calling the Brady Bunch, were calling for help. We were the closest vessel to them, but I had no intention of assisting them after their violent assault on my crew.

The next day, I decided to leave the Gulf of Saint Lawrence and set a course to the French islands of Saint-Pierre and Miquelon to refuel. From there, I planned to head to the Labrador Front to oppose the sealers there.

After refueling the *Farley Mowat*, I told the crew we were going to the Labrador Front. "The ice is thicker, the seas more treacherous, the sealing ships more numerous, the government more hostile, and the sealers more brutal. The last time we confronted them was in 1983, so let's do it again."

On April 9, we departed from Saint-Pierre and Miquelon for the waters off Labrador. We arrived on the sealing grounds of the Labrador Front on April 11. We immediately approached the sealing vessels *Labrador Sea*, the *Labrador Challenger II*, and the *Beccalina Mist*. These three were the only ships in the area—the rest had retreated into port because a storm was coming in.

The Canadian Coast Guard icebreaker *Henry Larsen* closed in. The authorities aboard the *Henry Larsen* informed the sealers that they were there to protect them from the *Farley Mowat*.

The opening day of the seal hunt was called off because of what was now a very angry storm. The sea was being whipped into a furious froth by shrieking winds. The ice, being tossed about by the sea, was "bubbling" on the surface—the water looked as if it were boiling instead of frigid.

Of the three hundred Newfoundland sealing boats, about two hundred were in the harbor. The other hundred were riding out the storm along with the Coast Guard and us. Some of the sealing vessels around us were whining on the radio to each other and cursing the *Farley Mowat* as a Jonah, noting that the weather had been just fine the day before we arrived and had been deteriorating ever since.

I got on the radio and said, "Hi, boys. This is Jonah. Wonderful day out here today, eh?"

The next day, the storm's intensity increased to hurricane-force winds. The Coast Guard was receiving dozens of calls from sealing vessels in trouble. The Coast Guard ships replied that they were busy elsewhere.

I picked up the radio. "Yes, they are busy watching us. But we're not in trouble, so apparently watching us is more important than rescuing you guys."

The third day was hellish. Our rudder stern tube ruptured and flooded our food storage area with hundreds of gallons of water. We ripped open the bulkhead and patched up the damage, which was quite a feat considering how we were being tossed about by the storm.

In these heavy seas, all I could do was turn eastward and literally surf away from the coast of Newfoundland for about one hundred miles, until we were more than two hundred miles offshore. The *Henry Larsen* was still following us and being tossed about just as we were. Despite the storm we were all very happy—no one was killing seals in this weather.

Finally, on April 16, the government opened the seal hunt. But by now the ice was broken up and driven far offshore, and the seals had scattered. The wind had died down, but it still made being on the ice quite dangerous. The seas and the wind prevented us from returning toward the coast.

I decided to head southward. As we voyaged across the Grand Banks of Newfoundland, I dropped dozens of net rippers that we had made from welding railway rails together. In the shallows of the banks, they would rip apart any dragnets that struck them.

We then went to Portland, Maine, for minor repairs. Next we moved on to Jacksonville, Florida, to dry-dock and make major repairs in preparation for a voyage through the Panama Canal, to the Galápagos Islands, and on to Australia to prepare for a campaign challenging the Japanese whaling fleet in the Southern Ocean.

2008

A Sack of Doubloons

GULF OF SAINT LAWRENCE

As soon as the *Steve Irwin* docked in Melbourne, Australia, I flew to Bermuda to join the *Farley Mowat*. Upon my arrival, I received a message from Transport Canada, the Canadian department of transportation.

> To: Master MY *Farley Mowat*,
>
> I have reasonable grounds to believe that your vessel is in contravention of international maritime conventions. The vessel must comply with International Maritime Organization (IMO) conventions, which include:
>
> - International Convention for the Safety of Life at Sea (SOLAS)
> - Standards of Training, Certification, and Watchkeeping (STCW)
> - International Convention for the Prevention of Pollution from Ships, 1973 (MARPOL)
> - International Tonnage Certificate requirements
>
> Based on information provided by the Netherlands registry, the vessel does not meet the requirements of the above conventions. Therefore, pursuant to Section 227 of the Canada Shipping Act, 2001, you

are hereby directed to not enter Canadian waters. If this order is not complied with, you will be subject to prosecution under Canadian law.

The Honorable Lawrence Cannon
Minister of Transport
Infrastructure and Communities

I immediately replied to the minister's letter and gave the order to finalize preparations for the ship to depart from Bermuda.

To: The Honorable Lawrence Cannon
Minister of Transport, Infrastructure, and Communities

Thank you for your notice denying the Sea Shepherd Conservation Society ship *Farley Mowat* into Canadian waters.

Although the *Farley Mowat* **will** be entering the Canadian economic exclusion zone next week, we will not be entering the twelve-mile territorial limit.

We dispute the "right" of the Canadian government to deny free passage of a Dutch-registered yacht into the waters of the Gulf of Saint Lawrence and the offshore waters of Labrador and Newfoundland.

The *Farley Mowat* is not engaged in economic activity, and therefore we will not be in violation of the economic exclusion zone. We have the right of free passage through these said waters.

Of course, the ship does not comply with all the IMO conventions because the conventions apply to a commercial ship, and the Sea Shepherd ship *Farley Mowat* is a registered yacht. The ship does not comply with SOLAS but does possess a tonnage certificate, an International Oil Pollution Prevention Certificate, and a Certificate of Financial Responsibility for oil pollution.

The ship will proceed into the Gulf of Saint Lawrence to defend seals from the violence and ecological recklessness of Canadian seal killers.

Sincerely,
Captain Paul Watson

I had to develop a strategy and an objective.

The objective was to raise publicity over the seal slaughter to support legislation in Europe to ban Canadian seal products. Defining the objective was the simple part.

The strategy was more complicated. The *Farley Mowat* flew a Dutch flag. Alex Cornelissen of the Netherlands would be her captain and Peter Hammarstedt of Sweden would be first officer. The crewmembers were from France, Great Britain, Australia, New Zealand, Canada, and Ecuador. I would not be aboard the *Farley Mowat*. Instead, I would coordinate from shore, so that the campaign would be represented mostly by European crewmembers.

I called the strategy the tar baby–Farley approach after the famous story of Bre'r Rabbit and the tar baby. We would entice the minister of fisheries to attack our ship and crew by saying that he did not dare stop us from protecting seals.

Fisheries minister Loyola Hearn was an easy target. We know that as a proud Newfoundlander and defender of the slaughter of baby seals, he wanted to come off as the hero of the sealers by being tough with Sea Shepherd.

The *Farley Mowat* departed from Bermuda on March 24, bound for the Gulf of Saint Lawrence. It wasn't long before Fisheries and Oceans began accusing us of being terrorists—the department declared that any interference with the killing of seals would not be tolerated.

I responded by publicly announcing that the minister did not have the guts to stop us. My intention was to make him angry and push him toward a confrontation.

Upon the *Farley Mowat*'s entry into the Gulf of Saint Lawrence, the ship's crewmembers were met by Canadian government surveillance flights. In addition, the Coast Guard was ordered out to intercept the *Farley Mowat*. At the same time, more than one hundred sealers on sixteen boats were pushing through the ice from the Magdalen Islands.

On March 29, the Coast Guard icebreaker *Sir William Alexander* responded to the distress call of one of these sealing vessels, the *L'Acadien II* (which had six sealers aboard), and took her under tow in heavy ice conditions. The decision for a large icebreaker to tow an aluminum vessel through thick ice was not a wise one. As the smaller boat was being towed, it hit a large floe of ice and overturned, dumping the crew into the frigid sea. Four sealers lost their lives.

The next day, the Canadian Coast Guard icebreaker *Des Groseilliers* ordered the *Farley Mowat* to stop filming the killing of seals.

The authorities on the *Des Groseilliers* radioed over to the *Farley Mowat*, demanding to know if her crew had a government permit to film the seals.

First officer Peter Hammarstedt knew that the Coast Guard knew we did not have a permit and replied by adapting a line from the 1940s movie *The Treasure of the Sierra Madre*: "We don't need no stinking permit."

When Peter refused to leave, the icebreaker approached and rammed the *Farley Mowat* near the port stern area. When Peter still refused to leave, the *Des Groseilliers* returned and rammed the *Farley Mowat* a second time, damaging plates on the starboard side of the hull amidships.

The same day, another sealing vessel—the *Annie Marie*—was crushed in the ice. Her crew was rescued by helicopter. When reporters contacted me to comment, I said, "Perhaps if the Canadian Coast Guard spent less time trying to prevent documentation of the seal slaughter and more time being concerned about protecting human lives, these people wouldn't be risking death."

One reporter asked me if I had sympathy for the sealers who died when the *L'Acadien II* capsized. I was not going to lie. "These men are sadistic baby killers," I said. I went on to say that sealers died while engaged in a viciously brutal activity. I referenced one sealer, who had said he'd felt absolutely helpless as he watched the boat sink, and then I continued: "I can't think of anything that defines helplessness and fear more than a seal pup on the ice that can't swim or escape as it is approached by some cigarette-smoking ape with a club."

The reporter pressed me. "Surely you have sympathy for these men."

The truth was that I did not, and I said so in a comment that made people in the government, the media, and the fishing industry quite angry: "The deaths of four Magdalen Islands sealers was a tragedy, a tragedy caused by the incompetence of the Canadian Coast Guard, but the slaughter of four hundred thousand baby seals is a far greater tragedy in my opinion. This is a seal nursery, and these men are sadistic baby killers, and that might offend some people, but it is the unvarnished truth—they are vicious killers who are now pleading for sympathy because some of their own died while engaged in a viciously brutal activity."

When the *Farley Mowat* berthed briefly in the French islands of Saint-Pierre and Miquelon, I flew there to meet with Alex, Peter, and the crew. The next morning, as the crew was preparing to depart, I caught a flight to Halifax. When I arrived, a TV crew from the CBC met me to ask what I thought of the *Farley Mowat* being attacked by fishermen in Saint-Pierre and Miquelon.

I was not aware of any attack, so I called Alex. He told me that as the crew was preparing to depart, a mob of angry fishermen had stormed the dock. Two French gendarmes arrived and did nothing as the fishermen cut the *Farley Mowat*'s mooring lines with axes, setting the ship adrift in the harbor and putting her in potential danger of colliding with other moored vessels. Fortunately, the engineers got the main engine started, and the *Farley Mowat* left the harbor as the angry fishermen shouted obscenities from the dock.

The Sea Shepherd crew continued to document the killing, and I continued to taunt the fisheries minister. We needed a high-profile international incident, and I intended to provoke Loyola Hearn into giving us one.

Finally, on April 12, Canada gave us what we came for.

At seven o'clock that morning, the *Farley Mowat* was attacked by a heavily armed Royal Canadian Mounted Police team from two Canadian Coast Guard icebreakers, the *Des Groseilliers* and the *Sir Wilfred Grenfell*.

Captain Alex Cornelissen informed the boarders that the *Farley Mowat* was a Dutch-registered ship in international waters and that Canada had no legal right to restrict the free passage of the vessel through international waters. The ship was in the Gulf of Saint Lawrence well beyond the Canadian twelve-mile territorial limit.

I was speaking by phone with *Farley Mowat* communications officer Shannon Mann when I overheard men screaming for the crew to fall to the floor. According to Mann, the men were carrying guns. I could hear them threatening the *Farley Mowat*'s crew. I was still speaking with Mann when suddenly the satellite phone went dead.

I called the media: "This is an act of war; the Canadian government has just sent an armed boarding party onto a Dutch-registered yacht in international waters and has seized the ship. Considering that the mission of the *Farley Mowat* was to document evidence of cruelty by sealers to support a European initiative to ban seal products, I can predict that the Europeans will not be very pleased with this move. Most likely, this move by Loyola Hearn will guarantee that this bill is passed. In other words, the minister of Fisheries and Oceans has just handed us the victory that we were looking for."

The *Farley Mowat* was towed to Sydney, Nova Scotia. All of the crew was arrested, but only Alex and Peter were charged with violating the Seal Protection Act.

The Mounties interrogated Alex and Peter in a hilarious nonconfrontation. Both Alex and Peter had read my book *Earthforce!* in which I write, "Nobody talks, everyone walks, and nobody signs, everything's fine."

Two Mounties escorted Peter into the interrogation room and sat him down behind a table with his back to the wall. Peter kept his head down and said nothing. He did not even make eye contact with the police.

The officer sitting across from Peter began with: "Incidents like this become polarized. And you know that's the thing I'm trying to tell you: they see you as being that Palestinian with the suicide vest. That's the problem here—they see you walking in with this big backpack full of nails, walking into a mall and detonating explosives. Unless I've got you all wrong and you're planning a 9/11 or something here, you must be vastly more intelligent than I am."

Peter said nothing, although he told me later he was thinking, *What the hell is this guy going on about?*

The second officer looked puzzled. "I'm looking at your emblems—it looks like a male mermaid with a dolphin. I don't understand. What is that?"

Peter said nothing.

The first officer asked, "Are you a martyr? What is your stance, what do you stand for? Even prisoners of war, if you ask them who they are fighting for, they tell you. I understand the cause—to a large degree, I find it to be a just cause. Look, the least you can do is to acknowledge that I am in the room here."

Peter still said nothing.

The officer continued. "Does your organization have a website? I'm not even certain of that."

This line of asinine questioning went on for two solid hours, yet Peter said not a word until the police finally gave up and told him to go back to his cell.

Peter got up. He told me later that as he left the room, he was tempted to say "Free Palestine" just to confuse them.

Alex took the same approach, refusing to even acknowledge the interrogators.

While this interrogation was going on, I arrived in Sydney to find that the rest of the crew had been put in a motel at the government's expense. They had not been charged with anything, but since the ship had been seized, the government provided overnight housing to keep an eye on everyone.

With Alex and Peter in jail, I needed to raise C$10,000 for their bail. Farley Mowat contacted me and offered to post the bond, saying to the media that the government's seizure of the ship was an act of totalitarianism.

Farley told the media that he was deeply honored that I had named the ship after him and that he was ashamed of the Canadian government when he saw the ship being towed under arrest into Sydney Harbor. "A gross miscarriage of justice has been perpetrated by Fisheries minister Loyola Hearn, and any Canadian with any conscience should try to rectify it," he said.

I went to the Bank of Nova Scotia to get the bail money. As I was standing in line for the teller, I was struck with an amusing idea.

"I would like to cash this check, please," I told the teller.

The teller took the check and asked, "In hundreds, fifties, or twenties?"

"Actually, I would like it in toonies," I said, employing the informal term Canadians use for their two-dollar coins. I've never understood why these coins are called toonies. The two-dollar coin has a bear on it, while the one-dollar coin has an engraving of a loon on one side and is called a loonie. It has always seemed to me that a two-dollar coin—since it is twice the value of a loonie—should be called a "double loon" or, even better, a "doubloon."

The teller looked at me strangely. "Toonies? Are you serious?"

"Absolutely," I replied. "I would like five thousand toonies, please."

The coins were brought out from the vault, all of them neatly organized in lines on a tray.

I opened a black bag made from recycled ocean plastic bearing the Sea Shepherd Jolly Roger logo and dumped all the coins into the bag.

The crew and I walked over to the courthouse to deliver the ransom.

The court clerk was not happy. "You can't post bail with coins."

"Why not?" I countered. "We consider the arrests of our two officers to be unlawful. They are being held against their will; we're here to deliver the ransom, and it's only right that we pay this pirate ransom with a sack of doubloons."

"Well, you can't post bond with coins."

"Really?" I said, surprised. "Is there a law that says we can't?"

"No, but you can't," the clerk said again.

"Oh, but we can," I replied. "Perhaps you should ask a judge. Money is money, and five thousand toonies are legal tender."

After some discussion with the prosecutor, the court agreed to take the coins but said they had to be counted. So we all went into the courtroom, where I dumped the contents of my bag into a big pile on the desk. Three court clerks sat down to count.

Counting the toonies took a while. Finally one of the clerks said, "It appears that the coins are short by two dollars."

"That can't be," I replied. "I am certain that the bank gave me exactly five thousand coins."

The clerks counted the coins a second time. Once again the count was short by two dollars.

I looked at the clerks. "Very strange. Let me check the bag."

I shook the bag and a solitary coin fell out and spun like a top on the table. "There," I said, "five thousand in doubloons."

And with that the order was sent to the prison to release Alex and Peter.

The court ordered both Alex and Peter deported and ordered the *Farley Mowat* to be seized. I was required to pay a fine of $75,000 to release the ship.

I informed the court that I had no intention of paying the fine.

The judge said, "If you don't pay the fine, we can't release the ship."

"That's okay, you can keep the ship. Maybe we will steal her back—you know, like pirates did back in the day."

What the court did not know was that it was my intention to retire the *Farley Mowat*, and I figured the best way to do that was to let the government seize her. But because I mentioned we might steal the *Farley Mowat* back, she was placed under twenty-four-hour guard at a secure dock. For a year the government was stuck with the bill. I called the situation Loyola's folly.

Alex and Peter were not allowed to reenter Canada by the country's immigration authorities, but they were tried in absentia and fined some $40,000. In the end, all the government got was a sack of doubloons—what we got was the passing of legislation in Europe banning Canadian seal products.

2010

Blue Rage

THE MEDITERRANEAN

In 2010, I made the decision to take the *Steve Irwin* across the Pacific, through the Panama Canal, and up to New York City to participate in fundraising activities. Afterward, I would cross the Atlantic to the Mediterranean.

Captain Locky MacLean brought the *Steve Irwin* to New York from the Panama Canal. Before entering New York Harbor, we were offered a berth in New Jersey to wait for the confirmation of a berth in New York.

The place was a metal-scrapping company and it was right out of *The Sopranos*. The owners were friendly but obviously had connections.

Locky tied up the *Steve Irwin* and went ashore to speak with the owner.

"How much do we owe you for the berth?" Locky asked.

In a thick New Jersey accent the man said, "Your money's no good here."

"Thanks," said Locky. "That's very generous of you."

The man smiled and said, "Fuggedaboutit."

A few hours later, the man came by the captain's cabin with a box of sausages as a gift. "Hey, Locky, my brotha owns a sausage factory. He sent these over for you."

Locky thanked him but said that the ship was 100 percent vegan.

Surprised, the man asked, "What the fok is a vegan ship?"

"No meat is allowed on the ship," Locky replied.

Mystified, the man responded, "Is this some sort of religious thing?"

"No," said Locky, "it's an animal rights thing."

Incredulous, the man took out his phone and called his brother.

"Yeah, Louie, you ain't gonna believe this. The ship is vegan. They don't allow any meat aboard."

He hung up, handed the box to Locky, and said, "Here—ain't nobody need to know about it."

It was nice to cruise past the Statue of Liberty and pay a visit to the Big Apple, but within a few days we departed for Gibraltar. Our objective was to stop the illegal fishing of the fast-diminishing numbers of bluefin tuna, one of the most amazing fish in the ocean. The bluefin is one of the world's fastest fish and one of the only warm-blooded fish in the sea. Bluefins are big fish and very expensive, especially in Japan where individual fish can sell for millions of euros.

We began the campaign in Malta and set out to search along the North African coastline for illegal fishing activities. It did not take long to find what we were looking for.

On June 17, our helicopter reconnaissance flight found two fishing vessels. One was engaged in transferring bluefin tuna into one of the two nets being towed by the other vessel. The bluefin fishery vessels were inside waters claimed by Libya and were about forty-two miles off the coast of North Africa. We moved in to check out the situation and discovered the Italian-flagged vessel *Cesare Rustico* towing two cages: one contained about eight hundred fish and the other was empty.

When we questioned him, the captain of the *Cesare Rustico* said that the tuna were caught on the morning of June 14 by the Libyan vessel *Tagreft*. When we replied that the number of tuna in the cage

Operation Blue Rage—freeing eight hundred bluefin tuna from a poacher's net off the coast of Libya.

exceeded the quota for the *Tagreft*, the captain said the cage also included tuna from seven other Libyan seiners. According to the captain of the *Cesare Rustico*, all the catches were caught on June 14, the last legal fishing day. He named off six of the other seven seiners: the *Khandheel II, Hanibal, Ozul II, Almadina, Morina*, and *Khaleej Eltahadi* (he could not name the seventh vessel).

The problem with this explanation was that on June 13 and 14, we had observed the *Khandheel II*—and she was not fishing. In addition, weather conditions for those two days made fishing virtually impossible. The extremely difficult conditions—coupled with the position of the cages, which were only forty miles off the Libyan coast when they should have been moving twenty-five miles a day— suggested to us that the fish were freshly caught within the last three days at most.

The captain's statement that all the catches were caught on June 14 sounded much too convenient, so we asked to examine the fish for juveniles. We were refused. I then put the bow of the *Steve Irwin* onto the floating cage so we could look into the cage from the bow to examine the fish.

Suddenly, the Maltese vessel *Rosaria Tuna* rammed the *Steve Irwin* on the aft port side and slid alongside the port rail, while a fisherman tried to violently gaff Sea Shepherd crewmembers with a long hooked pole.

The *Steve Irwin*'s crew retaliated with two gallons of rotten butter, forcing the fishing vessel to retreat.

At 3:30 p.m., the two fishing vessels circled their cages defensively, and the *Steve Irwin* stood off to notify the International Commission for the Conservation of Atlantic Tunas (ICCAT) of possible violations. The commission did not respond. We also learned that the *Jean Charcot*, the ICCAT inspection vessel, would not venture near our location.

With two fishing vessels full of angry Italian crewmembers, there were risks involved with getting into the water to assess the bluefin catch. But if the catch was illegal, Sea Shepherd divers knew they must cut the nets and free the fish. Sometimes, however, it is necessary to do what needs to be done despite the risks. We knew that the risk of losing the bluefin tuna as a species was far more important than the risks to our own lives and freedom. We decided to free the tuna.

At four o'clock, a five-person Sea Shepherd dive crew entered one of the two cages being towed by the *Cesare Rustico*. As the *Steve Irwin* held off the *Cesare Rustico* and the support ship *Rosaria Tuna*, the Sea Shepherd crew dove into the net to identify the size, age, and number of the bluefin tuna within. Once it was clearly established that the cage was overstocked and that a high percentage of the fish were juveniles, Sea Shepherd divers cut open the nets and freed hundreds of tuna.

A Sea Shepherd cameraman filmed the release of the fish from the center of the cage, and the divers confirmed that all of the tuna inside the enclosure were freed. "They shot out of that net like racehorses," said Canadian cameraman Simon Ager.

We returned to that same area in the summer of 2011. In July 2011, the Maltese tuna company that owned the net we had cut the year before had our ship impounded in Scotland, forcing us to raise nearly a million euros to secure her release. The story had a happy ending, however. After months of courtroom battles in Great Britain, we won the case and the Maltese tuna company paid us damages.

I still like to think of those eight hundred majestic fish we saved swimming freely in the sea.

Viking Shores

THE FAROE ISLANDS

I n 2011, I decided to launch our largest ship campaign to date in the Danish Faroes Islands. Toward that end, I mobilized the *Steve Irwin*, the *Brigitte Bardot*, and the Sea Shepherd helicopter. I had a land crew coming with two vans on the ferry from Denmark carrying essential supplies. I also recruited Animal Planet to shoot *Whale Wars: Viking Shores*.

The campaign got off to a rocky start when I arrived in the Shetland Islands to begin our push north toward the Faroes. The *Steve Irwin* was arrested and prohibited from departing because the Maltese company Fish and Fish Limited had filed a lawsuit in the United Kingdom seeking damages for our disruption of their illegal bluefin tuna fishing operations in the Mediterranean Sea a year earlier.

The Scottish court demanded that I post a £520,000 bond. Sea Shepherd simply did not have that kind of money. And although I could send the *Brigitte Bardot* alone, I needed the *Steve Irwin* because I needed the helicopter.

I decided to put out an emergency appeal to our supporters and on social media platforms. Within a week we had raised the bond and secured the release of the ship. At the same time, I sent the *Brigitte Bardot* ahead with an Animal Planet camera crew to do what they could to stop any attempts by the Faroese to kill whales.

The campaign suffered another a setback when the underwater acoustic devices that I needed to listen for approaching pods of pilot whales was discovered on the vehicles being ferried from Denmark. In addition, with the release of the *Steve Irwin*, I was preparing to depart from the port of Lerwick, Scotland, when I received a warning from the Faroese police: they had issued a warrant for my arrest. They did not say why, and I took it as an attempt to scare me off.

Upon arriving in Tórshavn, the capital of the Faroe Islands, we were cleared by Danish immigration. Although the police boarded the ship, they did not arrest me.

We received a tip that pilot whales had been spotted near Vestmanna, and both our vessels headed there to find an empty bay. At the same time, the Ólavsøka festival was being held in Tórshavn, and I sent the land crew there with displays of graphic images on the sides of the vans. That night the *Brigitte Bardot* was harassed in Tórshavn's harbor and her mooring lines were cut.

The next day we resumed our patrols with the two ships, our smaller inflatable boats, our helicopter, and our ultralight aircraft. The police informed us that ultralights were illegal in the Faroes and forced us to discontinue its use.

I had Chris Aultman fly Kelly Higgins and me to the top of one of the Faroese mountains. Chris left and returned with an Animal Planet crew to do some interviews.

While we waited, we marveled at the breathtaking view of the green mountains, numerous waterfalls, and deep, dark fjords running between the islands. After the interviews, as Chris was flying back with the film crew, it began to rain. There was a shepherd's hut nearby, and Kelly and I ran there for cover. Inside was a small stove, a table, and some chairs. We did not touch anything except to sit at the table, where I scrawled a note to thank the owner for the temporary shelter.

The natural beauty of the Faroes was contrasted by the tense conclusion of Sea Shepherd's campaign. A few of the crewmembers

In the Faroe Islands filming Whale Wars *Viking Shores* for Animal Planet.

were arrested and two of our Zodiacs were seized. The Royal Danish Navy followed the *Steve Irwin* to the Shetland Islands, and the British authorities allowed the navy to confiscate one of our inflatable boats from the ship. It was an illegal move and we petitioned for a court order to prevent it. The court order was issued but not before the boat had been removed. With the loss of two of our fast boats, I again petitioned Sea Shepherd supporters and we were able to raise $200,000 within the week to replace both boats.

Despite the challenges we faced during this operation, overall it was a success. There was not a single attempt to kill any whales while we were in the Faroes. The *Brigitte Bardot* was able to locate a couple of whale pods ten miles off the coast of the islands, and her crew was able to dissuade them from approaching the Faroes.

The Animal Planet producer informed me that the police had told him that there would be no whales killed while Sea Shepherd was in the area—they did not want the slaughter to be filmed by Animal Planet.

Sea Shepherd France president Lamya Essemlali was in the hotel in Tórshavn when she overheard a local whaler calling me out, demanding that I debate him. "Watson is a coward. He does not dare to debate me," the whaler declared.

Lamya called me, and then she called Animal Planet. I headed to the hotel with a cameraman. Lamya informed the whaler that I was on the way, but when I arrived, he was gone. He had dashed out the front door and driven off.

I publicly issued a challenge to any whaler that wanted to debate me, but there was no response. The whalers' excuse was that they did not wish to give me the publicity.

A Faroese reporter came to interview me, saying that the police and the whalers had decided to ignore Sea Shepherd and not kill any pilot whales while we were in the islands.

"Without a grind, you won't have a television show," the reporter said.

I smiled. "Why do you think we came to the Faroe Islands?"

"Well, I assume you want to stop the grind," he answered.

"Precisely," I replied. "And that is exactly what we have done. There is no grind."

"But without a grind, you won't have much of a show."

I laughed. "We have plenty of footage of this obscenity. We don't need more. There will be a show and the Faroese will not be looking so great—that I can guarantee."

Escape from Germany

On May 11, 2012, I boarded a Lufthansa flight in Denver, Colorado, bound for Nice, France, via Frankfurt.

The night before my flight, I had given a talk to a gathering organized by Sea Shepherd Denver. Now I was off to Europe for the Cannes Film Festival, as Sea Shepherd France had organized a major fundraising event to be held during the festival.

The event in Cannes would feature Sea Shepherd veteran crewmember Michelle Rodriguez. I was looking forward to seeing her again, as well as all the volunteers and crew in France. But I never made it.

Disembarking the airplane in Frankfurt, I proceeded to German customs, waited in line, and presented my American passport.

The German officer looked at me and said, "There is a warrant for your arrest. You will have to come with me."

"A warrant for my arrest? From whom?"

"Please come with me," he replied coldly.

The officer took me to an office and asked me to empty my pockets. "We will have to detain you."

"What are you detaining me for?" I asked.

"There is a warrant for your extradition."

"By whom?"

He did not answer.

My first thought was Japan. The nation had issued an Interpol Blue Notice for me, but that had never been cause for an arrest.

The officer was now joined by three more officers. They took both my US and Canadian passports, my cell phone, and my plane tickets. I was handcuffed and told to walk to a holding cell, where they uncuffed me and shut the door without any explanation.

I sat in silence for a few hours, trying to think of some reason to explain why I was there. It had to be the Japanese. But why would Germany cooperate with a nation illegally killing whales?

Hours later, I heard the lock turn. The door opened. There were three officers.

Surprisingly, one of the officers said, "I am sorry about this, Captain Watson. I heard you were here, and I wanted to meet you. I'm a big fan of yours, of Sea Shepherd, and of *Whale Wars*. I was wondering if I could take a selfie with you and get your autograph?"

"Sure, of course," I answered. I was surprised and somewhat confused.

She smiled and took the picture. She then asked another officer to take a picture of us.

"Danke," she said.

"My pleasure. But before you go, would you be able to tell me what I am being charged with?"

"Did no one tell you?"

"No, I have absolutely no idea."

"I'm sorry that you were left unaware of why you are being held," she said. "My understanding is you're not being charged with anything. There appears to be an extradition request for you from Costa Rica."

I was astounded. "Costa Rica? I have not been there for a decade—I can't think of any reason that I would be extradited to Costa Rica."

"It could be a mistake. I'm sure you will have more details in the morning."

The two other officers gestured toward the cell. I walked back in, the door clanged shut, and I heard them lock it.

It dawned on me that no one knew where I was, much less that I was being detained. At the Nice airport, my team was probably wondering what was going on.

It was then that jet lag hit me. I slept soundly until early the next morning.

Once again, the cell door opened, and I was handcuffed and escorted to a vehicle. I was placed in a tiny mobile cell without windows.

After a short time, I felt the vehicle stop. I heard the sound of a gate opening. The door of the vehicle opened abruptly. I was ushered out and into a prison reception area where I was stripped, searched, admitted, and escorted to a cell.

Once again, a heavy metal door slammed shut. Once again, I was alone in a cell in a German prison.

As prisons go, it was decent. Not as comfortable as Lelystad in the Netherlands, but much more comfortable than my brief stint in a Newfoundland jail and prison camp in 1994 for disrupting the illegal cod fishery, and much, much more comfortable than my two weeks in a cell in Iran in 1972 on a false charge of espionage.

Nine days later the prison doors opened, and I walked out with my lawyer—Oliver Wallasch—Captain Peter Hammarstedt, Scott West, and a few local supporters. But I was not exactly free. I had been placed under house arrest after posting a bond of €250,000. I thought that figure was a bit excessive, especially considering that the court held both my passports, but at least I was no longer behind bars.

Oliver had arranged for me to rent his girlfriend's apartment in Bornheim, a quarter of Frankfurt. Now I had to settle in and deal with the courts, the politics, and the daily reporting to the police station in Bornheim. Thankfully, though, Frankfurt is both a beautiful and friendly city, and my time was pleasantly spent doing Sea Shepherd business from my laptop and walking along the banks of the Main River.

I felt confident that all this would be resolved soon. So far, the judges and the prosecutors I'd spoken with were supportive and optimistic that the extradition request would all be dropped. There was only a request from Costa Rica. The country had not notified Interpol, so it was not a Red Notice that had flagged me at the Frankfurt airport. The unanswered question I grappled with was why Costa Rica would have directly put in an extradition request to Germany.

Oliver told me that the extradition request was for an incident in 2002 and that I was accused of a crime called shipwreck endangerment. I was completely baffled.

I spent two months in Frankfurt waiting for a decision on the Costa Rican extradition request. Every day I had to walk to the Bornheim police station to report that I was still in Frankfurt. During those two months, many Germans began supporting me and organized protests. The rock group Gojira brought me up on the stage at the Rock am Ring outdoor concert to address a crowd of some sixty-five thousand people. In addition, Pamela Anderson came to Frankfurt to hold a press conference with me to show her support. In Vienna at a fashion show, she wore a Free Paul Watson T-shirt. This caught the attention of fashion designer Cyrill Gutsch, who flew to Frankfurt to offer his support.

He asked me to come to a fashion show in Berlin to meet the mayor of Berlin and other celebrities. When I told him that I could not because I had to report each day to the police station, he chartered a helicopter to fly me to Berlin and back the next morning.

I was feeling confident. The judges I'd appeared before and the prosecutors that I had met with all were sympathetic and supportive. More than two hundred thousand signatures had been gathered and sent to Germany's Federal Ministry of Justice. Unfortunately, the president of Costa Rica, Laura Chinchilla, came to Germany to meet with Chancellor Angela Merkel and Federal Minister of Justice Sabine Leutheusser-Schnarrenberger. I knew this might make it more difficult for me as I tried to get the extradition request dismissed. I decided it was time to make an escape.

I left Frankfurt on Sunday, July 22, 2012.

That morning, I had walked into the small police station in Bornheim just as I had done for most of the past seventy-seven days. I knew all the German cops and greeted them with a smile and a cheery "Guten Morgen." Although they did not know it, this would be my last visit to their desk and the last time I would sign my name as part of the court order to report to this police station every day.

I knew something they did not, and my choice was a simple one. I knew that if I reported the next morning that I would be met with handcuffs and escorted back to that dreary prison cell where I had spent my first eight days of this visit to Germany. And after that it would be involuntary transport to Japan—and that was one place that I could not go if I had any hope for a future at all.

Japan had delivered a demand to Germany for my extradition while I was fighting extradition to Costa Rica. I knew that once Japan got hold of me, I would not be seeing freedom for a very long time, if ever again.

A reliable source in the German Ministry of Justice had contacted me to tell me that Monday would be the day—and it would not be Costa Rica that would be getting me. It would be Japan. The political decision had already been made, and the judicial decision would happen on Monday, which was the next day.

Of course, I knew it was Japan all along. The nation desperately wanted to shut me down in order to continue its illegal whaling activities in the Southern Ocean Whale Sanctuary.

My source in the German government had sent me a copy of the Japanese request to apprehend me on charges of ordering New Zealander Peter Bethune to board the *Shonan Maru No. 2* in 2010. I had done no such thing, but Bethune had traded the accusation that I had done so for a lenient sentence from the Japanese court. It was all the Japanese authorities had, but I knew that once they got me to Japan, they would exact their revenge for the tens of millions of dollars Sea Shepherd had cost their whaling operations in the Southern Ocean Whale Sanctuary over the past decade.

So, on July 22, after checking in with the police, I returned to my rented flat in Bornheim and quickly shaved my beard and dyed my hair brown. Alex Cornelissen had driven to Frankfurt from Amsterdam and Scott West had flown in from Seattle. They borrowed a car from a German supporter so that the three of us could take a road trip to Holland, where we met up with Sea Shepherd Netherlands director Geert Von Jans. Geert had rented a summerhouse where we stayed until the night before the *Columbus*, a French-flagged sailing boat, was due to arrive in Breskens, near the Belgian border.

On Thursday night, we switched cars, borrowing Geert's mother's car for the three-hour trip to Breskens. We rendezvoused with the *Columbus* in Breskens, and I boarded her at 6:00 a.m. on Friday, July 27. I bade Geert and Scott goodbye, the *Columbus*'s lines were let go, and I was headed seaward into the English Channel.

It was now six days since I'd left Frankfurt. Despite having both my passports confiscated, I was secure on the sailing boat as it cruised down the English Channel, on my way back to North America. Finally, after two and a half months of being restricted to German soil, I was now where I felt more secure and more comfortable than anywhere: on the water. Here at sea, I was beyond the reach of the politics and the laws of Germany, Costa Rica, and—most importantly—Japan.

The *Columbus* was a Sea Shepherd vessel, but she was not widely known as such. For the past three months, she had been doing educational tours in French ports. On the Sunday I left Frankfurt, Lamya Essemlali, the president of Sea Shepherd France, instructed the *Columbus*'s crew to cover up her Sea Shepherd markings and head straight for the Dutch port. The crew had no idea what their mission was, but they did not question Lamya's instructions.

Aboard the *Columbus* were four French citizens: Captain Jean Yves Terlain; his girlfriend, Lauren; a hired deckhand named Renaud; and Jacinthe Gould, a longtime Sea Shepherd supporter from Nice who was also a nurse. Lamya had recruited her to come along because I was suffering from a streptococcus infection in my right leg, for which I'd been taking antibiotics and painkillers. The infection was slowly clearing up, but it could be a dangerous affliction should it get out of control.

Although an arrest order had been issued in Germany only, I refused to take the chance of being stopped at any airport on the Costa Rican warrant. The Netherlands was the safest place to go after leaving Germany, because that country did not have any bilateral extradition agreements with either Japan or Costa Rica. Chances are I would not have been detained in France or Belgium—but if I were ever to be detained, the safest place would be the Netherlands.

Because I was without my passports, the only secure way to extract myself would be by sea. For this purpose Lamya had organized the voyage. The *Columbus* would take me across the North Atlantic to New York City, where I would be able to return home. Thankfully, I at least had a color photocopy of my passport plus a California driver's license to prove my US citizenship. Once again, I was one step ahead of the Japanese—but this time it had been very close.

Sea Shepherd was only four months away from launching Operation Zero Tolerance, our ninth and most ambitious campaign to the Southern Ocean. This time we would be taking a small fleet of four vessels—the *Steve Irwin*, the *Bob Barker*, the *Brigitte Bardot*, and our latest acquisition, the *Sam Simon*—our helicopter, and 120 international volunteers.

As I watched the white cliffs of Dover slide by on the starboard side of the *Columbus*, I felt a sense of amazement at where this long struggle against the Japanese whalers had brought me and the incredibly dangerous situations that my crew and I found ourselves in time and time again. Somehow we'd managed to make it through unscathed every time.

As we cruised past Dover, Jean Yves broke out a couple of bottles of wine, pulled down a big screen, and hooked it up to a television antenna. Suddenly we were watching the live opening of the Olympic Games in London. The moon sent sparkles of dancing lights across the water as I contemplated the long voyage ahead of us.

We passed by the Isle of Wight. With a storm approaching from the southwest, Jean Yves took us into the Isles of Scilly and dropped anchor. As we waited for the storm to abate, I slipped ashore to mail letters and walk about the town, relieved that no one recognized me.

From England, Jacinthe returned to France, leaving the four of us to make our way across the North Atlantic.

The *Columbus* was not a very comfortable boat. She was built as a racing yacht. A makeshift galley had been built on the open deck, and the one large accommodation area belowdecks was cold and constantly damp. If nothing else, it was an authentic way to cross the ocean, and although she was a motor sailing vessel, her skipper was inclined to not use the motor unless he absolutely had to do so. The skipper, Jean Yves Terlain, a sixty-eight-year-old grizzled sea dog, was quite the famous sailor, having competed in many single-handed races around the world. He was an old-fashioned sailor, resourceful, daring, and extremely skilled at his craft. He caught the tail of the storm and let it whip us up the coast of Ireland, using it to slingshot our course into the deep blue.

We passed under Iceland, and some eighteen days later I heard the surf pounding on the beach of Sable Island, well off the coast of Nova Scotia. The plan had been to head to Long Island, but when we were only a few days from arriving, I received another warning—this time from an American official—not to enter the United States. The Japanese had notified US authorities with a request to detain me for extradition.

I was astounded. Why would my country extradite a US citizen to Japan on such petty charges? I felt betrayed and disappointed.

A friend in Massachusetts offered to come get me, but I was reluctant to illegally enter the United States aboard the *Columbus*.

I was most disappointed because I had made plans to meet my brother Stephen at Niagara Falls. He lived in London, Ontario, and had been diagnosed with terminal cancer the month before. He did not have much time left. I called him to tell him how disappointed I was that I could not see him.

"Where are you now?" he asked.

"We're hanging off the coast of Nova Scotia, trying to figure out where to go from here."

"Then I'll come to you. You know I've always wanted to go on a Sea Shepherd campaign. You need to get to shore, so I'll get you to shore. It will be my contribution to Operation Zero Tolerance."

My relatives picked me up and drove to my hometown in New Brunswick on the border of Maine, where I easily slipped across the Saint Croix River into the United States. From there, two of my crew drove me across the country to California, where I met up with my fast vessel *Brigitte Bardot* off Catalina Island. I then set sail to the waters off American Samoa, where I took command of the *Steve Irwin*. I took the *Steve Irwin* to confront the Japanese whaling fleet in the Southern Ocean for Operation Zero Tolerance in December 2012.

2012-2013

Mobilizing Neptune's Navy

AUSTRALIA, UNITED STATES, AMERICAN SAMOA, NEW ZEALAND,
SOUTHERN OCEAN WHALE SANCTUARY

T he *Steve Irwin* departed from Williamstown, Australia, on November 5, 2012. The crew was overjoyed to see a pod of dolphins meet them at the Heads, the waterway that links Port Phillip and the Bass Strait—the dolphins seemed to be escorting the *Steve Irwin* for miles out into the Bass Strait. At ten o'clock in the morning, a whale breached alongside the ship as she turned to the east.

"It was a great sign," said Eva Hidalgo. "When I saw that whale breach at the beginning of our voyage, I knew this would be a great campaign."

At the same time, the *Brigitte Bardot* was moving southwest from Los Angeles, California. Both vessels were heading toward American Samoa from opposite directions. The *Steve Irwin* arrived in Pago Pago on Sunday, November 18, to take on fuel and provisions. She departed nine days later and headed to a waypoint two hundred miles east of Pago Pago.

On November 29, I saw our helicopter approach. It hovered overhead for a few minutes and then returned to the west. I knew that the *Steve Irwin* would be meeting the *Brigitte Bardot* within hours.

When the *Brigitte Bardot* was slightly more than two hundred miles east of American Samoa, I saw the outline of my flagship, the *Steve Irwin*, approaching and exhaled a great sight of relief. She was a beautiful sight. Captain Sid Chakravarty sent over one of the small boats to pick up Nick Taylor and me. The two ships had made the transit in just seventeen days.

I packed my bag, bade a temporary farewell to Luis Pinho and his crew on the *Brigitte Bardot*, and transferred over to the *Steve Irwin*. The *Brigitte Bardot* then proceeded onward to Pago Pago to refuel and take on new crewmembers. Luis would depart for Australia to take command of the *Sam Simon*, and Jean Yves Terlain from France would take over as the new skipper for the *Brigitte Bardot*.

I made it. It had seemed like an impossibility four months before, when I first stepped aboard the *Columbus*. We had crossed the North Atlantic, landed in Canada, crossed into the United States, and sailed the Pacific to rejoin the *Steve Irwin*—all without any papers or border clearances.

When I came aboard, Sid Chakravarty turned over the command of the *Steve Irwin* to me. We then waited for the *Brigitte Bardot*, and when the trimaran joined us, both vessels headed toward New Zealand.

The last time I'd seen Jean Yves Terlain, I was waving goodbye to him and his crew off the coast of Nova Scotia. It was nice to see him again, this famous French sailor aboard a ship with a famous French name.

Although it was early December, word from Japan was that the whaling fleet was still in port. Thus, we had a leisurely voyage toward Auckland, New Zealand, and the first few days of December were filled with positives: December 2 was my birthday, and on December 4, Sea Shepherd issued an official announcement that I had returned to my flagship, the *Steve Irwin*. It had taken me four months to come halfway around the planet.

On December 1, the *Bob Barker*, under the command of Captain Carlos Bueno Carbajal of Spain, left White Bay in Sydney, Australia, bound for Wellington, New Zealand. She arrived on December 5.

Mobilizing Neptune's Navy to stop the slaughter of whales by Japan in the Southern Ocean Whale Sanctuary.

The biggest surprise of the campaign came in Brisbane, Queensland. Captain Luis Pinho flew back to Australia from American Samoa to take command of a new ship. The ship had been newly registered under the Australian flag. Sea Shepherd had done an excellent job of keeping it a secret—but once the registry was granted, the ownership and the name became public knowledge. One thing we knew for sure was that the Japanese government and the Japanese whalers were going to be pissed.

It was no secret that the Japanese knew we were looking to secure another ship, but we made it obvious that the ship we wanted was in Germany. The last thing they expected was for Sea Shepherd to buy one of their own ships right under their noses.

Earlier in the year, we had received a special donation from Sam Simon, a man best known in the television industry for producing *The Simpsons*. He gave us $2 million for the purchase of a new ship. With the cash in hand we had registered a company in Delaware called New Atlantis Ventures, which in turn registered a company in Hong Kong. Then Florida-based Captain Locky MacLean, using the name Peter Riceman, negotiated the purchase of the ship through a brokerage in Australia. He had a Brazilian surveyor—Luis Gouveia, who was based in South Korea—fly to Japan to check out the vessel. The broker had no idea he was representing Sea Shepherd, and the sellers certainly did not realize who the buyers were—or they most certainly would not have sold the ship to us.

The ship was a research vessel constructed by Ishikawajima-Harima Heavy Industries in Tokyo in 1993 and originally named the *Seifu Maru*. She had been built for the Japanese government. She was originally a marine meteorological and oceanographic observation ship and one of four—along with her sister ships the *Chofu Maru*, *Kofu Maru*, and *Ryofu Maru*—operated by the Maizuru Marine Observatory for work in the Sea of Japan and the North Pacific. When the Argo research program ended in 2010, the ships were sold. The *Seifu Maru* was purchased by the Offshore Operation Company Ltd., which renamed her the *Kaiko Maru No. 8* in 2010; that owner in turn sold her to Sea Shepherd.

I liked her history. She hadn't been through a great deal of wear and tear, and she'd been retired after only seventeen years of duty. During the time the ship had been employed by the Japanese government, she had been engaged with research projects focused on greenhouse gases, ozone-depleting substances, heavy metals, and oils. Therefore, the surveyor had reported she was in excellent condition and had an abundance of spare parts.

At the time of purchase, she was sitting in the same dockyard as the Japanese whaling fleet. An additional annoyance to the Japanese whalers and government was the fact that Locky had even arranged for six Japanese crewmembers to deliver the ship to Cairns, Australia. He renamed the vessel the *New Atlantis* and put her under the temporary flag of Tuvalu.

"We did not have much choice, really. We could not have a Sea Shepherd crew fly into Japan and take command," Locky said with a laugh.

We understood that if we were discovered, the Japanese government would most likely seize our $2 million and the ship, so there were some anxious moments as we waited for the ship to depart.

The *New Atlantis* departed from Shimonoseki, Japan, on August 23 while I was making my way across the North Atlantic. We experienced more anxiety when we found out that the ship was weathering a typhoon passing through the South China Sea.

Our new ship and her six Japanese crewmembers arrived in Cairns on September 7 and were met by one of our engineers, Steve O'Leary, an Irishman living in the Philippines. The Japanese crew handed the vessel over to Steve, and he posed for pictures with them on the dock beside the ship. Steve told them the ship had been purchased for conversion to a mega yacht by a wealthy businessman named Peter Riceman.

Locky had printed up some nice white yacht shirts with the name *New Atlantis* under a silhouette of the ship. Steve and the Japanese sailors all proudly sported the shirts for the pictures. Locky had also arranged for the agent to give the Japanese captain a gift on behalf of Riceman: a bottle of eighteen-year single malt whiskey and a few cases of beer for the crew.

As soon as the Japanese crew departed for home, Locky brought up some crew from the *Steve Irwin* to convert the vessel to a Sea Shepherd campaign ship. Malcolm Holland arrived, along with Australian crewmember James Brooks, American crewmember Josh Trenter, and Italian crewmembers Giacomo Giorgi and Raffaella Tolicetti.

On September 30, Locky departed from Cairns for Brisbane, where he had arranged for the *New Atlantis* to be dry-docked and made ready for Operation Zero Tolerance. While she was in Brisbane, the ship would also reregister under the Australian flag as the *Sam Simon*.

Amazingly, from the time of purchase in August to late November, the fact that Sea Shepherd had acquired a new ship was a carefully guarded secret. I was proud of her crew's success in covertly preparing the ship for Operation Zero Tolerance.

Upon reaching New Zealand, the *Brigitte Bardot* went into Auckland to refuel and the *Steve Irwin* lingered offshore. The *Bob Barker* docked at Queens Wharf in Wellington and was joined by the *Brigitte Bardot*. Peter Hammarstedt resumed command of the *Bob Barker*, and both vessels spent time giving tours in Wellington in addition to being given an official blessing by the Maori.

Everything was going smoothly until mid-December. That was when the game changed dramatically. On December 18, our lawyer in Seattle, Charles Moure, called to say that the United States Court of Appeals for the Ninth Circuit had granted the Institute of Cetacean Research an injunction ordering Sea Shepherd not to approach within five hundred yards of any whaling ship and to refrain from throwing our stink bombs and using our prop-fouling measures. This was a complete reversal of the ruling in February 2012, when Judge Richard Jones had denied the Japanese request for an injunction, allowing us to continue our preparations to return to the Southern Ocean.

There were no details as to why the injunction had been granted, just a one-page email saying that it had. The injunction was enforceable against Sea Shepherd USA and against me personally.

As a US citizen I recognized that a federal injunction was enforceable against me and possibly against the Sea Shepherd directors in the United States, so it seemed logical that if there was no involvement from Sea Shepherd USA or me, the mission would be able to proceed without issue.

None of the ships involved in Operation Zero Tolerance—the *Sam Simon*, *Bob Barker*, *Steve Irwin*, and *Brigitte Bardot*—were flagged in the United States. Their captains were French, Indian, Australian, and Swedish. The ships departed from Australian and New Zealand ports with the objective of opposing Japanese-flagged vessels in the neutral waters around Antarctica.

I called Sea Shepherd Australia director Jeff Hansen to tell him the bad news.

"What has that got to do with us, Paul? What possible jurisdiction do the US courts have over us?"

"They don't," I answered, "but what it means is that I must step down as campaign leader and as captain of the *Steve Irwin*. All funding for the campaign from Sea Shepherd USA will be cut off. In other words, the only way this campaign can continue is under the direction of Sea Shepherd Australia."

"This is a hell of a thing, mate," said Jeff. "All the ships are at sea heading south, and I'm not going to call them back."

"It's out of my control, Jeff—my hands are tied. I will not continue in contempt of the court because I'm an American citizen. But the captains are not Americans and neither are you, so the call is yours."

Jeff Hansen had a meeting with Bob Brown and, at Jeff's request, Bob agreed to be expedition leader for Operation Zero Tolerance. Bob contacted the skippers of all four ships and told them to proceed south to wait for the whalers to arrive.

Because of my situation, I felt that I had no choice but to also resign from the board of Sea Shepherd USA and to quit my job with Sea Shepherd. My resignations took place on December 31. I also resigned from the board of Sea Shepherd Australia. Because I was specifically named, I felt I should not have any connections with Sea Shepherd either in Australia or the United States.

I called a meeting in the mess room of the *Steve Irwin* to inform the crew of the injunction and to tell them that I had no choice but to step down as expedition leader and captain. "Sid is now captain of the *Steve Irwin*," I announced. "I have asked all the captains to abide by the injunction, although they understand they are under no legal obligation to comply. However, I am under a legal obligation to do so, and thus I have requested of Sid—and he has agreed—that the *Steve Irwin* not approach any of the whaling ships while I am aboard. It is not possible for me to get off the ship, but I intend to abide by the injunction. It's a federal court order, so I don't have much choice. From now on, I am aboard strictly as an observer. Bob Brown is now the official expedition leader and Sid is now captain of the *Steve Irwin*."

What I had not anticipated was the paranoia of the majority of the Sea Shepherd USA board of directors. I received a message from the board requesting that we cancel the campaign completely.

We could not do that—the consequences, if any, be damned. Four ships, six rigid inflatable boats, a helicopter, two drones, and 120 crewmembers were prepared. We were now in the strongest position that we had ever been in, and I was not going to have this campaign derailed by judges in the United States who decided to side with the Japanese whalers.

I informed the US board of directors that the situation was now out of my hands and thus out of theirs. Operation Zero Tolerance would proceed.

On December 28, the *Brigitte Bardot* delivered our replacement helicopter pilot along with the film crew from Animal Planet.

On January 3, the *Brigitte Bardot* refueled in Christchurch and then departed to meet up with the *Steve Irwin* off Timaru, New Zealand.

On January 5, I transferred from the *Steve Irwin* to the *Brigitte Bardot*. The *Steve Irwin* headed to Timaru to refuel.

In Timaru, the *Steve Irwin* was boarded by customs and some police officers looking for me. They searched the ship. I certainly made the right decision not to trust the New Zealand authorities. New Zealand's minister of foreign affairs had made it very obvious over the past two years that he did not like Sea Shepherd, and I was sure he'd love to turn me over to the Japanese government.

The authorities asked Captain Sid Chakravarty if I was on his ship. When he replied that I was not and that I had transferred to another vessel at sea, they began a meticulous search of the entire ship. Their attempt to find me proved fruitless, however—at the time of the search of the *Steve Irwin*, I was swimming offshore with Hector's dolphins.

The *Brigitte Bardot* was drifting offshore when a government helicopter approached. The authorities claimed that someone had issued a distress signal, because we were observed not moving and the so-called caller had reported as an overturned yacht.

The helicopter hailed us and we did not answer. Instead, Captain Terlain headed seaward at full speed. The Coastguard South Canterbury and Maritime New Zealand publicly criticized us, saying, "There was no need for Sea Shepherd to behave like this."

Later I responded that I believed that the Coastguard South Canterbury officials were disingenuous with their bogus story about a caller reporting that we were an overturned yacht, since we had seen no other vessels and we could not be seen from shore.

When contacted by the media, I confessed that I left the *Steve Irwin* for the *Brigitte Bardot* because I was concerned that New

Zealand would acquiesce to the Japanese government's demand for my extradition. I told the media that if I were to enter New Zealand, I would be detained and thus would be unable to lead my ships to the Southern Ocean.

New Zealand was in a delicate position, and I think New Zealand's leaders were relieved that I did not enter the country. Civil rights lawyer Michael Bott told the media that governments "could and should act with discretion" regarding Interpol Red Notices. "He's not a war criminal and it's my understanding that the charges are historic and highly contested so . . . it could be seen as political," Bott stated. He went on to say that if the New Zealand government acted on the Red Notice, the action could be interpreted as New Zealand "trying to buddy up to Japan." New Zealand faced a "murky line" between legal requirements and politics, Bott added.

After refueling, the *Steve Irwin* departed from Timaru, and I transferred back to the Sea Shepherd flagship. The *Bob Barker* had departed Wellington on January 5 and met up with the *Steve Irwin* the next day.

It had not been until the end of December 2012 that our crew onshore in Japan relayed that the Japanese whaling fleet had finally departed. They had never left so late before, but now that we knew they were on their way, we began to make our slow cruise south. The *Brigitte Bardot*, the *Bob Barker*, and the *Steve Irwin* had a parley off the Auckland Islands on January 8 before heading toward Antarctica. The *Sam Simon* had gone from Brisbane to Hobart and, after refueling, had struck off for the Southern Ocean.

The *Steve Irwin*, *Brigitte Bardot*, and *Bob Barker* reached sixty degrees south on January 11. We saw our first iceberg of the season on January 12. The crew of the *Bob Barker* reported that a pod of pilot whales accompanied them across the line.

The *Sam Simon* had departed from Hobart just two days before, on January 10, reaching sixty degrees south on January 15. The crew happily reported being escorted over the line by a pod of hourglass dolphins.

The four vessels spread out across a hundred miles from one another in a line just south of sixty degrees to await the Japanese fleet. At last the Sea Shepherd fleet was ready and in place, waiting for the invasion of the Southern Ocean Whale Sanctuary by the Japanese whaling fleet. What had started in 2005 with one ancient and very slow trawler, the *Farley Mowat*, had evolved into four ships, a helicopter, and 120 crewmembers.

Before heading southward from New Zealand, all four vessels—including our new ship, the *Sam Simon*—came together so that the *Whale Wars* production crew could film them from the helicopter. It was a remarkable sight.

That year I had four new captains. Captain Sid Chakravarty of India was replacing me as captain of the *Steve Irwin*. Jean Yves Terlain from France had the helm of the *Brigitte Bardot*. Luis Pinho from Brazil was in command of the *Sam Simon*. And Peter Hammarstedt, despite being the youngest of the four, had the most experience. This was his eighth Southern Ocean campaign and he now had command of the *Bob Barker*.

We were now a navy—Neptune's Navy—and for the first time in thirty-five years, I was not leading a Sea Shepherd campaign. As an observer, I felt proud that the chain of command, which had evolved over the years, was now working perfectly.

2013

The Iron Wedge

SOUTHERN OCEAN

W e found the Japanese fleet just as we had every season since 2005. We had never been more powerful than we were now with four vessels, four crews, and a helicopter. We found the whalers and they began to run.

The chase finally ended on February 15. The *Bob Barker* traversed a wide circle into Prydz Bay, coming in from the west, while the *Shonan Maru No. 2* and the *Yushin Maru No. 2* stood guard to the east of the *Nisshin Maru*.

In his journal, Peter Hammarstedt had written:

When we found the *Nisshin Maru*, it was the result of some pretty good strategic thinking. Based on weather, it was quite clear that the whalers were likely operating in Commonwealth Bay. The *Steve Irwin*, which had a tailing vessel, therefore slowly searched along the coast east of Commonwealth Bay to give the whalers the false perception that we believed the fleet to be there. Further to that, it would ensure that the *Shonan Maru No. 2* searched for the *Bob Barker* east of Commonwealth Bay as well. That allowed the *Bob Barker* to approach from the west, where the bad weather was and the direction from which she was least expected. That's how we totally surprised the whaling fleet.

The previous night I gave the order to drift for the night. I presumed that they would be drifting as well; there were a lot of icebergs around and I didn't want to pick up a tailing vessel. As the sun came up, I made the decision to start sweeping the bay. It took no more than twenty minutes before we ran into the *Nisshin Maru*. They had been drifting just twenty-five miles away from us all night! We were able to approach within five miles and catch them completely by surprise. The *Steve Irwin* held down the rest of the fleet, ensuring that the *Nisshin Maru* was guarded by only one harpoon ship.

The whaling fleet had finally been run down at a distance of 2,245 miles southwest of Perth in one of the most hostile and isolated areas on the planet. There was now no way that the *Nisshin Maru* was going to escape, and the *Bob Barker* began to dog the factory ship. With the *Nisshin Maru* in plain view, the *Bob Barker*'s crew began their morning chore of knocking the thick ice from rails, small boats, machinery, and rigging. They happily observed numerous minke whales spouting nearby, and although the conditions were perfect for the Japanese to kill whales, the whalers were not hunting.

Upon locating the *Nisshin Maru*, Captain Hammarstedt radioed Captain Chakravarty of the *Steve Irwin*. The *Steve Irwin* set a course to intercept, with the *Yushin Maru No. 3* following close behind.

Peter increased the *Bob Barker*'s speed and headed toward the targets, which were five nautical miles away. But it soon became obvious that the whalers had spotted them. The *Nisshin Maru* got underway at maximum speed. The old whaler *Bob Barker*, which in the past had so often made this sprint to kill a whale, was now moving forward with the world's largest whaling ship in her sights.

The *Yushin Maru No. 2* closed in on the *Bob Barker* and began maneuvering in a dangerous zigzag pattern before the bow of the Sea Shepherd ship. Peter radioed to the *Yushin Maru No. 2* to desist. The whalers continued zigzagging but radioed back to the *Bob Barker* that she should desist from dangerous maneuvers, although she was simply maintaining her course.

By 1:30 p.m., the *Yushin Maru No. 2* had gone off the radar. Initially it was a mystery: Why was she abandoning her mother ship? The *Nisshin Maru* was now only three nautical miles away from the *Bob Barker*. Peter had the whalers and he did not intend to lose them.

Peter soon suspected that the *Yushin Maru No. 2* was intending to kill a whale. There were whales in the area, and this would be an opportunity for the whalers to test the resolve of the Sea Shepherd crew. When they reappeared on radar, it was clear that they were in a hunting pattern. At six miles away, Phil in the crow's nest saw the harpoon fired, too far away for the *Bob Barker* to directly intervene. All the Sea Shepherd crew could do was stick tight with the *Nisshin Maru* to prevent the whale from being transferred.

The *Yushin Maru No. 2* soon returned to the area, and the Sea Shepherd crew could see a slain whale strapped to the side of the killer and being dragged by her tail. The Japanese whalers had indeed killed a whale. They had not killed a whale near us since 2008. With the injunction in their hands, they intended to force the *Bob Barker* to violate the court order imposed by the Ninth Circuit Court of Appeals in the United States.

"What can we do?" Oona Layolle asked.

Peter looked across the water at the *Yushin Maru No. 2* and the whale lashed to its side. "That whale is dead because of the US courts. These bastards believe they can do what they want and that we won't interfere."

Peter paused, assessing the situation carefully. "We will not allow them to continue to kill whales illegally. This is a Dutch ship in Australian territorial waters. They have just illegally killed a whale. The United States has no jurisdiction here and none over us. Prepare to block any attempt to transfer that whale."

The *Nisshin Maru* began to trail longlines to prevent the *Bob Barker* from closing in. At seven o'clock that evening, Peter ordered one of the *Bob Barker*'s small boats, the *Gemini*, deployed. The *Gemini*'s crew quickly cut the port-side trailing line. When the whalers saw what had happened, they quickly began to retrieve the starboard trailing line. They did not get much of it back aboard before the *Gemini* crew cut that line too.

Preventing a fleet from refueling during our most successful year of opposing illegal Japanese whaling operations. Japan took only 10 percent of their quota.

The crew of the *Yushin Maru No. 2* hurled metal objects at the small boat's crew. A few of the large bolts and chunks of rusted steel landed in the boat or splashed into the water; fortunately, none of the *Gemini*'s crewmembers were struck.

The captain of the *Yushin Maru No. 2* could see that the *Bob Barker* was not to be deterred by the US court's injunction. He moved in recklessly. All three ships were in close proximity to our small boat's crew in the water. As the whaler crossed the bow of the *Bob Barker* at dangerously close range, the harpooner swung the whaling vessel's huge gun and aimed it at the crew standing on the bow of the *Bob Barker*. Not one of them moved. They simply looked straight at the harpooner, daring him to fire. One of the Japanese crew, who was standing with two other crewmembers on the deck above the dead whale, slowly slid his finger across his throat. The *Bob Barker*'s crew refused to be intimidated—they all stood fast and did not react.

For seven hours the *Bob Barker* successfully blocked the other ship's slipway, deterring twelve attempts by the whalers to transfer the dead whale. Finally, the loudspeakers on the *Nisshin Maru* boomed with a warning: "This is the first officer of the Japan Coast Guard aboard the *Nisshin Maru*. We warn you to not disrupt our operations. Stop. Stop."

On the bow of the *Bob Barker*, the crew stood in formation, watching the black-clad Japan Coast Guard officers glaring back at them from the stern of the factory ship.

On the whalers' thirteenth attempt to transfer their kill, the *Nisshin Maru* suddenly reversed, causing the *Bob Barker* to move forward along the starboard side of the factory ship. The *Yushin Maru No. 2* shot behind the *Bob Barker* on the port aft side, turning rapidly to starboard. The whalers quickly attached the towline to the whale before the *Bob Barker* could come about. As the *Yushin Maru No. 2* broke away, the whale's carcass was quickly pulled up the stern slipway. It was a reckless move, but it worked. They had transferred the whale. A loud cheer went up from the Japanese crew.

It was to be the whaling fleet's only victory, however. Despite the numerous whales in the area, that was the only whale killed for the next three days.

It was frustrating for me to be an observer during my own campaign on my own ship, but I was thrilled at how skillful Peter and Sid were in engaging the whalers. They were proceeding confidently and with great courage.

By February 20, the whaling fleet was desperate for fuel, especially the *Nisshin Maru*. That morning, we were certain the Japanese ships were preparing to refuel. Their internal radio transmissions were translated, and it was clear they were transferring their remaining fuel, getting the tanks ready.

The fueling ship *Sun Laurel* had been moving through chunks of ice all night. She was being followed closely by the *Sam Simon*. The whalers, followed by the *Steve Irwin* and the *Bob Barker*, were getting close to the tanker.

By 8:00 a.m., the *Sun Laurel* was the center of attention with all five of the whaling fleet's ships and the three Sea Shepherd ships surrounding her. A total of nine ships were slowly moving through the ice slope, warily eyeing one another's movements. The whalers were looking for an opening and the Sea Shepherd vessels were looking to block any opening.

The translator on the *Bob Barker* notified the *Nisshin Maru* that it was illegal to refuel south of sixty degrees and that the Sea Shepherd ships intended to stand their ground to prevent the *Nisshin Maru* from approaching the fuel tanker.

A few days before the refueling, Peter Hammarstedt had called a meeting with his crew to brief them on plans to disrupt any refueling attempts between the *Sun Laurel* and the *Nisshin Maru* south of sixty degrees. He advised the crewmembers that Sea Shepherd needed to take the opportunity to block this refueling, for if the refueling went ahead, the whalers would resume their hunting. He also gave the crew an opportunity to disembark if they were uncomfortable with what he called Operation Iron Wedge. Of the thirty-four crewmembers, no one asked a single question and no one asked to disembark.

All three Sea Shepherd ships were in position to block any attempt by the *Nisshin Maru* to come alongside the *Sun Laurel* to refuel. The *Steve Irwin* was on the port side of the *Sun Laurel* while the *Bob Barker* was on the starboard side. The *Sam Simon* was positioned ahead of the tanker, trailing more than eight hundred feet of line to keep the harpoon vessels from cutting across her stern. The small Sea Shepherd boats were also being lowered into the water.

At 10:35 a.m., the *Nisshin Maru* radioed the *Sun Laurel* to say they had completed the internal transfer of fuel into their own tanks. The Sea Shepherd crews prepared for the *Nisshin Maru* to attempt to come alongside the *Sun Laurel*. The ships moved slowly through the water, and it was plain to see that the *Nisshin Maru* could not find an opening.

Around noon, the *Nisshin Maru* suddenly sped up and headed away from the *Sun Laurel*, with the factory ship's harpoon vessels following obediently. The whaling fleet was underway and heading east.

The fleet returned eight hours later. The *Nisshin Maru* was moving fast and making a beeline for the *Sun Laurel*. The *Steve Irwin* blocked her stern, the *Sam Simon* her bow, and the *Bob Barker* covered the port side of the tanker. Two of the harpoon vessels and the *Shonan Maru No. 2* began moving in, their water cannons turned on. At the same time, the *Nisshin Maru* turned directly toward the *Bob Barker*. The *Yushin Maru No. 3* crossed the stern of the *Bob Barker*, aiming her water cannons at the aft deck.

The ships were all turning in different directions and near one another, each side attempting to intimidate the other. The *Sun Laurel*'s deck crew emerged and started preparing to position their huge Yokohama fenders for a docking with the *Nisshin Maru*.

The Sea Shepherd's small boats moved in. Tommy Knowles quickly began to cut one of the lines lowering a fender over the side of the tanker. A crewmember on the *Sun Laurel* thrust a long pole toward Tommy that glanced off his helmet. Undeterred, Tommy cut the fender free and it drifted toward the stern of the tanker.

The *Steve Irwin* was now between the *Nisshin Maru* and the *Sun Laurel*, taking a terrific pounding from two of the whaler's heavy water cannons. The water cannons were pointed straight down, and the Japanese vessel's black hull towered like a steel wall along the entire port side of the *Steve Irwin*.

Sid was holding the ship in place despite the pounding as the crew of the *Delta*, another of Sea Shepherd's small boats, worked to stop the *Sun Laurel*'s crew from deploying more fenders off the port side of the *Steve Irwin*.

In the *Delta*, a crewmember named Chad shouted, "It's useless! The fenders have been secured with heavy wire—we can't cut that!"

"Sure, we can," said Tommy as he reached down and pulled a huge bolt cutter from the floor of the *Delta*. The *Delta*'s crew managed to slice the wire, and the fender was set adrift, although still attached on the other side. But with one side cut, it was rendered useless.

The *Steve Irwin* was coming closer to the *Sun Laurel* as the *Nisshin Maru* continued to hit the ship with her heavy water cannons. The *Steve Irwin*'s crewmembers began to deploy her fenders on the starboard side in case the two ships were forced alongside each other. It looked as though the *Steve Irwin* was about to become the fender between the *Nisshin Maru* and the *Sun Laurel*.

Finally, at 9:45 p.m., the *Nisshin Maru* notified the *Sun Laurel* that she was retreating. The deck team on the *Sun Laurel* began to move off the deck and go back inside.

By 10:30 p.m., all the ships were underway again and moving at seven knots, with the *Nisshin Maru* having moved off half a mile. The *Steve Irwin* launched the helicopter to check out the *Nisshin Maru* and the whalers.

Peter radioed over to the *Steve Irwin* and the *Sam Simon*: "Great job, everyone. We stopped their refueling attempt for today, but they will try again in the morning. We need to keep our positions. No whales were killed today. Get some rest, everyone."

The next morning, we were all mystified: Why was the *Nisshin Maru* moving into thicker ice?

"It does not make sense," Luis radioed over to the other ships. "The whalers know we can go through the ice, but to navigate the tanker through these waters is lunacy."

Despite the ice, the huge factory ship began to move forward in an attempt to come alongside the *Sun Laurel*.

Captain Hammarstedt raced forward and placed his vessel between the two much larger ships, but the *Nisshin Maru* was not stopping.

From the deck of the *Steve Irwin*, I could see that the *Bob Barker* was now directly under the bow of the *Nisshin Maru*.

Peter and his bridge crew felt the crash as the huge bow of the *Nisshin Maru* hit the *Bob Barker* on the port side with all the whaling ship's water cannons aimed down. The whalers were trying to flood the funnel and the engine room of the *Bob Barker*.

With the *Nisshin Maru* pushing relentlessly against the port side of the *Bob Barker*, Andrea Gordon shouted over to Captain Hammarstedt. "They're on top of us now!"

Peter scanned the bridge and saw that everybody was looking at him. He had to make a decision. Would he stand fast, or would he move out of the way to allow the whalers to refuel?

Without hesitation, Peter gave the order not to move. I could see the bow of the whaler towering over the upper deck of the *Bob*

Barker, pushing against the aft mast, which came down with a crash. The *Bob Barker* was being pushed over hard to starboard and was colliding with the port side of the tanker. Meanwhile, the Japanese were throwing stun grenades, an incredibly stupid move alongside a fueling vessel.

Peter had positioned all nonessential off-duty crew in the mess to keep them out of harm's way. This approach also allowed him to know where everyone was at all times. The crew could see live images of the *Nisshin Maru* approaching on the *Bob Barker*'s security cameras.

"It must have been scarier for them there than for us on the bridge in many ways," Peter later reported. "They could feel the impact and they could hear the screech of buckling steel. They had their survival suits and were ready to abandon ship if the order was given."

The *Bob Barker* was literally being crushed between the massive factory ship on her port side and the giant tanker on her starboard side. It was becoming very clear to the Japanese skipper that the *Bob Barker* would not budge.

It was the *Nisshin Maru* that broke away and turned north. The fleet's whale killing was over for the season. We had prevented their refueling operation, and they were heading away from the Southern Ocean Whale Sanctuary.

2013

Exile at Sea

SOUTH PACIFIC

Operation Zero Tolerance was over. It was a magnificent victory: out of Japan's self-appointed quota, 932 whales had been spared the harpoon.

It was a long voyage for our three ships to travel from the middle of the southern Indian Ocean back to Melbourne. The *Sam Simon* passed the volcano on Heard Island. The *Steve Irwin* and the *Bob Barker* met up off the Kerguelen Islands, and the *Steve Irwin* took on some forty tons of fuel from the *Bob Barker*.

The French authorities on the Kerguelen Islands were notified that we were nearby. Any question of going ashore was ruled out when the authorities asked if I was aboard. With the refueling done, the two ships headed eastward again, following the *Sam Simon* home to Williamstown. Meanwhile, the *Brigitte Bardot* was being prepared in Hobart to rendezvous with the *Steve Irwin* and the *Bob Barker*.

On March 20, the three Sea Shepherd ships met up just west of King Island near the Bass Strait. Oona Layolle, Ryan Jones, and Josephine Watmore transferred to the *Steve Irwin* from the *Bob*

Barker. The *Sam Simon* and the *Bob Barker* then slowly headed off toward Port Phillip Bay on the coast of Australia.

Two hours later, the *Brigitte Bardot* arrived from the south and drifted close off the starboard quarter of the *Steve Irwin*. Oona, Ryan, and Josephine were joined by Tommy Knowles. In addition, I left the *Steve Irwin* and boarded the *Brigitte Bardot*. Captain Jean Yves Terlain handed over the *Brigitte Bardot* to Captain Oona Layolle and was ferried back to the *Steve Irwin*.

After four months aboard the *Steve Irwin*, I watched my flagship and her intrepid crew head north to follow the other two ships to Williamstown, where Bob Brown and Jeff Hansen had arranged a large public reception for the victorious anti-whaling fleet.

Already aboard the *Brigitte Bardot* were chief engineer Steve O'Leary, ship manager Simon Ager, cook Kate Garrison, and first mate Chantelle Derez.

I had appointed Oona as skipper for the *Brigitte Bardot* for two very good reasons: The first was that I could not officially be on the crew list. The second was that she was our most experienced sailor, and I needed someone who knew how to sail because I had arranged the purchase of a sailing yacht. We planned to rendezvous with the yacht in the South Pacific. Oona was twenty-nine, a French citizen who was raised in Colombia. Fluent in Spanish, French, and English, she had spent her childhood sailing with her family. She had been with Sea Shepherd as a deck officer for the past three campaigns, and I had no doubts about her abilities.

We decided not to cross the Bass Strait: that would have put the *Brigitte Bardot* well inside Australian waters. Instead, we went south around the bottom of Tasmania and worked our way up its eastern coast in very bad weather; so bad in fact that, despite the risks, we pulled into Slaughterhouse Bay to anchor and seek shelter.

Although considerably calmer than the outside waters, the bay was still rough. Conditions were so intense that we dragged anchor. The hydraulics broke on the anchor winch, and we found we could not raise the anchor. We had no choice but to cut it loose—we spent the night motoring in a circle until the winds died down.

The next day, we continued north toward Sydney Harbor. The *Brigitte Bardot* needed fuel, her lost anchor needed to be replaced, and her hydraulics needed to be repaired.

Two days prior, however, the *Steve Irwin*, *Bob Barker*, and *Sam Simon* had arrived in Williamstown to a warm welcome from hundreds of Sea Shepherd supporters. Bob Brown and Jeff Hansen were there, and Richard Dean Anderson and Peter Brown were also on the dock to greet everyone. The Australian Federal police did not show—just customs and immigration officials, who were very friendly. The ships were quickly cleared and the crew released to speak to the media and celebrate their victory in the Southern Ocean. None of the authorities asked about my whereabouts.

The problem with my being exiled at sea was that when a ship had to go ashore for fuel and provisions, I couldn't go with. The only solution, therefore, was to have two boats. When the *Brigitte Bardot* arrived off Sydney, I decided to stay offshore while Oona took the vessel in for repairs and supplies. My friend Rob Holden had chartered a fishing boat for me to stay on to allow Oona to enter Sydney with the *Brigitte Bardot*.

We expected the *Brigitte Bardot* to be searched when she reached Sydney; however, although the authorities may have suspected I might be aboard, they were not overly eager to find out. There were two customs officials on the dock, and they did not even step aboard the ship. They took the entry papers from Oona and left her and the crew to do the repairs and order the fuel and provisions. Two days later, the *Brigitte Bardot* returned from Sydney.

During this time, I finalized the negotiations with Roger Payne, PhD, and his group, Ocean Alliance, for the purchase of their sailboat the *Caribana*. In December the *Caribana* had left Gloucester, Massachusetts, for the Galápagos Islands via the Panama Canal. From the Galápagos Islands, she and her crew were now making their way to French Polynesia. And so, with the *Brigitte Bardot* fueled and provisioned once more, we departed from Australian waters and headed eastward to meet up with the *Caribana*.

The *Brigitte Bardot*, being faster than the *Caribana*, saw us arrive in Tonga two weeks before the sailboat. We spent a week anchored off the Tongan island of Ofalanga, and then we moved to Rose Atoll some two hundred miles east of American Samoa.

Although we didn't have much of a choice, I selected Rose Atoll for our rendezvous with the *Caribana* because it is an uninhabited island. In fact, it is illegal to visit it without a permit. Another reason for the restriction is to discourage the introduction of unwelcome invasive species, and we had none.

Tommy Knowles and I were put ashore at Rose Atoll, a very small, beautiful island surrounded by a spectacular reef and covered with birds. The *Brigitte Bardot* then turned back west to American Samoa to refuel and reprovision. The plan was that Tommy and I would be picked up the next day by the *Caribana*.

Rose Atoll was a fascinating place. The intense noise from a million seabirds was a constant cacophony. The birds filled the shrubs and the few coconut trees, covered the ground, and flooded the sky. Despite the never-ending bombardment of bird calls, we managed to finally get some sleep.

The next morning we saw the beautiful ketch *Caribana*. The delivery crew had departed the vessel when they reached Tahiti, leaving only Bob Wallace from Ocean Alliance aboard. Two of my crew—Mal Holland and Laura Dakin—had flown to Tahiti, where they boarded the vessel. Bob, Mal, and Laura immediately set sail for Rose Atoll. Perfect timing.

Mal and Laura came to the shore in the small red tender to pick up Tommy and me. We headed out the small channel through the reef to step on what would now be my new floating home.

She was a beautiful eighty-one-foot sailing vessel. Two masts, four sails, eight bunks.

"Damn, Mal, this is one nice boat," I said.

Mal smiled. "I thought you would like her. She's got two Caterpillar 250-horsepower diesel engines and a single screw that can give us ten knots—she can move faster under sail. She can hold five thousand gallons of fresh water and almost two thousand gallons of fuel."

The four of us then headed back to Ofalanga Island, where we dropped anchor to wait for the return of the *Brigitte Bardot* with new crewmembers and fresh supplies.

Once again, Tommy and I were dropped off on the shore to camp so that the *Caribana* could go into Nuku'alofa to clear Tongan customs. There Mal and Laura dropped off Bob and picked up Mal's brother, Cam Holland, who was to be the engineer on the *Caribana*.

In Tonga, we sorted out the crews, with Oona becoming captain of the *Caribana*, Josephine the cook, and Ryan the deckhand. Two new crewmembers were joining us as well: Miguel from Spain as engineer and François Martin from Réunion as mate. Mal took over as skipper of the *Brigitte Bardot* with Laura as cook and Chantelle Derez as mate. A new crewmember from France, Fabrice Destreguil, joined the crew of the *Brigitte Bardot* as engineer.

The *Brigitte Bardot* and the *Caribana* departed Tonga on June 10 to head toward northern Queensland. The *Bardot* was bound for Cairns and the *Caribana* for Mackay. The *Brigitte Bardot* made entry into Cairns first. Mal and Laura departed the ship from Cairns, and Carlos Bueno Carbajal came on as skipper. Afterward, the *Brigitte Bardot* rendezvoused with the *Caribana*. Miguel and I transferred to the *Brigitte Bardot* and Fabrice transferred to the *Caribana*.

I spent the last week of June and the first two weeks of July at anchor inside the remote Frederick Reefs on the northeast side of the Great Barrier Reef. Meanwhile, back in the United States, the lawyers for the Institute of Cetacean Research were threatening Sea Shepherd directors with severe penalties for contempt and deposing all the directors and some of the staff.

On June 26, Australia's case against the Japanese whaling industry finally commenced in The Hague before the International Court of Justice. Remarkably, the International Court of Justice had allocated two reserved seats for Sea Shepherd. Alex Cornelissen and Geert Von Jans would be attending each day's proceedings of the three-week trial.

My exile in the South Pacific lasted until October 2013. My lawyers managed to confront Peter Bethune about his deal with the Japanese prosecutor—he had accused me of ordering him to board the *Shonan Maru No. 2* in exchange for a suspended sentence.

Bethune signed an affidavit stating that he had lied to the prosecutor and that I had not ordered him to board the whaling ship. This made no difference to the Japanese. They insisted that I was guilty of ordering Bethune to board. Fortunately, the United States saw it differently, and US Secretary of State John Kerry allowed me to return Stateside.

The *Brigitte Bardot* brought me to San Pedro, California, where I was greeted by supporters, including Robert Kennedy Jr. When immigration officials came to clear the ship, they welcomed me back and asked if we had any T-shirts.

I then traveled north to Seattle, where Sea Shepherd was on trial for contempt of the federal injunction that had ordered us to stay away from the Japanese whalers. At the end of the ten-day trial, Judge Peter Shaw acquitted all of us.

Unfortunately, the US Ninth Circuit Court of Appeals overruled Judge Shaw, declaring us guilty and ordering us to pay damages to the Japanese whalers.

This was a surprise to the whalers. They had not asked for damages. In fact, they did not want damages. That would mean opening their books to the public—and they very much wanted to avoid that. Instead, they asked that we pay only their legal fees. That fee was $2.5 million.

We paid the fee, and we were glad to do so because, since the Japanese had brought this into a US court, they were now subject to a countersuit. We immediately charged them with piracy over the destruction of the *Ady Gil* several years earlier. This meant the whalers would have to open their books—if they did not, they would be held in contempt of court.

This forced the whalers to negotiate with us. We dropped the lawsuit and agreed that Sea Shepherd USA would not intervene in their whaling operations in exchange for a cash settlement in our favor. They also agreed that the actions of other Sea Shepherd groups were outside the control of Sea Shepherd USA.

With this settlement, Sea Shepherd Australia launched Operation Relentless. For the first time, I was forced to not participate personally in a campaign. The campaign was in good hands, though, and Operation Relentless helped save 599 minke whales and 50 fin whales.

The next season, in 2014—due to the verdict of the International Court of Justice—Japan for the first time did not commence whaling operations in the Southern Ocean, although the nation resumed in 2015.

I remained on the Interpol Red Notice list, wanted by both Japan and Costa Rica. Although I was safe in the United States, I was not free to travel outside the country—including to my native Canada: the Canadian government had made it quite clear that they would be very happy to extradite me to Japan.

2005-2017

The Whale Wars

SOUTHERN OCEAN

The ten annual expeditions to the Southern Ocean between 2005 and 2017 is too extensive a narrative to include in this book—perhaps someday these expeditions will fill the pages of another book.

Following are the years and names of Sea Shepherd's Southern Ocean campaigns:

2005–2006: Operation Minke

2006–2007: Operation Leviathan

2007–2008: Operation Migaloo

2008–2009: Operation Musashi

2009–2010: Operation Waltzing Matilda

2010–2011: Operation No Compromise

2011–2012: Operation Divine Wind

2012–2013: Operation Zero Tolerance

2013–2014: Operation Relentless

2016–2017: Operation Nemesis

The objective of the campaigns was to intervene with the illegal activities of the Japanese whaling fleet in the Southern Ocean Whale Sanctuary. The strategy was to obstruct the whaling operations and reduce the number of whales killed.

During my first campaign to Antarctica, in 2002–2003, I failed to track down the Japanese whaling fleet. The campaign taught me some valuable lessons, the most important of which was the need for a helicopter.

For Operation Minke, we secured a helicopter and confronted the Japanese factory ship twice. But my ship, the *Farley Mowat*, was not fast enough to keep up with the Japanese fleet.

For the 2004–2005 whaling season, the Japanese had set a quota of minke and fin whales. They actually caught six more whales than their self-appointed quota allowed.

The 2005–2006 quota was 850 minke whales, 50 fin whales, and 50 humpbacks for a total of 950 whales. The number killed was 856 minke whales, 10 fin whales, and zero humpbacks. Our pursuit and our brief confrontations slowed the whalers down a bit, and they fell short by 40 fin whales and 50 humpbacks.

After that campaign we docked in Cape Town, South Africa, where the local authorities (who had been alerted by Japan) harassed us, forced the removal of our Canadian flag, and prevented the *Farley Mowat* from departing. Three months later, we slipped quietly out of the harbor and set a course for Fremantle in Western Australia.

For Operation Leviathan during the 2006–2007 season, we secured a faster ship, the *Robert Hunter*. And this time, along with the *Farley Mowat*, we were able to track down the whaling fleet and disrupt their operations. That year a fire broke out on the *Nisshin Maru*, a Japanese factory ship. We were hundreds of miles away, fortunately, so we could not be blamed. The Japanese lost one crewmember and their whaling was ended for the season. The quota had been set at 850 minke whales and 10 fin whales. The Japanese killed 508 minke whales and 3 fin whales, falling 342 short of their quota for the minke whales and 7 short for the fin whales.

In 2007, I renamed the *Robert Hunter* as the *Steve Irwin* as a tribute to Steve Irwin, who was going to join us but tragically died months before we were scheduled to depart. The *Steve Irwin* and Operation Migaloo was the first season of filming for the Animal Planet series *Whale Wars*. Earlier that year, I had visited the head offices of major production companies with a proposal for a television show based on our pursuit of the Japanese fleet. Animal Planet decided to give it a go. Their film crew boarded the *Steve Irwin* in Melbourne, Australia.

I decided to send the *Farley Mowat* to Bermuda to prepare for another campaign to oppose the Canadian seal slaughter, and we took only the *Steve Irwin* south to the coast of Antarctica.

I had a fast ship, first-rate helicopter pilot Chris Aultman, and a helicopter. What I did not have was a fully dedicated crew, which was a source of many of the campaign's problems.

But two of my crew, Benjamin Potts from Australia and Giles Lane from England, were more passionate than the others and volunteered to board one of the harpoon vessels while at sea. Boarding the whaling vessel from an inflatable boat while moving at full speed was risky—but the attempt was successful, guaranteeing an international incident and maximum publicity. Predictably, the two men were detained, and I challenged the Australian government to intervene because an Australian citizen was being held hostage in Australian territorial waters. The controversy reached the offices of the prime ministers of both Japan and Australia. After three days, the two men were released back to the *Steve Irwin*.

For the first time, we were able to have a continuous intervention with the factory ship and were successfully able to impact Japan's quota for the season. This resulted in very close clashes, with the *Nisshin Maru* and the *Steve Irwin* racing side by side as the Japan Coast Guard officers aboard the *Nisshin Maru* threw flash-bang grenades and fired what they called warning shots. In retaliation, my crew threw bottles of foul-smelling butyric acid. One flash-bang knocked an Animal Planet cameraman flat on his back. I was struck by a bullet, which fortunately was stopped by my bulletproof vest. The Japanese denied shooting me, so on our return to Melbourne I requested that the Australian Federal Police conduct a forensic examination of the bullet. They refused to do so, citing the lack of jurisdiction. When I asked how Australian authorities could raid our ship, copy our logbooks, and access our computer hard drives if they did not have jurisdiction, the officer in charge said I would have to talk to the politicians about that.

The Japanese quota for that season was 850 minke whales and 10 fin whales. They killed 551 minke whales and no fin whales. Our interventions helped save 299 minke whales and 10 fin whales.

I decided to name the 2008–2009 campaign Operation Musashi in reference to a famous Japanese samurai hero, Miyamoto Musashi.

We left the port of Brisbane with actress Daryl Hannah aboard for the filming of the second season of *Whale Wars*. Once again, we blocked Japan's whaling operations by preventing the harpoon vessels from transferring dead whales to the factory ship. On January 6, 2009, the harpoon vessel *Yushin Maru No. 2* tried to transfer a whale, and I placed the *Steve Irwin* between the harpoon vessel and the factory ship. This maneuver resulted in a collision, which damaged the whaling vessel more than it damaged my ship.

The Japanese quota for that season was 850 minke whales and 50 fin whales. The whalers killed 680 minke whales and 1 fin whale. Our interventions helped save 170 minke whales and 49 fin whales.

The 2009–2010 campaign was called Operation Waltzing Matilda. This time I made the major mistake of allowing a third party to become involved when Peter Bethune volunteered with his fast trimaran *Earthrace* (which had been renamed the *Ady Gil*). It was also the year we had secured a second ship, the *Bob Barker*, something that we did not reveal until she tracked down the *Nisshin Maru*.

I was some three hundred miles away when the factory ship was located. The primary task for Bethune and his boat was to find the Japanese whalers. Despite failing to do so, he raced to where the *Bob Barker* and the whalers were located and began to intimidate and harass one of the harpoon boats in a very reckless manner. He underestimated the ruthlessness of the whalers and foolishly stopped in the path of the *Shonan Maru No. 2*. The harpoon vessel deliberately turned in to the *Ady Gil*, causing a collision that literally cut the trimaran in half.

As a result, the whaling fleet escaped, and we were forced to address the rescue of the heavily damaged vessel's crew. Fortunately, no one was injured; however, the vessel was a total loss.

We eventually relocated the whaling fleet, and the *Bob Barker*—a former Antarctic whaling ship—and the *Steve Irwin* were able to successfully interrupt the whaling activities.

However, the campaign was to face another challenge. Against my advice, Bethune had boarded the *Shonan Maru No. 2* and was arrested. The *Shonan Maru No. 2* then set a course back to Japan with Bethune as a prisoner. He was charged with trespassing and spent a few months in jail awaiting trial. While incarcerated he'd made a deal with the prosecutor: if he said I ordered him to board the *Shonan Maru No. 2*, he would receive a suspended sentence. He'd lied—even though he knew Animal Planet had filmed me advising him not to board the Japanese ship. Bethune was released and Japan filed charges against me for conspiracy to trespass.

The Japanese quota for that difficult season was 850 minke whales and 50 fin whales. The Japanese killed 507 minke whales and 1 fin whale. Our interventions helped save 343 minke whales and 49 fin whales.

Operation No Compromise was the fourth *Whale Wars* season. We departed from Hobart, Tasmania, with three ships—the *Steve Irwin*, the *Bob Barker*, and the *Gojira*. The date was December 2, 2010—my birthday. The *Steve Irwin* was under my command. Captain Alex Cornelissen was master of the *Bob Barker*, while Captain Locky MacLean was master of the *Gojira*. The total number of international crewmembers on the three ships was eighty-eight.

Our opposition was comprised of just four Japanese ships that year: the *Nisshin Maru* and the harpoon vessels *Yushin Maru, Yushin Maru No. 2*, and the *Yushin Maru No. 3*. We were able to find and intercept the whaling fleet on December 31, before they killed a single whale. The *Nisshin Maru* escaped, and two of the harpoon boats were assigned to tail the *Steve Irwin* and the *Bob Barker* to prevent our relocating the *Nisshin Maru*. This kept two of the three killer boats out of action for more than a month.

Operation No Compromise was an intense three months of pursuit through ice and storms. But because we kept the whaling fleet on the run, their quota was severely impacted. The Japanese quota for the season was 850 minke whales and 50 fin whales. Out of that

The campaigns to stop illegal whaling in the Southern Ocean Whale Sanctuary were featured on *Whale Wars*.

quota, 171 minke whales and 2 fin whales were killed. Our interventions helped save 679 minke whales and 48 fin whales.

Operation Divine Wind took place the next season, during 2011 and 2012. Despite the *Gojira* breaking a pontoon and having to be towed back to Fremantle by the *Steve Irwin*, we were still able to intercept, harass, and disrupt whaling operations.

The Japanese quota for the 2011–2012 season was 850 minke whales and 50 fin whales. The whalers killed 266 minke whales and only 1 fin whale. Our interventions helped save 584 minke whales and 49 fin whales.

Operation Zero Tolerance was our most effective campaign. I sent four ships: the *Steve Irwin*, the *Bob Barker*, the *Sam Simon*, and the *Brigitte Bardot*. We blocked the whaling fleet's refueling operations, severely hampering Japan's ability to hunt whales. The whalers' quota that season was 850 minke whales and 50 fin whales. They killed 171 minke whales and no fin whales. We helped save 679 minke whales and 50 fin whales.

Operation Relentless began in 2013. It was the first campaign that I could not participate in. Japan's quota was 850 minke whales and 50 fin whales. The Japanese killed 251 minke whales and no fin whales. We helped save 599 minke whales and 50 fin whales.

No whales were killed by the Japanese in the Southern Ocean during the 2014–2015 season.

Operation Nemesis was our last campaign. In 2016, for our final effort, I sent the *Ocean Warrior* and the *Brigitte Bardot*. The Japanese quota was 333 minke whales and zero fin whales. The Japanese whalers killed 335 minke whales. In 2017, they killed 333 minke whales.

In 2018, Japanese whalers killed 334 minke whales. One of the reasons that we did not confront them in 2018 was because we needed to give Japan the opportunity to save face and back out voluntarily. It became obvious to me that as long as we were harassing the whalers, they would be forced by their nationalists to continue to spite us—and that meant more whales would die.

Whatever challenges these expeditions faced, however, the reality is that thousands of whales were saved:

Minke whale quota between 2005 and 2016: 7,983
Minke whales killed between 2005 and 2016: 4,269
Total minke whales saved: 3,714

Fin whale quota between 2005 and 2013: 380
Fin whales killed between 2013 and 2018: 18
Total fin whales saved: 362

The Antarctic whale wars was a long-fought series of ten campaigns in the Southern Ocean Whale Sanctuary between 2005 and 2017, eight of which I commanded on my own.

After Operation Zero Tolerance and the betrayal by Peter Bethune that forced me into exile, I appointed my very competent captains—Peter Hammarstedt, Wyanda Lublink, and Adam Meyerson—to lead the last two campaigns, Operation Relentless and Operation Nemesis.

In 2017, we decided not to contest the Japanese whalers in Antarctic waters. The growing opposition from members of the International Whaling Commission made it clear that Japan would not be able to get the approval from the organization that it had been seeking.

I knew that Japan would never surrender to us, so we decided not to return to the Southern Ocean in 2017. We indicated that we could not prevail against Japanese technology, and it would not be worthwhile to continue.

This gave Japan the opportunity to have one more whaling season. For the first time in a decade, the Japanese could hunt whales without our opposition. They could now withdraw without losing face.

As I anticipated, on December 26, 2018, Japan announced their withdrawal from membership in the International Whaling Commission and ceased all further whaling operations in the Southern Ocean Whale Sanctuary.

After a decade of confrontations, the whale wars in the Southern Ocean were finally over. The whales in the Southern Ocean Whale Sanctuary were now—finally—safe.

1992 & 2008

The Ships That Wouldn't Sink

PACIFIC AND ATLANTIC COASTS

In 1992, after the North Pacific drift-net campaign, I was returning to Seattle with the *Sea Shepherd II* and *Edward Abbey*. As we
were transiting along the coast of Vancouver Island, I was ordered
into the port of Ucluelet by the Royal Canadian Mounted Police.

I could have ignored the order and continued on to Seattle, but
I decided to comply. My team and I had nothing to hide, and we
knew this was just another case of harassment following a complaint
from Japan.

A pilot was compulsory for Ucluelet, so after the pilot boarded
we headed in for the inspection. It was a full-blown affair, complete with plenty of Mounties and Canadian Coast Guard personnel
(some of whom I recognized from my time in the Coast Guard), a few
dogs, a handful of cameras, and customs and immigration officials—
all of whom had been flown in from Victoria, the capital of British
Columbia, just to welcome us.

We were released two hours later, the authorities having found
nothing. I was preparing to depart when the pilot handed me a bill
for $7,500.

"What's this for?" I asked. "The Mounties ordered me in—they can pay it."

"That's not how it works," the pilot replied. "You can't leave without paying the pilotage bill."

"I think this bill is quite excessive considering you were on the ship for about ten minutes and all you did was watch me bring her in."

"Nonetheless," he said, "you can't leave until you pay the bill."

I looked at him for a moment and then said, "Then I guess we're not leaving. I have no intention of paying this bill."

Flustered, the pilot repeated, "If you don't pay the bill, you can't leave."

I smiled. "Yes, I heard you the first time. We're not leaving."

So, with a few members of the crew, I headed to the pub. When we entered the establishment, some of the locals harassed us about how we were going to lose our ship. Most of them were loggers, and they were not very friendly. One of the loggers got in my face and said, "I hope you lose your fucking ship."

I laughed. "Be careful what you wish for."

When I returned to the ship, I noticed a seaplane landing nearby. On the plane was the president of the Pacific Pilotage Authority.

He introduced himself and presented the bill to me once again.

"Yes, I already have a copy of that bill," I responded. "Not paying it."

He looked at me and said, "If you don't pay this bill, this ship can't leave the harbor."

"Is that right?" I replied.

"Yes, that's the deal. Pay or stay. You don't pay, you don't leave."

"What's to stop me from leaving?" I asked.

"You need a pilot to leave."

"No, I don't. I did not need a pilot to get in here."

Somewhat angry now, he said, "The Coast Guard has orders to stop you if you attempt to leave."

I laughed. "You mean our Canadian Coast Guard, the guys with no guns and no real authority? You mean *that* Coast Guard? I've played chicken with the Soviet navy. Do you think I'm intimidated by the Canadian Coast Guard?"

Even angrier now, he threatened, "The Mounties will back up the Coast Guard if need be."

This back-and-forth was fun. I could not resist saying, "Oh, *now* I'm scared. The Mounties, that's another thing altogether. Well, I guess we won't be leaving now. But one thing is for certain: I'm not paying this bill."

After the Pacific Pilotage Authority president left, I called the crew together to tell them it was time to retire the *Sea Shepherd II*.

"We've had a good run with this ship—I've had her since 1980—and she's weathered campaign after campaign. But the annual upkeep has become more costly than the ship is worth. Retiring a ship is always expensive, so I think we'll just leave the old girl here."

The *Edward Abbey*, being much smaller, did not require a pilot. I planned to pump all the fuel from the *Sea Shepherd II* into the *Edward Abbey* and remove everything of value. The *Abbey* would then transport the valuables and us to Seattle.

It took three return trips to offload everything from the *Sea Shepherd II*. I removed the ship's wheel, the bronze portholes, the tools, and everything else that was useful. I also cut the mahogany boards from her deck.

Before leaving the *Sea Shepherd II*, I left a message for the loggers. From the pub on the hill they could clearly read the large yellow letters on the side of the vessel's black hull: Stop Clear-Cutting.

And there the *Sea Shepherd* sat. That winter, a storm caused the *Sea Shepherd II* to drag anchor. She almost took out a local yacht marina.

A few months later, I received a message on my answering machine from a lawyer named Jay Straith. He identified himself as the president of a diving club and wanted to know if I would be interested in having the ship sunk as a dive site.

I called him back, reached an answering machine, and left a message: "Hi, Jay. This is Paul Watson. Absolutely, you can sink the ship. All I would like is a video of the ship being sunk."

Apparently, I had gotten the wrong number and the machine did not belong to Jay Straith but to a young man who told his father about the message. His father excitedly called the police about my wanting to sink a ship.

Soon afterward, a journalist called and wanted to know why the Mounties were asking questions about me. I replied that I had no idea.

Finally, after spending thousands of dollars on the "investigation" without bothering to ask me about it, the Mounties knocked on the door of Jay Straith to ask if he knew me and anything about sinking a ship. The newspapers got wind of the story, and it was quite embarrassing to the police.

The people at Pacific Pilotage Authority still wanted their pound of flesh, so they sued me. They spent more than $60,000 in legal fees to force me to pay their bill of $7,500.

I simply refused to show up for court. The judge ruled against me but qualified the amount, saying I owed only half that fee because it was to cover entry and departure—and I hadn't departed.

The president of the Pacific Pilotage Authority called me to say he had a court order for me to pay $3,750.

"That's nice, but I'm not paying."

"You must pay. It's a court order."

I replied, "It may be a court order, but I am a stone. You can't sue me, because I don't own anything in Canada. There is nothing to seize. Bottom line: I'm not paying."

The next year, when I took the *Edward Abbey* up to Tofino to help protect the old-growth forest of Clayoquot Sound, I stopped at Ucluelet to see the *Sea Shepherd II* still at anchor. I went aboard and saw plants, including a couple of saplings, that had taken root on the deck.

I decided to visit the pub again, and this time I ran into a man who asked me if I still legally owned the ship. When I replied yes, he asked me if I would like to sell it. I said sure. He offered $5,000, and I drew up a contract to sign the ship over to him. Apparently, he wanted to fix it up and turn it into a floating hostel. The *Sea Shepherd II* was no longer my legal responsibility. Unfortunately, however, the man died in a kayak accident shortly after the transaction. But I still had the contract proving the ship was not my property.

Ten years later, the Canadian Coast Guard called me about the ship, saying it had become a problem and could sink in the harbor unless attended to.

Setting out on the *Farley Mowat* during the 2005 campaign.

"Well, I guess you should attend to it," I replied. The Coast Guard was surprised when I stated I was no longer the legal owner.

Transport Canada had the ship towed from Ucluelet down to Victoria, where the vessel was scrapped. The cost for doing so exceeded a million Canadian dollars. All because the Canadian government wanted to charge me $7,500 for pilotage after forcing me into port to harass me.

After that years-long experience, one would think the government had learned its lesson.

In 2007, it was evident that the *Farley Mowat*, which I had purchased in 1997 in Scotland, had reached the age of retirement. The ship had served us well in Antarctica, the Caribbean, Africa, and the North Atlantic. But she was becoming more costly to maintain.

The *Farley Mowat* was in Bermuda when I decided on the tar baby–Farley approach, the deliberate sacrifice of the ship to help further our efforts to ban seal products in Europe.

Fast-forward to 2008. Sea Shepherd's last campaign to defend seals resulted in the arrest of the *Farley Mowat*. To punish us for disrupting the seal slaughter by violating the Seal Protection Act, a Canadian court ordered me to pay a fine of $75,000.

I laughed. "You're kidding! You want me to pay a fine for a ship I actually no longer want?"

The court was not kidding. "If you don't pay the fine," I was told, "you don't get the ship."

To tease the authorities a bit, I said, "We'll just steal it back. I'm not paying a fine."

The government's response was to move the ship to a secure dock with twenty-four-hour security.

And there she stayed for an entire year, racking up a bill of half a million Canadian dollars for berthing and security costs, until the government was able to convince the court to order the confiscation of the ship. Loyola Hearn, the minister of Fisheries and Oceans, was taking every precaution to keep us from stealing the ship. Once the *Farley Mowat* was confiscated, he declared that the ship would be sold at auction.

When it came time for the auction, I could have put in a bid under an assumed company name—but I was afraid that I would win. The ship was sold for $5,000. The buyer was Green Ship LLC of Oregon. The company had the *Farley Mowat* towed to Lunenburg, where it announced that the ship was going to be converted into an Arctic research vessel.

That plan did not pan out, however, and by 2010, the ship had racked up some $90,000 in unpaid berthage charges. The ship was seized by the port of Lunenburg and sold again in 2013 at a sheriff's auction to a man named Tracy Dodds, the owner of Eastern Scrap and Demolition Services, for $9,200.

Dodds ran up a berthage fee he did not pay, and he was ordered to move the ship from Lunenburg. In September 2014, the *Farley Mowat* was towed to Shelburne, Nova Scotia.

On June 25, 2015, *Farley Mowat* sank at her berth and came to rest on the bottom of the harbor. The vessel was then refloated so that 528 gallons of pollutants could be removed. The Canadian Coast Guard incurred costs of more than C$500,000 for the cleanup effort. Owner Tracy Dodds was found to be in contempt of court for failing to remove the vessel or pay C$10,000 in penalties and fees. On August 3, 2016, Dodds was arrested in Wolfville, Nova Scotia, on contempt charges. He subsequently served twenty days in jail.

As of December 29, 2016, the hulk of the *Farley Mowat* remained docked in Shelburne, carrying with her more than C$130,000 in docking fees. On July 26, 2017, the hulk was towed away by Atlantic Towing under contract with the Canadian Coast Guard to be broken up at Liverpool, Nova Scotia.

Afterword

I n 2014, I was living in Vermont, but I had a problem. I had been corresponding with a lovely woman in Paris. She was Russian but had been living for ten years in France, where she was studying and working as an opera singer. Because she was Russian, she could not come to the United States, and because of an Interpol Red Notice, I could not go to France.

The president of Sea Shepherd France, Lamya Essemlali, once again came to my rescue. She contacted Nicolas Hulot, a prominent French environmentalist and an advisor to President François Hollande. He said I wouldn't have any problem traveling to France and that France would not extradite me to Costa Rica or Japan. (Japan's leaders believed I had humiliated their country, and they were seeking revenge.)

In June 2014, we had an international Sea Shepherd summit in Vermont, hosted by a supporter on his farm. Hundreds of people came from around the world to attend and to celebrate our achievements in protecting whales in the Southern Ocean.

Right after the summit, I decided to fly to France. After corresponding with Yanina Rusinovich (Yana) for eight months over the internet, I was finally able to meet her in person. She was there to greet me when I arrived at the airport.

I had no intention of returning to the United States without her, and we began the very long process of applying for a visa. However, I also had to consider my own risks if I returned to the United States. Although I had been allowed in previously, I still had the Interpol Red Notice against me, which would trigger an alert if I tried to re-enter the country and could result in my detainment.

It was amusing on one level. The Interpol Red Notice is for major criminals, most notably war criminals, drug traffickers, or serial killers. As far as I know, I am the only person ever to be placed on that list for the charge of conspiracy to trespass. It is also amusing that Sea Shepherd and I have partnered with Interpol to stop poachers on the high seas. I think I also may be the only person ever to have an Interpol Red Notice while simultaneously working with Interpol.

In France I gave lectures and wrote books. A French publisher asked me to write a children's book and a book on climate change. I also was invited by Nicolas Hulot to give a presentation to the UN Climate Change Conference in Paris in 2015.

In the fall of 2014, I proposed to Yana beneath the Eiffel Tower. We were married in the fourth arrondissement of Paris on February 14, 2015. Nicolas Hulot invited us to use his home on Corsica for our honeymoon.

We lived in Paris close to Notre Dame for a year and a half. We then spent six months in the small town of Cogolin in southern France, where Patrice de Columbe had invited us to stay at his castle, which was once the home of Antoine de Saint-Exupéry, the author of *The Little Prince*. That is where Yana became pregnant. Finally, after jumping through countless hoops, and with the help of senator John Kerry, she was given a visa to come to the United States as my wife.

We arrived at Dulles International Airport in early August with a small dog and a cat and a bad case of nerves. We were met by an immigration official, who escorted us to the desk where passports are checked.

As the officer at the desk inserted my passport, he said, "Ah, there seems to be . . ."

Another officer quickly jumped in and said, "Ignore that."

And so we got through and were back in the States.

My friend Cyrill Gutsch met us at the airport and drove us to New York City. A few days later we moved on to Vermont. Our son Tiger was born in late September 2016.

Sea Shepherd had evolved from an organization centralized in the United States to a global movement in numerous countries with the ships coordinated out of the office of Sea Shepherd Global in Amsterdam. I could not have been happier. It had become the global movement I had always wished it to be, and it was no longer under my sole control. Now it was in the very capable hands of directors in other countries and our captains and officers on ships working all around the planet.

In 2019, director Leslie Chilcott released her film *Watson*, the third and, in my opinion, best documentary on my life. Leslie had directed the film *An Inconvenient Truth*, featuring Al Gore, so I was thrilled to participate. However, not everyone else was equally thrilled. There were some people in Sea Shepherd who saw the film as counter-productive and complained that I had come off as "too radical."

Organizations change, and as Sea Shepherd grew, it had attracted development directors, administrators, merchandise directors, and fundraisers. The downside of this is that they wanted me to be more mainstream, less confrontational, and less controversial.

By nature, I'm naively trusting, so it was easy for them to gradually marginalize me. In 2019, the Sea Shepherd USA board of directors asked me to voluntarily step down from the board because, they said, my reputation and history were obstacles to their acquiring directors' insurance. I was assured that I would still be part of the decision-making process. Foolishly, I agreed. However, I only consented to do this after the board hired my friends Captain Alex Cornelissen (as CEO) and Captain Peter Hammarstedt (as Director for Campaigns). Nevertheless, other friends, such as Captain Oona Layolle, Captain Locky MacLean, and my assistant, Omar Todd, were slowly being dismissed. The turning point came in early 2022 when I was told that I could not participate in a meeting because they were having a Zoom conference with US government officials and my presence would not be acceptable.

In April 2022, Alex Cornelissen and Peter Hammarstedt resigned from Sea Shepherd USA, citing micromanagement by the board. In June 2022, I was invited to a board meeting where I was informed that Sea Shepherd would be changing direction, becoming more mainstream, and working toward partnerships with governments. I was told that its priority would now be research and cooperation with governments, and that my style of confrontation was no longer acceptable. I replied that I could not support nor participate in this course change for Sea Shepherd, at which point the board informed me that I was an employee and that they expected me to do what I was told. In response, I resigned.

Sea Shepherd USA removed my name as founder and deleted my profile and photographs. Basically, they erased me from my own organization, which I had founded in 1977. I was still a director for Sea Shepherd Global. Sea Shepherd Global's director, Alex Cornelissen, was not a fan of the USA board, so I assumed I would continue to work with the Global board. What I did not know was that the US board had covertly registered trademarks worldwide for the name "Sea Shepherd" and the logos that I had designed. I was told that I could no longer wear the logo or anything with the name "Sea Shepherd" on it.

Sea Shepherd USA then used these trademarks to threaten Sea Shepherd Global to submit to their authority. One of their demands was for my dismissal. So in early September 2022, I received an email from Alex Cornelissen informing me that I was dismissed. There was no meeting, no discussion, and no vote. Lamya Essemlali, who supported me, was also not allowed to vote.

Strangely, I was not bitter. I actually felt liberated and more motivated than ever. Now I was free to be myself. I established the Captain Paul Watson Foundation and formed a coalition with Sea Shepherd France, UK, Germany, Austria, New Zealand, and Brazil to continue the Sea Shepherd legacy.

In truth, Sea Shepherd was not an organization; it was a movement. While the US board may try to stop one individual or usurp one branch, just like a tree, Sea Shepherd will survive, as its remaining branches are still strong and healthy.

Aside from the ongoing drama, I was personally very happy. I've never been inclined to suffer stress. Plus, I had the support of my family: my wife, Yana; my daughter, Lani (born in 1980 and the mother of my two beautiful grandchildren); and my son, Tiger. In August 2021, six years after the birth of Tiger, we welcomed our second son, Murtagh, into the world.

I have been criticized for being an environmentalist who has children. I don't believe that not having children is a solution to much of anything. We need children to inspire us, to motivate us, and to teach us. However, people who decide to be parents must be ready to embrace the huge responsibility it entails. No children should be brought into this world without their parents pledging to love, nurture, guide, and educate them until adulthood.

Having children is not the source of the world's problems. Rather, problems begin when people have children irresponsibly. Unwanted, unloved, malnourished, and uneducated children grow into adults who are incapable of empathy, unable to appreciate the beauty of the natural world, and devoid of the desire to live a peaceful and loving life.

Of course, there are exceptions. I am the product of an abusive parent and was forced to fend for myself as a child. Although I was fortunate to have a loving mother, she also was a victim of my father, and when she died, my brothers, sisters, and I had to survive the best way we could. For my brother Stephen, survival became an art that guided him. My sister Sharyn took refuge in the love of a man she met at age seventeen, to whom she is still married a half century later. I found solace in nature, animals, and the sea.

Because of my background, I believe it is vital to give my children love and protection and to encourage them to be whatever they wish to be. Whenever people ask me what they should teach their children, I always reply, "Nothing." Parents don't really need to teach children much beyond the basics, as youngsters have an intuitive understanding of the natural world around them. Instead, our task is to guide them, listen to their ideas, respect their dreams, and above all else, love them unconditionally.

What began in 1977, when I established Sea Shepherd, became the world's largest conservation navy and, in my opinion, the world's most effective marine anti-poaching movement. After having cofounded Greenpeace and founding Sea Shepherd and the Church of Biocentrism, I'm moving on with my foundation.

Now in my seventies, I am still as excited about life and nature as when I was a boy. Aside from my achievements at sea over the last five decades, the lives saved, and the ecosystems protected, the one thing I am most proud of is creating a global movement that is now independent of me and will continue to grow and be increasingly more effective in the future.

I don't believe in retirement, so I won't be retiring. When I was younger, I felt that the perfect job was something a person could do without pay, seven days a week, every day of the year, without ever retiring. It turns out, I have the perfect job! I rejected being a highly paid impotent figurehead for Sea Shepherd USA, and I now get great satisfaction as head of my foundation with two newly acquired ships and a loyal crew who have served with me through the years, a crew of men and women who share my belief that we can change the world through passion, imagination, and courage.

After all these years, the following are the ten most important things I have learned:

1. Never be deterred. Always follow your heart, with confidence and honesty. Ignore criticism without anger or resentment.

2. Focus on the present: this is where our power lies. What we do in the present will define the future.

3. We each have the potential to change the world. Find your passion and harness it to the virtues of courage and imagination.

4. Be passive-aggressive when dealing with bureaucracy. Agree to comply with the bureaucrats and then proceed to do what you wish.

5. The greatest legacy is preventing the extinction of a species or the destruction of an ecosystem.

6. The answer to an impossible problem is to find the impossible solution.

7. When you lose the fear of death and failure, you can accomplish anything.

8. Life is to be enjoyed. Have an adventurous life filled with purpose and accomplishment.

9. Be kind always. Show consideration toward every living thing, plants and animals alike. They are the engineers that maintain the life-support system that is responsible for the survival of us all.

10. Never forget: if the ocean dies, we all die!

paulwatsonfoundation.org

ABOUT THE AUTHOR

C aptain Paul Watson is a marine conservationist, master mariner, author, educator, and poet. He is the founder of both the Captain Paul Watson Foundation and the Sea Shepherd Conservation Society and cofounder of the Greenpeace Foundation. Born in Ontario, Canada, Captain Watson currently resides in New York City.

PHOTO CREDITS

Cover photo: Jo-Anne McArthur

Text photos courtesy of the following:

Animal Planet, page 273

Chris Aultman, pages 268, 285, 321

Mary Bloom, page 71

David Garrick, page 134

Jeff Goodman, page 143

Marcus Halavi, page 79

Bob Hunter, page 214

Al Johnson, pages 59, 126

Jones, page 103

Patrick Moore, page 52

Eric Swartz, page 90

unknown, pages 83, 153, 224, 229

Paul Watson, pages 162, 195, 207, 238, 251, 296, 314

Rex Weyler, page 42

INDEX

A

Abbey, Edward, 108
Activism. *See also* Protests; Sea Shepherd campaigns
anti-trapping efforts during childhood, 8–9
against atmospheric nuclear tests, 27–28
for baby seals (1977), 55–60
blocking Norwegian sealing ship, 52, 53–54
blocking Russian whaling fleet in North Pacific, 38–39, 40–44
Christopher Columbus protest, 183–190
against clear-cutting on Vancouver Island, 200, 202–203
Greenpeace whale campaign, 38–39
against Hegins pigeon massacre, 178–182
paint bombing Soviet spy ship (1982), 111–115
painting seal pups, 85
to protect wolves in Peace River Valley, British Columbia, 130–135
release of lobsters during childhood, 4–5
releasing cows and pigs at slaughterhouse, 13–14
releasing monkeys in Saint George, Grenada zoo, 118–119
rescuing rabbits with Animal Liberation Front, 166–169
"Save the Seals" sign, 85–86
Sierra, hunting down and ramming of, 74–80
tree-spiking, 106–109, 200–201
against underground nuclear testing, 24–27
for whitecoat seals (1976), 50–54
for wolves (1984-1985), 130–135
Wounded Knee resistance, 32–35
Ady Gil, 307, 312
Africa, 61–66
African Elephant Conservation Act (1988), 61
Ager, Simon, 269, 303
Alberta, Canada, proposal to exterminate wood buffalo in, 170–177
Alberta Fish and Game Association, 172
Alexandria, Virginia, 87
Aligat (ship), 184, 187, 188
All Seasons Park (People's Park), 23–24
Almadina (Libyan seiner), 268
Amchitka Island, 21, 24–26
American Indian Movement (AIM), 33
Amin, Idi, 64–66
Amory, Cleveland, 67–68, 69, 75, 179
Amsterdam, Netherlands, 192–193, 221, 234–235, 326
Amundsen (Canadian Coast Guard icebreaker), 250, 252, 254

Andenes (warship), 193–195, 196–199, 223
Anderson, Pamela, 278
Anderson, Richard Dean, 249, 250, 304
Anderson, Will, 225
Angola, 75
Animal Liberation Front, 166–169
Animal Planet. *See Whale Wars* (television program)
Animals, kindness to, 3–4, 7
Annie Marie (sealing vessel), 260
Apartheid, 19
Arctic Explorer (sealing ship), 53
Around the World in Eighty Days (Verne), 28
Arrests. *See also* Prisons
  Faroese police issuing warrant for (2011), 272
  in Germany (1997), 221
  in Gulf of Saint Lawrence (1983), 122, 127
  Gulf of Stain Lawrence (1979), 70, 72
  at Newfoundland Grand Banks, 208–209
  for occupying a construction site near Stanley Park (1970), 23
  for paint-bombing Soviet ship, 115
  at protest against Hegins pigeon massacre, 178, 179, 180, 181
  of Sea Shepherd crew in Gulf of Saint Lawrence (2005), 254
  Simon Fraser University occupation (1968), 17
Astral (boat), 27, 28
Astrid (pirate whaler), 80
Athens, Greece, 36–38
Athens Polytechnic University (National Technical University of Athens), 36, 37
Atlantic Towing, 323
Auckland, New Zealand, 284, 287
Aultman, Chris, 272, 311
Australia, 18, 29, 256, 257. *See also* specific locations in Australia
Australian Federal Police, 311–312

Azores, Portugal, 76

B

Baby seals
  blocking Norwegian ship for (1976), 52, 53–54
  campaign in Gulf of Saint Lawrence for (2005), 250–255
  campaign to disrupt slaughter of (1981), 81–86
  Canadian Coast Guard icebreaker harming, 122
  Canadian government biologists putting dye on, 51
  efforts to save (1977), 55–60, 59
  painting, 67–73, 85
  research on using hairs from, 212–219
  tourism and, 212
Bail money, in toonies, 263–264
Bale, Christian, 232
Ballem, Peter, 57
Ballestero, Jorge, 243
Bandar Shahpur, Iran, 18, 29
Bangor Base, Washington, 112
Banks, Dennis, 34
Bardot, Brigitte, 58, 59, 227
Barnard, Neal, 179–180
Barrett, Dave, 155
Barrett, Pam, 172
Batchelor, Jon, 253
BBC, 139, 140, 143
BB rifles, 9
Beavers, 1, 5–6, 7–9
Beccalina Mist (sealing vessel), 255
Behr, Andrew, 75, 80
Beilenson, Anthony, 61
Beira, Mozambique, 20
Belle Isle, 53–54, 55
Bering Sea, 88, 159
Bermuda, 75, 257, 258, 259, 311, 322
Bethune, Peter, 279, 306–307, 312
Bikini Atoll, Marshall Islands, 24
Billboards, fur company, 46–47

Bill, Tony, 232
Bison (wood buffalo), 171–177
Bissonette, Pedro, 35
Black Creek Valley, 12
Black Elk, Wallace, 35
Black Harvest (documentary), 143
Blair, Cherie, 227
Blanc-Sablon, Quebec, 55
Bluefin tuna, 267–270
Bluenose (schooner), 204
Bob Barker, 284, 293–294, 295
    after Operation Zero Tolerance, 304
    Neptune's Navy and, 287–288
    Operation Compromise and, 313
    Operation Waltzing Matilda and, 312, 313
    Operation Zero Tolerance and, 281, 291–292, 293–299, 296–297, 300–301, 314
    returning from Operation Zero Tolerance, 302
Booth, Bronwen, 227
Bornheim, Germany, 277
Boston, Massachusetts, 68
Bott, Michael, 291
Bouchard, Donald, 219
Bounties, 100, 242
Bovine brucelosis disease, 171, 172–173
Boycott, of Japanese products, 104
Brady Mariner (sealing vessel), 252, 253, 255
Brave Heart, Dewey, 35
Breskens, Netherlands, 280
Brigitte Bardot
    after Operation Zero Tolerance, 302, 303–304
    arriving in American Samoa, 283–284
    arriving in Sydney, Australia (2013), 304
    crew of (2013), 306
    in Faroe Islands campaign (2011), 271–272, 273
    meeting up with *Caribana* (sailboat), 304–305
    Neptune's Navy and, 287–288
    Oona Layolle as skipper for, 303

    Operation Zero Tolerance and, 281, 282, 290, 291–292, 314
Bris (carrier), 21
Brisbane, Queensland, 285, 287
Brooks, James, 287
Brower, Kenneth, 81
Brown, Bob, 289, 304
Brown, Peter, 102, 304
Brucella abortus, 171, 172
Brummett, Anthony, 130, 135
Brune, Michael, 248
Bryde's whales, 74, 75
Bunting, Bruce, 61
Busch, Marc, 87, 93, 95–96, 98
Butyric acid, 147, 181, 207, 311

C

Cabot Strait, 69, 71, 123, 125
Cachalot (sperm whale), 40, 41–44
Cairns, Australia, 286, 287, 306
Calgary Herald, 172, 173
California, releasing rabbits in, 166–169
Canada Packer slaughterhouses, 12
Canadian Cattlemen's Association (Canadian Cattle Association) (CCA), 170
Canadian Coast Guard, 38, 72
    apprehended by (1979), 69
    in Gulf of Saint Lawrence (2005), 250–251, 252, 253
    in Gulf of Saint Lawrence (2008), 259–265
    Newfoundland blockade (1983) and, 120–121
    pilot bill and (1992), 318–319
    Sea Shepherd II and, 320–321, 323
    Sir Wilfred Grenfell ship, 205
    during storm in the Labrador Front (2005), 255–256
Canadian Federation of Humane Societies, 174
Canadian Fisheries and Oceans, 69, 204, 205, 206, 211, 259
Canadian Red Ensign, 12, 164

Canadian Sealers Association, 213
Canadian Seal Protection Act, 69, 86,
    128, 250, 252, 322
Canadian Wildlife Service, 171
Canary Islands, 75, 80
Cannes Film Festival, 275
Cape Fisher (pirate whaler), 80
Cape Knox, 163
Cape Roger, 205, 206
Cape Town, South Africa, 310
Captain Paul Watson Foundation, 327
Carbajal, Carlos Bueno, 284
Caribana (sailboat), 304–305, 306
Carlais, Bernard, 124
Casey, Brian, 210, 211
Casino, 87
Cate, Dexter, 100–101, 104
Cattle industry, 171–177
Cavendish Beach, 84
CCGS Camsell, 38
Cedarleaf, Wally, 107
Cembrero, Carlos Pérez, 237
Cesare Rustico (Italian-flagged vessel),
    267–268, 269
Chakravarty, Sid, 284, 289, 290, 292,
    294, 297
Chamblin, Dottie, 224, 225, 228, 229
Charleston, South Carolina, 163, 245
Charlottetown, Prince Edward Island,
    82, 83, 84, 86, 254
Chester (sealing ship), 121
Chilcott, Leslie, 326
Chinchilla, Laura, 278
Chocolate pie cannons, 143
Chofu Maru, 286
Church of Biocentrism, 328
Citytv, Toronto, 161
Clayoquot Sound, Vancouver Island,
    200, 320
Clear cutting, 106–109, 200–203
Cleveland Armory, 205–211
Clorox, 248
Coastguard South Canterbury, 290
Cocos Island, Costa Rica, 164, 237–243
Cod fishery, 204–211
Cogolin, France, 325
Cohen, Leonard, 37

Columbe, Patrice de, 325
Columbus (Sea Shepherd boat),
    279–282, 284
Columbus, Christopher, 183
Conley's Lobster Factory, 4
Cormack, John, 24, 39
Cornelissen, Alex, 259, 261, 262–265,
    279, 306, 313, 326, 327
Coronado, Rod, 142, 143, 148–154
Costa Rica
    campaign to protect sharks in
        (2002), 237–243
    extradition request from, 276,
        277–278, 279, 308
Costa Rican Ministry of the Environ-
    ment and Energy, 239
The Cove (documentary), 235
Cows, at slaughterhouse, 12–13
Craven, Wes, 232, 233, 234
Cronkite, Walter, 23
Crow Dog, Chief, 34–35
Cuba/Cubans, 118, 206–207, 211
Cummings, Bob, 58
Curio shop, in Nairobi, Kenya, 62–63
Cusack, John, 232
Custer, George Armstrong, 32

D

Dagblad, 158
Dakin, Laura, 305
Dam, Atli, 138
Damgaard, Nels, 172
Darnell, Bill, 25
David, Bobby, 116
A Death Feast in Dimlahamid (Glavin),
    184
Defenders (magazine), 61
Defenders of Wildlife, 61
DeJoria, John Paul, 227
Delta, 299
Denmark, moratorium on commercial
    whaling and, 139
Derek, Bo, 131
Des Groseilliers (Canadian Coast
    Guard icebreaker), 259–260, 261

Destreguil, Fabrice, 306
Devonian Harbor Park (All Season's
    Park), 23–24
Diehl, James, 181
Discovery Channel, 235
Divine Wind, 159
Documentaries, 139, 143, 235, 237–
    238, 326
Documentation
    of drift-net fishing, 160–161, 163
    of experience with *Varadero I*, 241
    of illegal Russian whaling opera-
        tions, 88–98
    of poachers on Cocos Island, 164,
        237–238, 239
    on release of bluefin tuna, 269
    of seal slaughters to support ban
        on seal products, 258–265
    of violations by sealers, 250, 252
Dodds, Tracy, 322, 323
Dolphins
    campaign to protect slaughter of,
        101–105, 110
    clubbed and speared in Japan,
        99–100
    Dexter Cate releasing captive,
        100–101
    drift netting campaign and, 160–161
    grindadráp and, 136
    Sea Shepherd crews seeing, 283, 291
Don't Make a Wave Committee, 24, 25
Doran, Jerry, 77, 78
Douglas-Hamilton, Iain, 61
Drift-net fishing, 159–163
Dr. Strangelove (film), 36
Duck hunts, 9
Dudka, Stanley, 70, 72
Dufort, Pierre, 215
Durban, South Africa, 19
Dutch prison (Lelystad), 221–226
Dyson, Freeman, 81
Dyson, George, 81, 86

E

Earth First! (newsletter), 108

Earth First! (organization), 108
Earthforce! (organization), 61
Earthforce! (Watson), 262
Eastern Scrap and Demolition Services,
    322
East, Ken, 174
Eco-Hawks, 175–177
Ecoterrorism, tree spiking and, 107
Ecuador, 239
Edgewater Fortune, 25
Edinburgh, Scotland, 220
Edmonton Journal, 173
Edward Abbey, 163–164, 317
    for Clayoquot Sound campaign
        (1993), 200, 320
    drift-netting campaigns and, 159
    at Neah Bay (1995), 228
    Sea Shepherd II and, 319
Edward Cornwallis (Canadian Coast
    Guard icebreaker), 252, 254
Einarsson, Hallvardur, 154, 158
Elephants, 20, 61–62, 65
Elliott, John, 130, 133
Elsie (typhoon), 20–21
Employment
    as a deck boy on a Norwegian
        merchant vessel, 17–21
    as deckhand on CCGS *Camsell*, 38
    at Expo 67, 15
    at Pappas Bros. Furs, 45–49
    as tour guide in Turkey, 38
    for Vancouver Park Board, 36
    during youth, 16–17
Ernst Haeckel, 205
Ernst, Manfred, 221
Essemlali, Lamya, 274, 280, 324, 327
Eurich, Richard, 206
European Economic Community, 205
Expo 67, 15

F

Fagan, Tina, 213
Farley Mowat, 165
    attached by Royal Canadian Mount-
        ed Police (2008), 261–262

in Cape Town, South Africa, 310
fishermen's attack on (2008), 261
in Gulf of Saint Lawrence (2005),
250–255
in Gulf of Saint Lawrence (2008),
259–265
IMO conventions and, 257–258
inspected by customs authorities, 249
in Labrador Front (2005), 255–256
Operation Minke and, 310
retirement of, 265, 321
in Saint-Pierre and Miquelon, 261
sent to Bermuda (2007), 311
unpaid berthage charges and,
322–323
Faroe Islands, 136–143, 149, 234,
271–274
FBI, 33, 193
Film rights, 232–236
Fin whales, 307, 310, 312, 313, 315
First Nations, people of the, 12
Fishing
childhood experience of, 7
cod, 204–211
drift net, 159–163
illegal fishing of bluefin tuna,
267–270
Sierra Club's support for, 245
Flash-bang grenades, 311
Flemming, Aida, 1–2, 84
Flemming, Hugh John, 1
Flynn, Colin, 210, 211
Force, Lisa, 245
Foreman, Dave, 108
Forretningsbanken of Trondheim, 75
Fort Nelson, British Columbia, 131
Foxhunting, 144–147
France
atmospheric nuclear tests in the
South Pacific, 27–28
Cannes Film Festival (2012) in, 275
Watson's travel to (2014), 324–325
Frank, Francis, 201
Frankfurt, Germany, 242, 275–282
Fraser Canyon, 16
Frederick Reefs, 306
Fredericton, New Brunswick, 1, 84

Free Paul Watson t-shirt, 278
Friend, Robert, 102
Friends of the Wolf, 130, 131
Fukuda, Mina, 103–104
Fund For Animals, 67, 75
Fundraising
during Cannes Film Festival, 275
marathon swim, 110–111
to protest underground nuclear
testing, 24–25
to purchase Zodiac boats, 39
Fur industry, 45–49

G

Gaede, Marc, 161, 215, 216
Galápagos Islands, 239, 256, 304
Galápagos Marine Reserve, 239
Galatée Films, 232, 236
Gallon, Gary, 61
Gamble, Ray, 225
Garrick, David, 33, 35, 51, 54, 106, 132
Garrison, Kate, 303
Gary, Romain, 65
Gavril Sarychev (ship), 112
Geist, Valerius, 173
Gelbaum, David, 246
Gemini, 295
George, Paul, 201–202
Georgia Straight, 19, 22, 28, 51
German bear hunter, 202–203
Germany, 220–221, 242, 275–282
Gibraltar, 267
Giorgi, Giacomo, 287
Gitxsan Nation, 184
Glasgow Hunt Sabs, 143–144
Glavin, Terry, 184
Glenn, Scott, 232
Gojira (rock group), 278
Gojira (ship), 313, 314
Golden Rule (sailing yacht), 24
Goodman, Jeff, 139, 143
Gordon, Andrea, 300
Gore, Al, 326
Gould, Jacinthe, 280, 281
Gouveia, Luis, 286

Gray seal hunt, banning of, 105
Great Barrier Reef, 306
Green, Derek, 211
Greenhouse gas emissions, 14
Greenock, Scotland, 81
Greenpeace
  Amchitka expedition
  founding of, 26
  in Iceland, 138
  origin of name, 25
  on painting seals, 53
  seal campaign (1977) and, 58–59
  Sierra campaign and, 75
  on tree spiking, 107
  Watson's resignation from, 59–60
Greenpeace (ship), 25
Greenpeace Too (ship), 25–26
Greenpeace VII, 50
Grenada, West Indies, 116–119
Grindadráp, 136, 234
Grouse Mountain, British Columbia,
  106–109, 201
Guatemala, 237, 240, 241
Gulf Clipper (sealing vessel), 251
Gulf of Saint Lawrence, 227
  2008, 257–265
  blocking sealing ships in, 121–129
  campaign to protect seals in (2005),
    250–255
  painting baby seals in, 69–73
Gutsch, Cyrill, 278, 326

H

Haber, Gordon, 131
Halal laws, 18–19
Haley, Adrian, 253
Halifax, Nova Scotia, 249
Hambley, Sarah, 149, 150
Hammarstedt, Peter, 277
  as Director of Campaigns for Sea
    Shepherd USA, 326
  Farley Mowat and, 259
  interrogated by Mounties, 262–263
  Operation Relentless/Operation
    Nemesis and, 315

Operation Zero Tolerance and, 288,
  292, 293–294, 295, 297, 316
  refueling of Japanese whaling ships
    and, 297, 298, 300–301
  resigning from Sea Shepherd USA,
    327
  sealing campaign in Gulf of Saint
    Lawrence (2008) and, 259, 260,
    261, 263–265
Hanibal (Libyan seiner), 268
Hannah, Daryl, 312
Hanscom, Marcia, 245
Hansen, Jeff, 288, 304
Harrison, Roy, 94
Hartop, Bart, 174
Hauer, Rutger, 222–223, 232
Heard Island, 302
Hearn, Loyola, 259, 262, 263, 322
Heche, Anne, 234
Hegins, Pennsylvania, 178–182
Helicopters
  for Southern Ocean campaigns, 310
Henry Larsen (Canadian Coast Guard
  icebreaker), 255–256
Hermannsson, Steingrimur, 154
Hidalgo, Eva, 283
Higgins, Kelly, 272
HMCS *Saskatchewan*, 112
Hoka hey, 34
Holden, Rob, 304
Holder, Stan, 33
Holland, Cam, 306
Hollande, François, 324
Holland, Malcolm, 287, 305, 306
Hollywood, 232–236
Horses, 3–4
House arrest, 277
Howitt, David, 149–154
Hulot, Nicolas, 324, 325
Humanitarian relief work, 116–118
Humpback whales, 74, 310
Hunter, Bob, 22–23
  Astral, 27
  campaign to block Norwegian
    sealing ship, 51, 52, 53
  campaign to oppose*grindadráp*,
    234

Christopher Columbus protest and, 183–184, 187, 188
drift-net fishing campaign and, 161
George Dyson and, 81
Greenpeace name and, 25
Greenpeace whale campaign and, 38–39, 41
media conference at Lelystad prison, the Netherlands, 223
reports from Wounded Knee to, 33
Huntermer, John, 164
Hunting
Sierra Club and, 245, 247–248
speaking out against, in childhood, 7
Wood Buffalo National Park, 172
Hunt Saboteurs Association, 143–144
Hunt Without Pity (film), 84
Hvalur 6 (whaling ship), 151–152
Hvalur 7 (whaling ship), 151–152

I

Iceland
delegates at International Whaling Commission (IWC) reception/meeting from, 225
International Whaling Commission moratorium and, 139, 148
Sea Shepherd campaign against whaling in (1986), 148–158
whaling regulations and, 137–138
Ides, Jeff, 224, 228, 229
Iki Island, Japan, 99–105, 110
Immigration, 246–247
Indigenous people
extermination of wood buffalo and, 171, 172–173
protest for Columbus celebration and, 183–190
whaling by Makah Indian tribe, 228
Inishkea Islands, 105
Institute of Cetacean Research, 288, 306
International Court of Justice, 306, 307
International Maritime Organization (IMO) conventions, 257–258

International Whaling Commission (IWC), 229
approval of Japan, 316
Japan withdrawing membership from, 316
meeting in Malmö, Sweden (1986), 139
meeting in Monaco, 223
Norwegian whaling and, 193, 220
reception for (1997), 225–226
Russian whaling operations and, 89, 96
Sierra operating in defiance of, 74
Interpol Blue Notice, 276
Interpol Red Notice, 277–278, 291, 308, 324, 325
Interpol warrant, 221, 242, 277–278
Iran, 18–19, 29–30
Ireland, 105, 224
Irish Sea, 105
Irwin, Steve, 311
Isba I (whaling ship), 80
Isba II (whaling ship), 80
Ishikawajima-Harima Heavy Industries, 286
Islam, halal laws and, 18–19
Ivory trade, trip to investigate, 61–66

J

Jacksonville, Florida, 256
Jail. *See* Prisons
Japan
Bethune's deal with prosecutor of, 306–307
bluefin tuna and, 267
campaign to end slaughter of dolphins in, 99–105, 110
delegates at International Whaling Commission (IWC) reception from, 225–226
demand for Watson's extradition to, 279, 282, 290–291
drift netting campaign and, 159–163
first trip to, 21
Makah whalers and, 224, 228–229

Sea Shepherd ship obtained from, 286–287
slicing flag of, 101
Taiyo Fishery Company, 75
Watson's extradition and, 276, 279, 280, 282, 324
Japan Coast Guard, 297, 311
Japanese consulate, 101, 163
Japanese whalers/whaling. *See also* Operation Zero Tolerance (2012-2013)
in 2014 and 2015, 307–308, 315
federal injunction ordering Sea Shepherd to stay away from, 288–290, 307
International Court of Justice trial on, 306, 307
lawsuit against, 307
moratorium on, 139
quotas, impact of Sea Shepherd campaigns on, 302, 310, 312, 313, 314, 315
Sea Shepherd campaigns against (2005-2017), 309–316
Sea Shepherd's lawsuit against, 307
withdrawing membership in International Whaling Commission, 316
Japanese whaling boats, 21
Jarl R. Trapp (Swedish Bulk carrier), 29
Jean Charcot (ICCAT inspection vessel), 269
Jeanne D'Arc (helicopter carrier), 27–28
Jericho Beach, 110, 111
John A. MacDonald (icebreaker), 122, 123, 124, 126
Johnson, Al "Jet"
activism for whitecoat seals, 51
assault on *Sea Shepherd II*, 1983 and, 126
Astrid/Cape Fisher and, 80
fundraising swim and, 111
fur company billboards and, 46–47
in Japan with Mina Fukuda, 103
jet fuel and, 54
kayaking campaign (1981) and, 81–82
"Save the Seals" sign and, 85–86

Soviet spy ship and, 112–115
tree spiking by, 106
trip to Africa, 61, 62, 64–65
visit with Aida Flemming, 1, 84
Jones, Richard, 288
Jones, Ryan, 302, 303, 306
Jordan, Bill, 68

K

Kaas, Elisabeth, 193
Kaga, Marilyn, 45, 51
Kaiko Maru No. 8, 286
Karle, Marsha, 172
Kayaks, 81–83, 100
Kechika River, 133, 134
Keen, Bob, 131
Keflavík, Iceland, 149, 156
Kennedy, Robert Jr., 307
Kenyatta, Jomo, 62, 64
Kenyatta, Mama Ngina, 64
Kenyatta, Margaret, 64
Kerguelen Islands, 302
Kerry, John, 307, 325
Keystone XL pipeline, 248
Key West, Florida, 164, 184, 190
Khaleej Eltahadi (Libyan seiner), 268
Khandheel II (Libyan seiner), 268
Khorramshahr, Iran, 29–30
Kindness Club, 1–2, 7
Kingsborough Greenlight Pictures, 232, 234
Kirchoff Bedding Fabrics, 213–214
Kirchoff, Tobias, 213–214
Knowles, Tommy, 299, 303, 305, 306
Kofu Maru, 286
Kruger National Park, South Africa, 19
Kurszewski, George, 172–173
Kuwait, 30

L

Labrador, 50–54, 55–60, 255–256
Labrador Challenger II (sealing vessel), 255

Labrador Sea (sealing vessels), 255
L'Acadien II (sealing vessel), 260
Lacitis, Erik, 111
La Follette, Doug, 245
Lake Union, 110
Landis, Tate, 110–111
Lane, Giles, 311
Lawrence, R.D., 174
Lawsuits, 129, 137, 271, 307, 320
Layolle, Oona, 295, 302, 303, 304, 306, 326
Leask, Peter, 23
Le Coeur des Bois (The Heart of the Woods), 200
Legislation/laws. *See also* Regulations
    banning gray seal hunt in Irish Sea, 105
    European banning Canadian seal products, 258, 265
    on importing ivory, 61
    on landing of helicopters near sealing operations, 55
    on photographing/filming seal hunt, 69
    sheep and halal (Muslim), 18–19
    on spiking trees, 107
    on whaling, 139
Lelystad prison, the Netherlands, 221–226
Lerwick, Scotland, 272
Leutheusser-Schnarrenberger, Sabine, 278
Libya, 267–268
Lindos, Greece, 37
Little Green Holm, Orkney Islands, 105
Liverpool, Nova Scotia, 250, 323
L.J. Kennedy (sealing ship), 254
Lobsters, 4–5
Lofoten Islands, Norway, 191–199, 223
Logging and loggers, 106–109, 200–203, 318, 319
Logo, Sea Shepherd, 327
London, Ontario, 14, 282
Loring, Arthur, 188, 189
Lorino, Soviet Union, 88–90
Los Angeles Times, 246
Lublink, Wyanda, 316

Lum, Starlet, 67, 135
Lunenburg, port of, 322

M

Maassen, Theo, 234
MacLean, Locky, 266–267, 286, 287, 313, 326
Madrid, Rocque, 34–35
Magdalen Islands, 73, 121, 212–219, 259–260
Magdalen Islands Sealers Association, 214–215
Maizura Marine Observatory, 286
Makah Indian tribe, whaling by, 224, 228–231
Malmö, Sweden, 139, 148
Malta, 267–270
Mandela, Nelson, 19
Mann, Shannon, 261–262
Marble Arch Productions, 232
Marcel, Pat, 173–174
Margarine, smuggling, 9
Marining, Rod, 23, 27–28, 106
Martin, François, 306
Martin, Pamela, 132
Massacre of the Little Bighorn, 32
McCarthy, Spencer, 229
McColl, David, 136
McLeod, Dan, 28–29
McLuhan, Marshall, 22
Means, Russell, 34
Meat industry, 14
Mech, David, 131
Media. *See also* Documentaries
    attack on whaling operations in Iceland and, 154, 155, 158
    in Boston (1979), 68
    Bridget Bardot and, 58
    campaign to sink/disable Norwegian whaling ship and, 194, 198
    at Christopher Columbus protest, 189–190
    on confrontation with police in Faroe Islands, 139–140
    on Cuba and Grenada, 118

debate about exterminating wood
  buffalo in, 172–174
drift-net fishing and, 161, 163
Icelandic, 138
in Japan, 102
on Japan's demand for Watson's
  extradition, 290–291
at Lelystad prison, the Netherlands,
  222–223
Makah whalers and, 228–229
Marshall McLuhan on, 22
"Save the Seals" message, Prince
  Edward Island and, 86
sealer violence on Magdalen Islands
  and, 215, 218, 219
showing Japanese fishermen killing
  dolphins, 99–100
Sierra Club and, 246–247
sinking of Norwegian whaling ship
  and, 192, 193
sinking of *Sea Shepherd II* and, 320
on sinking of whaling ship in Iceland, 150
on Soviet whalers, 50
on sympathy for sealers who died,
  260
on tree spiking in North Vancouver,
  107
Washington Post article on Hegins
  pigeon massacre, 178
on Watson's lecture about Eco-
  Hawks, 176
wolf campaign (1984-1985) and,
  130–131, 132–135
Mediterranean, campaign to stop illegal
  fishing of bluefin tuna in, 267–270
Mercier, Yvon, 82, 127, 128–129, 136
Merkel, Angela, 278
Meru National Park, 61
Messier, Francois, 174
Meyerson, Adam, 316
Millardair, 84
Millard, Madeleine, 84, 86
Millard, Wayne, 84, 86
Miller, John, 110–111
Ministry of Agriculture, Canadian,
  170, 171

Minke whales, 307, 310, 312, 313,
  315
Miquelon (French island), 261
Mitchell, Joni, 24–25
Miwa, Thomas, 109
Moises, Lisa, 253, 254
Monaco, 223–225
The Monkey Wrench Gang (Abbey),
  108, 163–164
Montreal, Canada, 15, 31
Moore, Patrick, 51, 54, 58
Moratorium, on killing of whales, 139
Morina (Libyan seiner), 268
Moulin Rouge, Beira, Mozambique,
  20
Mountainfilm festival, Telluride,
  Colorado, 244
Mounties. *See also* Royal Canadian
  Mounted Police
  arrest in 1983 and, 127
  assault on *Sea Shepherd II* (1983),
    125–126
  confrontation with, Gulf of Stain
    Lawrence (1979), 69–70, 72
  in Fort Nelson, British Columbia,
    131
  kayaking trip, Prince Edward Islands
    (1981) and, 82–83
Movie(s), 232–235
Mowat, Farley, 227, 263
Mozambique, 19, 20
Muir, John, 247–248
Mururoa Atoll, French Polynesia, 27
Musashi, Miyamoto, 312
Mussomeli, Josephine, 126
Mustang Survival suits, 84, 85, 89

N

Nairobi, Kenya, 61–62
Nakamura, Tadahiko, 226
Nanaimo, British Columbia, 110–111
National Geographic, 235
Neah Bay, Washington, 228–231
Neptune's Navy, 283–292
Netflix, 235

Netherlands, the, 74, 221–226, 234–235, 280
Net rippers, 228, 256
New Atlantis, 285–287
New Atlantis Ventures, 286
New Brunswick, Canada, 1, 3–10, 14, 82, 282
Newfoundland. *See also* Labrador
    blockade of sealing ship in (1983), 120–121
    cod fishing in, 204–211
    protecting seals in (1976), 51–54
Newfoundland Leader, 250
Newkirk, Ingrid, 179, 180
New York City, 266, 281, 326
New Zealand, 284–285, 290–291
Niigata, Japan, 21
Niña (ship), 184, 188
Ninth Circuit of Appeals, 288, 295, 307
Nisshin Maru (whaling ship), 293–295, 297, 298–300, 301, 310, 311, 312, 313
Nonviolence, Greenpeace and, 59
Nordengen, Arvid, 77, 78
Norfolk, Virginia, 164
Northern Regional Research Laboratory, Peoria, Illinois, 109
North Pacific Ocean, 39, 40–44, 50, 159–163
North Vancouver, British Columbia, 106
North Vancouver Garden and Arbor Club, 106–107, 201
North York, Toronto, 12
Norway
    blocking sealing ship of, *52, 53*–54
    delegates at International Whaling Commission (IWC) meeting/reception from, 225
    Makah whalers and, 224
    moratorium on commercial whaling and, 139
    Sea Shepherd's confrontations with whalers in, 220–221
    sinking whaling ships in, 191–199, 223
    warrant for extradition by, 221

Norwegian merchant marine, 17–21
Nuclear weapons testing, 21, 24–28
Nuu-chah-nulth people, 201–202, 228
Nuu-chah-nulth Tribal Council, 201
Nybraena (ship), 192, 223

O

Ocean Alliance, 304
Ocean Warrior (ship), 234, 235, 239, 240–241, 315
Ochs, Phil, 24–25
Ofalanga (Tongan island), 304–305
Offshore Operation Company Ltd., 286
Oglala Nation of Wounded Knee, 35
Oglala people, 32
Old-growth forest, clear-cutting, 200–203
O'Leary, Steve, 287, 303
Olivur Haglur (coast guard patrol ship), 140–142, 141–142
Operation Divine Wind (2011-2012), 309, 314
Operation Iron Wedge (2013), 298
Operation Leviathan (2006-2007), 309, 310
Operation Migaloo (2007-2008), 309, 311
Operation Mink (2005-2006), 309
Operation Musashi (2008-2009), 309, 312
Operation Nemesis (2016-2017), 309, 315, 316
Operation No Compromise (2010-2011), 309, 313–314
Operation Relentless, 307, 316
Operation Relentless (2013-2014), 307, 309, 315, 316
Operation Waltzing Matilda (2009-2010), 309, 312–313
Operation Zero Tolerance (2012-2013), 281, 282, 309
    accomplishments from, 314–315
    blocking refueling attempts by Japanese whalers, 297–301

blocking transfer of dead whale
during, 295–297
Bob Brown as expedition leader
for, 289
public reception following, 303, 304
running down Japanese whaling
fleet, 293–295
ships returning from, 302–303
success of, 302
U.S. court injunction and, 288–290,
295, 296
vessels for, 283–288, 291–292
Oporto, Portugal, 76, 79
Orca sounds, 230
Orkney Islands, 105
Osaka, Japan, 102
Osborn, Robert, 88, 89–93
Overpopulation, 246–247
Oxfam, 116–117
Ozul II (Libyan seiner), 268

P

Pacelle, Wayne, 179, 180
Pacheco, Alex, 76, 179
Pacheco, Claudio, 239–240, 241
Pacific Pilotage Authority, 318, 319,
320
Pago Pago, American Samoa, 283, 284
Paha Sapa, the, 32
Paintballs, 164
Paint-bombing Soviet spy ship (1982),
111–115
Panama Canal, 86, 87, 117, 164, 228,
256, 266
Pappas Bros. Furs, 45–49
Paris, France, 324, 325
Paris Match, 58, 227
Parks Canada Agency, 171
Passamaquoddy Bay, 4
Payne, Roger, 304
Peace River Valley, British Columbia,
130
Pelton, Austin, 135
Penn, Sean, 232
People's Park (All Seasons Park), 23

Percé, Quebec, 127
Perrin, Jacques, 236
Pezwick, Paul, 124, 128, 129
Phyllis Cormack (seiner), 24, 25, 39
Pie cannons, 164
Pigeon massacre, 178–182
Pilot bill, 317–321
Pilot whales, 136
Pineiro, Santiago Bolivar, 189
Pinho, Luis, 284, 285, 292, 300
Pinta (ship), 184, 188
Plaster Rock, New Brunswick, 83–84
Poachers, 164, 237–238, 239
Poetry, 37
Police. *See also* Royal Canadian
Mounted Police
Australian, Operation Migaloo
and, 311–312
in Bornheim, Germany, 277,
278–279
at Christopher Columbus protest,
188, 189–190
confrontation with, in Gulf of Stain
Lawrence (1979), 69–70, 72–73
in Fairo Islands, 139–140, 142
in Nairobi, Kenya, 63–64
sealer violence on Magdalen Islands,
215–216, 217–218
sinking of Norwegian whaling ship
and, 193
Pope, Carl, 244, 246, 247, 248
Population growth, 246
Portland, Maine, 120, 256
Port Phillip Bay, Australia, 303
Portugal, 75–80
Potts, Benjamin, 311
Precious, Ron, 54
Prescott, Heidi, 179
PRETOMA, 243
Prince Edward Island, 81–86, 127,
254
Prisons
in Germany (2012), 242, 275–277
in the Netherlands (Lelystad prison),
221–226
in Percé, Quebec, 127
in Reykjavík, Iceland, 158

in Saint John's, Newfoundland,
209
Protests
by American Indian Movement
(AIM), 33
in Athens, Greece, 37
against Christopher Columbus celebration, 183–190
by fisherman supporting Paul Watson, 208
against Hegins pigeon massacre,
178–182
against Keystone XL pipeline, 248
by Newfoundland fisherman, 205
against nuclear testing on Amchitka
Island, 24–26
opposing Four Seasons hotel near
Stanley Park (1970), 23
at University of British Columbia
(UBC), 17
The Province (newspaper), 132
Puerto Rico, 183–190, 184, 186–187
Puerto San Jose, Guatemala, 240–241
Puntarenas, Costa Rica, 240, 241, 243

Q

Quakers, 21, 24, 39
Quebec, Canada, 82, 127–128. See
also Magdalen Islands
Quebec Court of Appeal, 82, 129, 136
Quebec provincial police (QPP),
215–216, 217–218, 219
Queen Charlotte Islands, 39
Queen of Oak Bay (ferry), 111
Quinn, Aidan, 232, 234

R

Rabbits, 166–169
Rainier III, Prince of Monaco, 223–224,
225
Ramsay, Gordon, 243
Ray, Dixie Lee, 9
Regenstein, Lewis, 82

Regulations
banning broadcasting of orca
sounds, 230
of International Whaling Commis-
sion, 96, 148, 193
on photos or film of seal hunts
(Canadian Seal Protection
Regulations), 69, 89, 250, 252
on tonnage tax in Grenada, 117
Renfrewshire, Scotland, 144–147
Reservations, Sioux Nation, 32
Reykjavík, Iceland, 138, 148–158, 156
Rio Las Casas, 206, 211
Riverdale Zoo, Toronto, 3, 11–12
Robert Hunter, 310, 311. See also Steve
Irwin
Robichaud, Ian, 253
Rodriguez, Michelle, 275
Rogers, Cliff, 124, 125–126
Rogers, Warren, 110
The Roots of Heaven (Gary), 65
Rosaria Tuna (Maltese vessel), 269
Rose Atoll, 305
Roselle, Mike, 108
Royal Canadian Air Force, 112
Royal Canadian Mounted Police. See
also Mounties
cod fishing campaign and, 207–209
Farley Mowat attacked by, 261
harassment in Ucluelet from, 317
interrogation of Farley Mowat crew
by, 262–263
pilot bill (1992), 318–319
reacting to violence from sealers
(1977), 56
Sea Shepherd II and, 165, 317
at Simon Fraser University (1968),
17
tree spiking and, 107
Royal Society for the Prevention of
Cruelty to Animals (RSPCA), 68
Rubin, Jerry, 17
Rusinovich, Yanina, 324–325, 328
Russia. See Soviet Union
Russian whaling, 38–39, 40–44, 50
Ryerson University (Toronto Metropolitan University), 175

Ryofu Maru, 286
Ryoun Maru 6, 161

S

Sable fur, 89
Saint Andrews, New Brunswick, 1, 4
Saint Anthony, Newfoundland, 51, 53, 54
Saint Croix River, 8, 282
Saint Exupéry, Antoine de, 325
Saint George, Grenada, 117, 118
Saint John's Lockup, 209
Saint John's Newfoundland, 120, 121, 208, 209, 210
Saint-Pierre (French island), 255, 261
Sam Simon, 284, 287
    after Operation Zero Tolerance, 302, 303, 304
    Operation Zero Tolerance and, 281, 291–292, 297–298, 299, 314
Sanctuaries, 105
Sanderson, Neil, 88, 93, 94, 95, 97
Sandoy (island), 141
San Francisco, California, 29, 50, 244–248
San Francisco Chronicle, 246
San Jose (longliner), 239
San Pedro, California, 307
San Salvador, Bahamas, 184
Santa Maria (ship), 184, 188, 189
Schwartz, Eric, 88, 89–93
Scotland
    disrupting killing of seals in, 105
    Farley Mowat and, 321
    foxhunting in, 143–147
    purchase of *Sea Shepherd III* in, 220
    Sea Shepherd II and, 81
    Sea Shepherd ship impounded in, 270
Seal products, Europe banning Canadian, 258, 262, 265
Seal Protection Act. *See* Canadian Seal Protection Act
Seal pups. *See* Baby seals
Seals and sealing
    banning gray seal hunt, 105

blocking Newfoundland sealing ship to protect, 120–121
    campaign to disrupt slaughter of (1981), 81–86
    death of sealers in Magdalen Islands, 259–260
    in Gulf of Saint Lawrence (2008), 259–265
    interfering with Irish fisherman to kill gray, 105
    Labrador Front storm (2005) and, 255–256
    protecting in the Gulf of Saint Lawrence (1983), 121–129
    questioning sympathy for dead, 260–261
    sanctuary on island of Little Green Holm for, 105
    "Save the Seals" sign in Prince Edward Island, 85–86
    whitecoat, 51, 59–73, 212–219
Sea of Shadows (documentary), 235
Sea Shepherd
    changing direction of, 326–327
    Dutch citizens recruited in, 223
    federal injunction against (2012), 288–290, 295, 296
    as a global movement, 326
    growth of, 326, 328–329
    international summit (2014) in Vermont for, 324
    Japanese whaling delegate wearing shirt of, 226
    lawsuit against Japanese whalers, 307
    purchase of Little Green Holm, Orkney Islands, 105
    sealers assaulting members of, 253–254
    Watson asked to step down from board of (2019), 326
    Watson's resignation from (2012), 289
    working with Costa Rican government, 239–240
Sea Shepherd (ship), 68, 69, 71, 75–80
Sea Shepherd Australia, 288–289, 307

Sea Shepherd campaigns. *See also*
Operation Zero Tolerance
(2012-2013)
attack on Icelandic whaling operations (1986), 148–158
to defend pilot whales in the Faroe
Islands, 136–143
disrupting killing of seals in Ireland
and Scotland, 105
documenting evidence of seal
slaughters to support a ban on
seal products, 258–265
documenting illegal Russian whaling operations (1981), 88–98
first campaign: painting baby seals,
67–73, 85
intervening against poachers around
Cocos Island, 237–239
intervening whaling by Makah
peoples, 228–231
Operation Relentless, for whales,
307
to oppose and shut down high-seas
drift netting, 159–163
opposing *grindadráp*, 136, 234
to protect dolphins in Japan, 101–105
protecting seals in Gulf of Saint
Lawrence (2005), 250–255
protection of whales in Faroe Islands
(2011), 271–274
to protect seals in the Gulf of Saint
Lawrence (1983), 120–129
Sierra (1979-1980), 74–80
sinking and disabling Norwegian
whaling fleet, 191–199
in the Southern Ocean (2005-2017),
309–316
to stop illegal fishing of bluefin tuna,
267–270
against whaling in Iceland, 148–158
Sea Shepherd Denver, 275
Sea Shepherd France, 275, 280, 327.
See also Essemlali, Lamya
Sea Shepherd Global, 326, 327
Sea Shepherd II
assaulted by Mounties (1983),
125–126

drift net campaign and, 159, 160,
163
in the Faroe Islands, 137–138, 139
funding fuel and canal fee for
(1981), 86–87
inspected at Ucluelet, 317–318
intercepting replicas of Christopher
Columbus's ships, 184
lawsuit against government for
damages to, 129, 136
Newfoundland blockade (1983)
and, 120–121
pilot bill and, 317–321
purchase of, 81
returned by Canadian government,
136
searched by Royal Canadian
Mounted Police, 165
Soviet Siberia invasion and, 88–98
taking supplies for Oxfam to Grenada, 116–119
Sea Shepherd III, 220, 223–224,
227–228
Sea Shepherd: My Fight for Whales
(Rogers), 110
Sea Shepherd Netherlands, 279
Sea Shepherd USA, 307
Alex Cornelissen and Peter Ham-
marstedt resigning from, 327
dismissing and erasing Paul Wat-
son from the organization, 327
lawsuit against Japanese whalers,
307
Operation Zero Tolerance and,
288, 289
Operation Zero Tolerance federal
injunction (2012) for, 288, 289
resignation from, 327
"Sea Shepherd" logo and, 327
Watson resigning from, 289
Seaspiracy (documentary), 235
Seattle Times, 111
Sebastian, Gordon, 184, 185, 189
SEDNA, 230
Seeks, Chief Wii, 184
Seifu Maru (ship), 286
Selassie, Haile, 15

Senet (ship), 193
Shalom, Lisa, 253
Sharks, 161, 237–243
Sharkwater (film), 237–238, 242
Shaw, Peter, 307
Sheen, Martin, 214, 215, 219
Sheep, 18–19, 29
Shelburne, Nova Scotia, 322, 323
Shimonoseki, Japan, 287
Shonan Maru No. 2, 279, 293, 299, 306, 312, 313
Shunyo Maru 8, 160, 161
Siberia, 88–98
Sidler, Bernard, 227
Sierra (whaling ship), 74–80, 111, 232
Sierra Agency, 75, 79
Sierra Club
    debate with Carl Pope of, 244
    donations received by, 245, 248
    food served at meetings of, 245–246
    protest against nuclear weapons testing (1969), 21
    social justice issues and, 247
    Watson on board of directors of, 245
Sierra Fishing and Trading Company, 75
Siesta Conversation and Gourmet Club, 245
Sifaoui, Brigitte, 225
Simon Fraser University, 17, 22, 25
Simon, Sam, 285–286
Singapore, 18, 29
Sioux Nation, 32
Sirius, 138
Sir Wilfred Grenfell (ship), 205, 207, 261
Sir William Alexander (sealing vessel), 124, 125, 259
Ski resort, Grouse Mountain, 106–109
Skunk, childhood incident with a, 7
Slaughterhouses, 12–13
Small, Mark, 213
Smith, Brian, 154–155
Snapping turtle, released from Riverdale Zoo, 11–12
Snorkeling, 37
Social justice issues, Sierra Club and, 247
Sony, 232–233

South Africa, 19, 75, 80, 310
South China Sea, 20, 287
South Dakota, 32–35
Southern Ocean, Sea Shepherd's campaigns in (2005-2017), 309–316. *See also* Operation Zero Tolerance (2012-2013)
Southern Ocean Whale Sanctuary, 235, 279, 301, 310. *See also* Japanese whalers/whaling; Operation Zero Tolerance (2012-2013)
Southern right whales, 74
South Korea, 286
South Pacific
    nuclear tests in the, 27–28
    Watson's exile in the (2013), 302–307
Soviet Union
    campaign to document whaling in (1986), 88–98
    confronting ship of, in Strait of Juan de Fuca, 111–115
Spain, 80, 183–190, 185
Sperm oil, 43–44, 109
Sperm whales, 40–44
Spice Isle, 117
Spong, Paul, 39
Spy ship, Soviet, 111–115
Stanley Park, Vancouver, 23
Star-Phoenix, 174
The Starship and the Canoe (Brower), 81
Steve Irwin, 257, 271, 272, 273
    after Operation Zero Tolerance, 304
    Animal Planet series and, 311
    for campaign to stop illegal fishing of bluefin tuna, 267–270
    departing Williamstown, Australia, 283
    in New Jersey and New York, 266–267
    Operation Compromise and, 313
    Operation Migaloo and, 310–311
    Operation Musashi and, 312
    Operation Zero Tolerance and, 281, 282, 289, 290, 291–292, 293, 294, 298, 299–300, 314

returning from Operation Zero Tolerance, 302
Watson stepping down as leader of, 288, 289
Stewart, Rob, 237–238, 242
St. Giles, 81
Stink bombs, 164, 211
Stockyards, in Toronto, 12–14
The Storming of the Mind (Hunter), 22–23
Storms, 255–256, 281
Storrow, Marvin, 210
Straith, Jay, 319, 320
Strait of Juan de Fuca, 111–115
Students for Democratic University (SDU), 17
Stun grenades, 301
Stun guns, 216–217, 218
Sun Laurel (fueling ship), 297–300
Supreme Court of Canada, 115, 136
Susan I (whaling ship), 80
Swahili, 62
Sweeney, D. B., 232
Swim, fundraising marathon, 110–111
Sydney, Australia, 304

T

Tagreft (Libyan vessel), 267–268
Tagus River, 80
Tahiti, 305
Taiji, Japan, 105
Tail of the Grand Banks, 204
Taiwanese drift netters, 159
Taiwanese longliners, 241–242
Taiyo Canada Ltd., 75
Taiyo Fishery Company, 75
Tanzania, 66
Tar baby-Farley approach, 259, 322
Taylor, James, 24–25
Tear gas, 125, 142, 143, 211
Techno Venture (sealing ship), 121
Teeuwen, Hans, 234
Television program. *See Whale Wars* (television program)

Terlain, Jean Yves, 280, 281, 282, 284, 290, 292, 303
Theresa III (whaling ship), 80
Theriault, Gilles, 215, 217
Thomas Carleton, 205
Thompson, Alberta, 224, 225, 228, 229, 231
Timaru, New Zealand, 290, 291
Time, 55
Tobin, Brian, 211
Todd, Omar, 326
Tofino, British Columbia, 200–203, 320
Tolicetti, Raffaella, 287
Tonga, 304–305, 306
Tonnage tax, 117–118
Toronto, Canada, 3, 10, 11–15, 84, 86, 175
Tórshavn, Faroe Islands, 141, 234, 272, 274
Tourism, baby seals and, 212
Transport Canada, 257–258, 321
Trapping/trappers, 8, 133
Trashing the Planet (Ray), 9
Treaty of Fort Laramie, 32
Tree planting, 16–17, 24
Tree spiking, 106–109, 200–201
Trenter, Josh, 287
Trials
 for Gulf of Saint Lawrence campaign (1983), 128–129
 for interfering with cod fishing, 210–211
 against Japanese whaling industry, 306
 in the Netherlands (1997), 223
 Sea Shepherd on (2013), 307
Tsavo East National Park, 62
Tsushima Island, 100
Tuna, bluefin, 267–270
Turkey, 38
Typhoons, 20–21, 287

U

Ucluelet, British Columbia, 165, 317, 320, 321

Uganda, 64–66
Underground testing of nuclear weapons, 21, 24–27
UNESCO World Heritage Site, 174
United Nations Conference on the Environment and Development, Rio de Janeiro, Brazil, 165
United Nations Conference on the Environment, Stockholm (1972), 26
United Nations Conference on the Environment, Stockholm (2015), 325
United Nations Environmental Liaison Center, 61
United States. *See also* Sea Shepherd USA; US Coast Guard
Makah whalers in Neah Bay, Washington, 228–231
Operation Zero Tolerance and court injunction from, 288–289, 295, 296
plan to detain Watson for extradition to Japan, 282
protest against pigeon massacre in, 178–182
releasing rabbits with Animal Liberation Front in, 166–169
returning to, after exile (2013), 306–307
Sierra Club and, 244–248
Wounded Knee, South Dakota resistance, 32–35
University of British Columbia (UBC), 16–17
University of Calgary, 172, 173
Urase, Mr., 102, 104
Ursford, Bjorn, 198
US Coast Guard
Columbus Day protest and, 185
drift-net campaign and, 163
inspection of *Farley Mowat*, 249
Makah whalers and, 230, 231
Soviet spy ship and, 111
US Customs, 184
US Marshals, 33, 34
US Navy, 164, 186, 187

V

Vancouver, Canada, 16–17, 21, 23–24, 29, 39, 45–49, 106–109
Vancouver City College (Vancouver Community College) (VCC), 16, 17
Vancouver Island, 165, 228, 317. *See also* Tofino, British Columbia
Vancouver Sun, 23, 33, 132
Van Kooten, Kim, 234
Varadero I (fishing vessel), 237, 240–241, 242, 243
Vasic, Jonny, 253
Vermont, 324
Verne, Jules, 28
Vidal, John, 234
Viking Shores (*Whale Wars* series), 271–274
Vlasak, Jerry, 253, 254
Vogel, Carroll, 112–115, 124, 126
Voight, Jon, 232
Von Jans, Geert, 279–280, 306

W

Wallace, Bob, 305
Wallasch, Oliver, 277, 278
Wallerstein, Peter, 137, 138–139
Wall, Patrick, 101
Ward, Cliff, 61, 62–63
Warner Brothers, 232
Washington Post, 178, 181
Water cannons, 125, 138, 143, 164, 299, 300
Watmore, Josephine, 302, 303, 306
Watson (documentary), 235, 326
Watson, Lilliolani (Lani), 135, 328
Watson, Paul
activism by.*See* Activism
arrests.*See* Arrests
beaver experience in childhood, 5–6, 7–9
Captain Paul Watson Foundation, 327
childhood in New Brunswick, 3–10
childhood in Toronto, 11–14

on children and parenting, 328
children of, 325, 328
debate with Carl Pope, 244
documentary on, 235, 326
education, 11, 16, 17, 22
80 days on 80 dollars challenge,
28–31
employed as deckhand for Canadian Coast Guard, 38
employment by.*See* Employment
escape from psychiatric hospital,
14–15
exiled at sea, 302–307
father, 4, 7, 9, 10, 14
fishing experience in childhood, 7
grandfather of, 3–4
as "hitman" for the Kindness Club,
1–2
on Hollywood, 232–236
Interpol Red Notice and, 308, 324,
325
lecture at Ryerson University,
175–177
living in France, 324–325
marriage to Yani, 325
mother, 9–10
photos of, 52, 59, 126, 134, 273
in prison.*See* Prisons
resignation from Sea Shepherd,
288–289, 327
selling feature film rights, 232–236
siblings, 328
on Sierra's board of directors,
244–248
skunk incident in childhood, 7
stepping down from Sea Shepherd
USA board of directors, 326
struck by a bullet (2007), 311–312
on ten most important things he
has learned, 329–330
travel to East Africa (1978), 61–66
travel to Greece (1973-1974), 36–38
travel to Turkey, 38
writing by, 11–12, 19
Watson, Sharyn, 328
Watson, Stephen, 282, 328
Watson, Tiger, 325, 328

Weasel, experience during youth with,
8
Weiss, Norm, 172
Wellington, New Zealand, 284, 287,
288, 291
Westella (ship), 68, 75
Western Canada Wilderness Society,
107, 201
West, Scott, 277, 279
Wet'suwet'en Nation, 184
Wet'suwet'en peoples, 184
Whalers, debate with local, 274
Whales and whaling. *See also* Japanese
whalers/whaling
attack on Icelandic operations
for illegal whaling activities,
148–158
blocking Russian whaling fleet
in North Pacific for, 38–39,
40–44
cachelot (sperm whale), 40–44
documenting illegal Russian operations with, 88–98
Faroe Islands campaign (2011) and,
271–274
grindadráp practice and, 136, 234
killed for sperm oil, 43–44
Makah Indian tribe and, 228–231
moratorium on, 139
paint bombing Soviet spy ship
against killing, 111–115
Quakers and, 39
regulations, 137–138, 193
Sierra campaign, 74–80
World Council of Whalers, 228
Whales Forever (ship), 193–199
Whale Wars (television program),
235, 271–274, 292, 311, 312,
313–314
White, Ben, 124–125, 127
Whitecoat seals, 51, 69–73, 212–219
Willem Barendsz (Dutch factory ship),
74
Williamstown, Australia, 283, 303,
304
Wolfe (icebreaker), 70, 72
Wolke, Howie, 108

Wolves, 130–135, 171
Wood buffalo, 171–177
Wood Buffalo National Park, 170, 171–177
Woof, Peter, 77, 78, 79–80
Worker, Dwight, 191–199
World Council of Whalers, Vancouver Island, 228
Wounded Knee, South Dakota, 32–35, 130

Y

Yellow Journal, 22
Yellowstone National Park, 172

Yushin Maru No. 2, 293, 294–295, 296–297, 312, 313
Yushin Maru No. 3, 299, 313

Z

Zodiac inflatable boats, 39, 41, 88, 91, 187, 273
Zoo(s)
    grandfather taking Watson to the, 3
    releasing monkeys in Saint George, Grenada, 118–119
    school newspaper article on Riverdale Zoo, 11–12
Zuckerman, Benjamin, 245, 246

GROUNDSWELL BOOKS
SOLUTIONS FOR A SUSTAINABLE WORLD

For more books that inspire readers to create a healthy,
sustainable planet for future generations, visit
BookPubCo.com

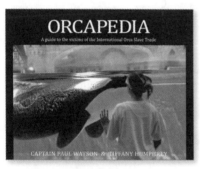

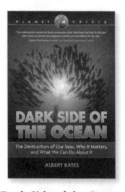

Orcapedia:
*A Guide to the Victims of the
International Orca Slave Trade*
Captain Paul Watson and Tiffany Humphrey
978-1-57067-398-6 • $24.95

Dark Side of the Ocean:
*The Destruction of Our Seas, Why It Matter
and What We Can Do About It*
Albert Bates
978-1-57067-394-8 • $12.95

Transforming Plastic:
From Pollution to Evolution
Albert Bates
978-1-57067-371-9 • $9.95

Cookin' Up a Storm:
Sea Stories and Vegan Recipes
Laura Dakin
978-1-57067-312-2 • $24.95

Purchase these titles from your favorite book source or buy them directly from:
Book Publishing Company • PO Box 99 • Summertown, TN 38483 • 1-888-260-845
Free shipping and handling on all orders